The Humor of Irony and Satire
in the *Tradiciones peruanas*

The Humor of
Irony and Satire
in the *Tradiciones peruanas*

Roy L. Tanner

University of Missouri Press
Columbia, 1986

Library of Congress Cataloging in Publication Data
Tanner, Roy L.
  The humor of irony and satire.
  Bibliography: p.
  Includes index.
  1. Palma, Ricardo, 1833-1919—Humor, satire, etc. 2. Palma,
Ricardo, 1833-1919—Style. 3. Palma, Ricardo, 1833-1919.
Tradiciones peruanas. I. Title.
PQ8497.P26Z89   1985   863   85-1013
ISBN 0-8262-0448-1

∞™ This paper meets the minimum requirements of
the American National Standard for Permanence of Paper
for Printed Library Materials, Z39.48, 1984.

To Joann

Preface

After many years of studying Ricardo Palma and the *Tradiciones peruanas,* I finally decided to write what was obviously lacking—a detailed analysis of Palma's humor as related to irony and satire. In the process I have happily been obliged to fill a gap in our knowledge of Palma's style, given the distinct interdependence of humor and style in the prose of the *tradiciones.* Curiously, despite the enormous bibliography that has grown up around the Peruvian writer's famed works, these two facets of his expression have continually eluded detailed examination. Though frequently applauded, and touched on in part by such scholars as Alessandro Martinengo, Alberto Escobar, José Miguel Oviedo, Luis Alberto Sánchez, Luis Hernán Ramírez, Ventura García Calderón, Dora Bazán Montenegro, Shirley Arora, William Russell Wilder, among others, Palma's use of irony and satire have never been studied closely. The present work, though humble, makes a concerted effort to do just that.

As the reader will note on thumbing through the book, my effort has not been totally analytical. The richness and vastness of Palma's narrative contribution have long demanded a more illustrative approach, such as that employed by Rosenblat and Hatzfeld in their studies of Cervantes' language. Accordingly, I have endeavored to buttress each point of analysis with a representative variety of examples. This format, of course, permits the reader to skim the examples and to focus on the analytical observations if the latter is of prime interest to him. He will, however, miss much of the real flavor of Palma's humor, which often requires contemplation to be fully enjoyed.

I have used Edith Palma's 1968 Aguilar edition of the *Tradiciones peruanas completas* for this study. All quotes are as they appear in that volume, with the exception of accent marks over such monosyllabic verb forms as *fui* and *dio,* which I have eliminated. Palma frequently emphasized particular terms by using italics, and, as a consequence, many of the quotes in this book contain italicized words. Any parts italicized by me are indicated either immediately following the quote or prior to a series of citations. All translations of critical commentary are mine.

This book has been made possible by a Sesquicentennial Associateship awarded by the Center for Advanced Studies at the University of Virginia. I am very grateful for the full-time research assignment provided by the grant, which permitted me to complete the basic text of the book. Special thanks go to Professors Chad Wright and Merlin Compton for their careful reading of the manuscript. Their suggestions have proved highly valuable. Professor Daniel C. Scroggins enabled access to the portrait of Palma reproduced on the jacket. I would also like to thank my excellent typists, Lorraine Quillon and Cindy Burnett. A grant from the Committee for Small Grants aided in the cost of the typing. Finally, I wish to recognize with deep appreciation the understanding and support of my wife and six children during the course of the project.

R. L. T.
May 1985

Contents

1

Introduction

Historical-Literary Context

This book is a treatment of humor as practiced by the Peruvian author Ricardo Palma (1833-1919) in his famed *Tradiciones peruanas*. As a step leading to that analysis, I would like to examine briefly from several perspectives the literary context within which that humor took its enduring shape and to summarize Palma's overall importance in Latin American literary and cultural history.

For a starting point, let us consider Palma in his relationship to the Spanish race and thus as a benefactor of the genius and character embodied in the great literature of that people. In particular, he was greatly influenced in style and spirit by the Golden Age masters of the language, Cervantes and Quevedo.

Second, as a Latin American author, Palma harmonizes well with some of the constants of the literature of that land. I refer especially to a well-embedded and continuous vein of satire and to a general tendency to condemn hypocrisy and guile while sustaining the dignity of man.

A third context within which Palma finds congenial company is the chronicles. On at least three counts he ties in with this rich heritage of colonial literary creation. As is well known, many a fictitious gem lies inset in the history of the chroniclers. In a sense the *tradicionista*, who gave birth to an imaginative prose gingerly moistened in historical reality, stands as a culmination of the tendency to tincture history with fiction. In addition, Palma not only re-created scenes and encounters typical of the chronicles but also drew heavily on them for his sources and descriptions (el Inca Garcilaso de la Vega, for example). It is also significant that the presence of humor and piquancy in those antecedent works—Bernal Díaz, *El carnero*—finds echo and expansion in the *Tradiciones peruanas*.

Fourth, one notes Palma's place in a continuum of coastal, Limean writers, all of whom relied heavily on satire and/or irony. Beginning with the poetry of Mateo Rosas de Oquendo (circa 1559-1621), author of *Sátira a las cosas que pasan en el Perú, año de 1598*, we perceive a steady satiric tone through the poetry of Juan del Valle y Caviedes (circa 1652-1697), author of *Diente del Parnaso*, the poetry of Esteban de Terralla y Landa (late 1700s), author of *Lima por dentro y por fuera*, and in *El Lazarillo de ciegos caminantes* by Alonso Carrió de la Vandera (1775-1776). Palma was heavily influenced by many of these works, and the *Tradiciones peruanas*, although uniquely independent as a whole, maintain the spirit of *lisura* so inbred in the Peruvian literary tradition, as discussed in the next section.

A fifth perspective from which to view the humor of Palma's masterpiece deals with romanticism and *costumbrismo*. In the early 1850s Don Ricardo's pen enthusiastically fathered an array of romantic verse and drama, and the later precursors of the mature "tradition" clearly reflect that initial immersion. Although for Palma romanticism was only a passing infection, certain key aspects of that movement did take permanent hold in his character and works, thus figuring among the cornerstones of the *tradición*. I refer to enthusiasm for the national past, an attitude of independence, support for individual freedom and justice, and a desire for social and political progress.

Palma is a significant figure in an important manifestation of romanticism in Latin America known as *costumbrismo*. The *tradición* embodies many aspects typical of that form, especially satire with its social and political themes, its criticism, and its desire for reform. Several Peruvian *costumbristas* precede Palma and exert some degree of influence on him. Of particular importance in this regard are Felipe Pardo y Aliaga, who cultivated, among other things, the satiric *letrilla* to promote political ideas, and the popular dramatist Manuel Ascencio Segura, who took the young Palma under his wing and with him wrote a play in 1859 entitled *El santo de Panchita*. Thus, although the *tradiciones* are much more than sketches of customs, their author may be viewed to advantage in the context of the nineteenth-century *costumbristas*, many of whom resorted to the humor of satire so rife in the *Tradiciones peruanas*.

Sixth, we must also consider Ricardo Palma in light of the genre he created. The *tradición* embodies many significant features but in its essence comprises a historical anecdote blending a sketch of customs; the historical data of the era; the warm ironic presence of a very visible narrator; and a singular style, a mixture of pure Castilian phraseology, archaisms, and vernacular expressions and sayings; all abounding in humor and satire. Although related to the historical fiction of Sir Walter Scott, this genre is unique in theme, style, and tone. The first series of *tradiciones* appeared in 1872, followed by nine others during the next thirty years. The number of imitators spawned by Palma's creation was large. However, none could reproduce the tone and the style forged by the master.

Finally, the humor of the *Tradiciones peruanas* can be more fully appreciated when viewed within the context of Palma the lexicographer. Don Ricardo was a master of the language. During his lifetime he published two works—*Neologismos y americanismos* (1895) and *Papeletas lexicográficas* (1903)—dealing with words that he considered worthy of inclusion in the official dictionary of the language. This dominion over the language contributed greatly to his achievement as a humorist of irony and satire, for, as we shall observe frequently in this book, style and mirth commingle throughout the *tradiciones*.

To assess Palma's overall importance, we must consider both the past and the present. During his own lifetime he was one of the most widely read penmen of Latin America. With minimal exaggeration Enrique de Gandía avers that there was no one, not "a scholar, a simple reader, or even a housewife, who did not have Palma's *tradiciones* on hand."[1] He maintained a vast correspondence with the important writers of his day—peninsular and Spanish American—and was extensively known and respected. In the minds of many he constituted one of the most significant elements of Peruvian culture and in his later years was constantly sought out by visitors to Lima.

Over sixty years later his consequence and standing remain stable, and his manifold contributions to Peruvian and Latin American literature and culture remain clear and eminent. Perhaps foremost among the contributions is the creation of a new genre, which stimulated many other writers in Mexico, Guatemala, Argentina, Chile, and Peru to enhance their own cultures in a similar vein. However, as noted, "Palma has remained the master whom all others have sought to follow, although it is only right to say it, at no time has anyone surpassed him, for there has not been anyone who has displayed such brilliant diction, such elegance in the telling of a story, and such variety in the scenes he was able to portray."[2] His other enduring achievements include forging a unique and masterful style—a linguistic masterpiece—preserving and enlivening many elements of Peruvian history, enriching the mother tongue, restoring the National Library, and, with the humor of indirect expression, crystallizing in literary form the Limean spirit.

Humor and Palma

To write about humor in the *Tradiciones peruanas* is akin to writing about water in the sea, so omnipresent is it in that collection of historical anecdotes. Rarely does a critic of Ricardo Palma fail to comment on at least one of its facets. "Our great humorous epic, our human comedy," "the comical epic of our history"—such references abound, along with allusions to Palma's "salty, earthy humor," to his "ironique légèreté" and to "his humorous vision of the past."[3] Ventura García Calderón maintains that "to laugh and to make us laugh is the preferential mission of the chronicler," while Palma's granddaughter, who prepared the Aguilar edition of his complete works, asserts, and with justifiable admiration, that her grandfather sometimes "conducts himself as the most consummate humorist, in a way that has no parallel in the Spanish literature of his time."[4] In full agreement with such analyses, the *tradicionista* himself has confessed: "Mi idiosincracia literaria es humorística, y quizá algo volteriana."[5]

Still lacking, however, despite many analytical considerations already in existence, is a comprehensive, detailed study of the techniques instrumented by Palma in the creation of this Limean *Libro de buen humor*. Such an undertaking constitutes my objective in the following pages. As the reader will soon see, however, the breadth of this objective will lead beyond a limited stylistic analysis to a consideration of many features of Palma's writing, including, for example, the relationship between the reader and the text. Thus, at various points, we will be involved in what might best be called rhetorical or even discourse analysis.

We have seen that as a master of humor, irony, and satire Ricardo Palma descends from an illustrious lineage of European and Latin American writers. "Supreme geniuses of the most sublime stock, and in the most agitated or grandiose ages, attended out of preference, like him, to the smiling and comical side of life." José de la Riva Agüero, author of those words, goes on to signal as worthy and obvious antecedents Boccaccio, Chaucer, Froissart, Archpriest of Hita, Rabelais, Ariosto, Cervantes, Quevedo, and La Fontaine, among others.[6] An indication of the suitability of Palma's inclusion in such company appears in a letter written to him by Miguel de Unamuno.

> Soy hombre de cara dura, es decir, de fisonomía poco movible, y así, siendo alegre de espíritu . . . rarísima vez me río, por mucha gracia que una cosa me haga. Acababa un día de acostarme, cuando a poco entra mi mujer en el cuarto, alarmada al oírme reír de tal modo, en carcajada contenida—por no despertar a los niños—que creyó que me había dado algún accidente, y ello era que acababa de leer el chistosísimo cuento del inglés.[7]

Santiago Vilas affirms that humor has been the main source of inspiration for the great artistic works of the past, including the novel, painting, sculpture, music, and poetry.[8] Although perhaps a little overstated, the insight certainly holds true for Ricardo Palma.

It has been suggested that "a humorist, as an artist, is born with that gift; strictly as a writer, he makes himself, he polishes, and at the same time 'makes' his attitude."[9] Palma exemplified this observation by Vilas explicitly. Though born a legitimate heir to Peruvian *lisura*, "that graceful maliciousness" that constitutes "the Peruvian way of making literature," and with an apparently innate genius for that clever Limean wit, he had to apply himself diligently in order to find the appropriate aesthetic pathway along which to channel it.[10] He worked and reworked his stories with great patience while acclimatizing and immersing himself in the lexicon and the spirit of the language, especially as manifest in classical Spanish authors. Later he returned to his initial *tradiciones,* retouching and revitalizing them with the humor, irony, and spontaneity so typical of his mature style.

Therein lies one of the keys to his success. In order to achieve its greatest effect, particularly in the spoken tongue, humor requires a spontaneity and a natural wit often lost in belabored writings.[11] Palma's anecdotes, however, though exceedingly polished and reconsidered by the author, are alive with the naturalness of a conversational tone essential to the full expression and conveyance of humor.

Within limits one can find "a certain distinctive individuality that marks the humor of each country."[12] Palma's humor exhibits two veins, as suggested earlier in this chapter—Peruvian *lisura* and a particularly Spanish hue. As a disciple of Miguel de Cervantes, he became saturated with the latter's mode of speech as well as with the speech of Quevedo. In a fashion those great masters guided him in the solidification of his style and his humorous perspective of life. One must underscore as equally significant the influence of Peruvian satire. It informs his perception and, guided by the examples of the Spanish classicists, asserts itself in every facet of his work.

Raúl Porras Barrenechea suggests, "Palma, the most representative spirit of our literature, of necessity had to be a wag. His humor originated from that bubbling Creole vein, of wholesome and jovial laughter, of unmistakable mischievous cunning, which had its cheerful origin in the seventeenth century, in Juan del Valle y Caviedes, the poet of the river bank."[13] There exists a book entitled *España en sus humoristas*. With equal facility a volume entitled "Perú en sus lisuristas" could be composed. In such a case the singular form would suffice because Ricardo Palma, from his waggish, aesthetic-philosophical promontory, encompasses and synthesizes most of the historic moments of his country.

A genuine humorist fulfills simultaneous roles as a critical spectator of life and as an artist. As spectator, he contemplates and interprets the whole gamut of human activity from a set philosophical perspective. Having viewed and experienced life, he has adopted "an attitude toward life," a weltanschauung, that for him constitutes "an art for existing."[14] Master of his perspective, he discerns the imperfections in humanity and the seeming paradoxes of existence and responds to them artistically, sometimes suggesting solutions (humorist-moralist), sometimes limiting himself to pure aesthetic delight (humorist-artist).[15]

Palma takes both stances. He criticizes, ironizes, satirizes, or trivializes as occasion and his "comic muse" demand, but always with a strict awareness of the stylistic mold in which he wishes his humor cast. Federico de Onís, in evaluating the novels of Galdós, could also be speaking of Palma's anecdotes when he says, "There is always present as a permanent characteristic of unity a tone in the expression and a way of seeing the world and of feeling life that have a clearly humorous character, a simple, natural, juicy, human humor that resembles that of Cervantes more than does that of any other author." Thus, filtered through the eyes of the *tradicionista*, the colonial era, the Republic, and, in effect, humanity in general take on life and substance under Palma's ironic burst.[16]

The perspective of the humorist derives in part from a firm posture of independence. Like other humorists, Palma championed freedom of conscience and thought. And while he basked in the broader opportunities for expression afforded by ironic humor, Palma, the "unobserved observer," scrutinized and illuminated the multifarious activities of Peruvian society—past and present—according to the free-flowing inspiration permitted by his conception of life. The precise nature of that conception or ideological stance vis-à-vis both the viceroyalty and the republic will become clear as we proceed in our analysis. A true *humorista,* Palma sought "through a realistic vision of existence . . . the exaltation of the human spirit in its free will."[17] In part, however, his recourse to humor and to irony also functioned as a defensive measure. Palma was sensitive to criticism and to his possible lack of popularity; as Jean Lamore points out, "That particular sensitivity to the criticisms and barbs of younger authors is combated by humor."[18]

In addition, the assassination of President José Balta in 1872, the Sánchez Carrión-Monteagudo affair of the same decade, and the loss of his home and library in 1881, along with other disquieting experiences, had led him to seek further refuge both in the past and in the light skepticism of humorous irony and satire. Each orientation enhanced his role as an independent spectator, relatively free from the barbs of contemporaries and from the philosophical uneasiness that would have accompanied a more serious evaluation of life's inconsistencies and incompatibilities. Of course, another motivation in the adoption of humor as the mainstay of his style and his tone relates to his avid desire to disseminate Peruvian history among his compatriots; his way of sweetening the pill, as he phrased it, so that the *pueblo* would not flee from the imprint of its past.

Few would refute that such humor is a universal and essential element of human nature. Even fewer agree as to its definition, although theories and explanations abound. Rather than enter into the labyrinthian competition, our effort will be served more fruitfully by taking advantage of Vilas's excellent work, *El humor y la novela española contemporánea,* wherein he distills and synthesizes his study of some three hundred treatises dealing with the subject.

After analyzing the word *humor,* as many others have done, noting its original usage in connection with the fluids of the body and its rise to modern employment in the eighteenth and nineteenth centuries, Vilas proceeds to lay out carefully a number of classifications of the element *humor.* The latter tends to occasion reflection and enjoys as its most important components "benevolence, talent, subtlety, tolerance, humanity, forgiveness, critical understanding; and as possible ingredients there stand out a sharpness of wit, irony, contrast, philosophical poppycock, . . . and also ingenuousness."

Vilas categorizes humor as either *humorismo* or *humoricidad*. As an attitude and philosophy, *humorismo* evidences relativity, *perspectivismo,* and skepticism, along with intuition and maturity or experience. Often, this is accompanied by melancholy, irony, and contrast. In short, "it is the maximum philosophical and aesthetic expression that humor can produce." *Humoricidad,* in contrast, constitutes the common, practical, realist aspect of humor "without the artistic, philosophic, or aesthetic uneasiness that characterizes *humorismo.* It is the funny, the jocose, the festive 'without height,' the joking, the waggish, the bantering." Its nature is determined by two basic ingredients, "the greater or lesser dose of ironic, satirical, and even sarcastic criticism with wit, and of ambition for reform; and the intentional . . . quality of the *humoricista.*" This shade of humor lacks intellectualization, generally does not stimulate deeper thought or emotional reaction, and tends to interest due to the social, economic, or political immediacy of its themes. "It is the ingredient normally indispensable in comedy, caricature, and joking."

Deriving from *humoricidad* is *comicidad,* whose most expressive configuration is comedy. This type of humor lacks serious emotion, plays with incongruities, mocks the ridiculous, and produces laughter. Vilas then highlights *ingenio,* or wit, which amounts to little more than mental juggling. It is independent and cold but can be accompanied by either *humorismo* or *humoricidad* to take on a variety of hues.

The last five categories include irony, satire, *socarronería, chiste,* and sarcasm. Vilas simplifies irony tremendously but helpfully, designating it as intentioned wit, which can derive from either good or bad aspirations. Irony borders on satire, which he terms "an inflexible, implacable, cold, offensive, insulting, didactic criticism because of its interest in reforming, educating, or correcting." Stemming from *ingenio* is *socarronería,* what Unamuno called "pure Castilian humor." It embodies irony of lesser intellectual force but of an essential subtle quality and requires witty touches and extraordinary mental quickness. The *chiste* involves only technique, no intellectual depth. It constitutes opportune but artificial wit. Sarcasm reaches the limits of humor, of which it is mostly devoid, presenting, rather, a caustic, cruel nature, "the grotesque gibe."[19]

As can be seen, humor offers a very slippery surface. Some even maintain that any attempt to encase it in a tight definition can only lead to "its own undoing" while supplying proof of a "want of a true sense of humor."[20] Nevertheless, in order to discern more distinctly the nature of Palma's humor in its diverse forms, we need a theoretical foundation like the one just provided, which I will now expand further.

Humor, especially *humorismo,* and to some degree *humoricidad,* involves a degree of sympathy on the part of the humorist. Different theorists amplify the involvement to include tolerance, generosity, love, optimism, and benevolence. Julio Casares has called humor the "supreme formula of comprehension," which is a definition of the kind of humor that finally evolved from the satire and sarcasm of the Middle Ages to the profound humanity embodied in the tone of *Don Quijote.*[21]

Being deeply human, humor incorporates a blend of the serious and the comic, the tragic and the happy. The humorist laughs, but he also cries, for he, as a human being, partakes of the same nature that so readily lends itself to his comic perspective. The plays of the Golden Age exemplify this aspect of humor.

Humor is also frequently accompanied by an ethical or moralizing air, particularly in Spanish. As Helmut Hatzfeld explains, "everyone knows that the humor reflected in the Spanish language is, above all, a humor that concerns spiritual and moral life as well as ecclesiastical institutions." Max Eastman tells us that for some, humor constitutes "not only an art, but also an ethics and a philosophy of life."[22]

Within this realm, satire and irony enter the domain of humor, intermixing and cross-pollinating in almost infinite variations and indefinable degrees. Opinions vary as to their exact relationship. David Worcester, in *The Art of Satire,* regards satire and irony as belonging to the same family and being made of the same stuff, although he specifies later in the book that "irony is a form of criticism and all irony is satirical, though not all satire is ironical." Shifting the perspective somewhat, D. C. Muecke, author of *The Compass of Irony,* avers that "irony is not essentially related to satire, and when it is related in practice it is a relationship of means to end," thus seconding Wayne C. Booth's conclusion that "irony is

used in some satire, not in all; some irony is satire, much is not."
George Meredith seems to exalt the comic spirit when he observes
that "humorist and satirist frequently hunt together as ironists in
pursuit of the grotesque, to the exclusion of the comic." Humor,
satire, and irony together pounce on human folly as their common
prey; "the Comic Spirit eyes, but does not touch it." Michael Nimetz
informs us that "throughout literary history, the encasing of satiric,
moralistic and ironic intentions within a humorous mold has been
standard procedure." Vilas categorizes irony as an element of *humorismo,* while placing satire as a limit of irony. Others differentiate
between humor and satire, relating sympathy with the one, scorn
with the other.[23]

The truth of the matter must be seen in light of the manifold hues,
shapes, and functions each of these approaches can take. Humor
may exude pure aesthetic joy. Irony may draw little, if any, mirth.
Satire may steer clear of any ironic stance. However, very frequently,
ironic comments or situations prove highly comic, while with much
regularity irony functions in the service of satire, often with a great
degree of joviality. What we have, then, are three interrelated terms
capable of independent existence but usually tapping each other for
added dimension and significance.

Now, what can we say concerning the humor of the *Tradiciones
peruanas?* First of all, Palma, rather than presenting a single signal,
offers a full spectrum of tonalities. From a central attitude that
engenders within him a tendency to detect readily in all things "the
jocose side of life," his "waggish muse" radiates in all directions.
Almost every adjective in the critic's arsenal has been or could be
applied to his humor. On the one hand, the *tradiciones* smack of
humoricidad, with an abundance of jests, jokes, frivolous asides, and
a regular light banter, an inclination to make light of everything
under the sun. As Esmeralda Gijón Zapata has said of Tirso de
Molina, his humor "allows nothing to escape which has any handle
on which to attach laughter." On the other hand, there hovers over
the *tradiciones* a veil of irony that infuses nearly all of them with
what Juan Remos terms "a subtle, penetrating humor."[24] This pervasive irony oscillates between pure *socarronería* and biting satire
and frequently evidences both spontaneous wit and substantive perspective. Indeed, perhaps more than any other single facet, Palma's
mastery of ironic constructions endows his writing with its distinctive quality. The present study tends to bear this out.

Humor lies latent in all things, but it takes the rays of a singular humorous attitude to awaken the comic potentiality therein. As Palma focused his own festive, smiling, Creole perspective on the intimacies and the surface features of Peruvian history, he enlivened them with the grade of comicity or *humorismo* they naturally elicited from him. A majority of his comments, however, are couched in a spirit of benevolent sympathy and tolerance that often renders his barbs harmless. Palma's humor breathes this aura of basic human understanding, making it less caustic in general than otherwise might be the case. The *tradiciones* merge tenderness and mordacity, cultivating "the happy doctrine of the joke that does not quite mistreat, of the irony that slides in the midst of a cascade of words that play among themselves testing hues."[25]

Nevertheless, all is not libertine laughter or sportful evocation.[26] The humor of the *Tradiciones peruanas* is designed to teach, to instruct, to motivate, and to criticize at various levels. At the most obvious, Palma wields humor as a bait to attract his countrymen to the perusal of Peruvian history. On another level, as an ironist-satirist with a sympathetic vein, he seeks to call attention to many deficiencies, follies, and injustices by evoking amusement, smiles, or scorn. It is to this level that some point as proof or justification of their perception of Palma as subversive or as antiestablishment. The question is a significant one, and I will comment on it here and then expand on it in subsequent chapters.

Over the years Ricardo Palma's works have elicited cries ranging from anti-republic to anti-Spanish, with many gradations in between. In a letter written to Vicente Barrantes in 1890 Palma called attention to Barrante's persistent allusions to his "anti-españolismo" and then interjected, "Por Dios, señor don Vicente! En mi tierra me acusan de lo contrario."[27] Principal among the latter accusers was Manuel González Prada, who, beginning in 1886, launched an energetic campaign to discredit on many fronts the preceding generation, Palma included. While belittling the latter's style, he pounded on the absence of ideas of present and future significance in the *tradición,* in essence terming it a monstrous falsification of history created by a reactionary.[28] Rufino Blanco Fombona perpetuated this view in his prologue to *Páginas libres* in 1915 and in his own work, *Grandes escritores de América,* two years later. "Palma is a Hispanizer, a retarder, a servile spirit, a man of the colonies" who seeks to preserve the memory of domination in his yearning for chains and for the whip. (Of course, Palma's irritating marginal notes in one of Blanco Fombona's books in the National Library did not help matters any.) At the opposite end of the pendulum stand Haya de la Torre, Mariátegui, Luis Alberto Sánchez, and others who underscore the critical portrayal of both the viceroyalty and the republic by the *tradicionista*. Says Mariátegui: "His gibing cheerfully gnaws at the prestige of the viceroyalty and the aristocracy. He translates the waggish discontent of the *creole demos* . . . Palma harbored a latent rancor against the reactionary aristocracy of yore."[29]

In addition to these two perspectives, there are many critics who place greatest emphasis on Palma's nationalism, lauding his exaltation of the native land. These critics tend to play down his liberalism and skepticism, sometimes intentionally, sometimes because they have not analyzed carefully enough. This variance between those who pass over his freethinking spirit and those who stress it was brought to light in 1933 on the occasion of the hundredth anniversary of his birth when a lecture by Jorge Guillermo Leguía on Palma's liberal tendencies was eliminated from the collection of papers published as a tribute to him at that time.[30]

The truth of the matter naturally draws and blends assertions from both parties, discarding their respective singleness of focus. Palma, a true mestizo, was pulled and influenced by a number of attitudes. On the one hand, he loved the colonial era for its historical and human dimension as a key antecedent to present nationality. On the other hand, he used the *tradición* to chide and to attack folly and injustice, both in the viceroyalty and among his own contemporaries. Palma was stiffly jolted by reality on many occasions. As the victim of venomous attacks in public, of "gossip, envy, everyone's looking out for himself," and as a witness of "the meanness of national life, public immorality, ingratitude, and the misunderstanding of the people," the Peruvian author had been wounded deeply in his sensitivity.[31] These experiences led to a disenchantment that manifested itself in the irony and the ironic satire that constitute such a significant component of his style and tone.

As several critics have touched on briefly and as I illustrate in detail later, the *Tradiciones peruanas* reveal to the careful reader an abundant number of between-the-lines statements that ironically and/or satirically draw comparisons between the private and public deficiencies of the viceroyalty and those of the nineteenth century. To label Palma a subversive on the basis of these allusions, however, is to employ an overly harsh and unduly connotative term. Palma's liberal, reformist, patriotic, freedom-loving stance is never placed in question. Democracy and republican independence are clearly not abandoned. However, the various power elites in Lima deserved upbraiding on many points, most of which were echoes of injustices of the colonial past. Palma's irony and satire humorously but clearly denounce these shortcomings. Nevertheless, his irony does not suggest subversion in the sense of overthrow; rather, it admonishes repentance, adherence to basic morality and wisdom, and true democratic progress.

In addition, as further manifestation of his fundamental perception of right and wrong, and despite his epicurean bent, the Peruvian author almost exclusively underscores in his anecdotes the triumph of virtue over vice or at least the punishment and the remorse associated with evil acts.

The *Diccionario de la Real Academia Española* defines *humorismo* as "estilo literario en que se hermanan la gracia con la ironía y lo alegre con lo triste." In Palma the combination of the tragic and the comic presents two exteriors. On the one hand, the anecdotes themselves depict a myriad of tragic scenes or events. These Palma attenuates in "clouds of irony," as each *tradición* flows "without shrillness, softening drama with smiles, tragedy with jests, gravity with elegance." Osvaldo Crispo Acosta has articulated it best: "In Ricardo Palma there is such a deeply rooted tendency to joke that he even seasons the toasted flesh of the Inquisitorial fires with the salt of his wit."[32]

Another angle to this blending lies in the weltanschauung of the *tradicionista*. As noted above, behind the frolicking, mischievous facade beat the heart of a man who had experienced, often very personally, the joys and discouragements of human existence. Palma scanned humanity with a knowing, sympathetic eye, maturely having opted to project a humorous ironic image throughout his works as well as in his life, that is, to stress the mirthful side of life, despite the pessimism and the mordacious invective to which the abundant ugliness of human nature could have led him. This stance, however, never materialized in the shape of a philosophical treatise. Rather, it constituted a natural, somewhat unconscious result or reaction of his particular makeup. His vocation lay elsewhere. "Palma was neither a thinker nor a philosopher." Consequently, as Miró Quesada Laos describes, "he did not explore deeply in his depictions" in the sense of an organized, systematic metaphysical scheme. The philosophic perspective was there in what Luis Avilés calls lay language, but Palma left it to his critics and his readers to extract and to articulate it.[33]

As mentioned before, Palma's humor partakes of many of the characteristics normally associated with the Creole nature, particularly in its coastal, Limean variety. In varying grades and shades both approaches to humor—Creole and Limean—embody *lisura,* satire, irony, *socarronería,* and irreverence presented in a mocking, mischievous tone. Manuel Beltroy, on the occasion of the *tradicionista*'s death, sums up the relationship in this way: "The Peruvian creole temperament, bantering and happy, sly and frivolous, epicurean and fanatical, frolicsome and versatile, found its finished, complete concretion in Palma's temperament and its most faithful expression in the 'Tradiciones Peruanas.' "[34] All this, however, took time to develop. Early *tradiciones* (in their original versions) reveal little of the subtle irony and light mocking laughter of the majority of the anecdotes. As he matured in his perspective and ability, Palma not only wrote in a more jovial and biting vein but also went back to earlier *tradiciones,* infusing them with the same spirit. The final result, as I have sought to highlight, was the merging in Palma of "wittiness, truth, goodness and poetry," the four cardinal points of humor.[35]

At this juncture we can now look closely at two key areas: the basic material of human existence upon which Palma's humor and irony operate and the techniques adopted to extract most felicitously the comic potential of that material. Constituents of the former include the Catholic religion and spiritual life; marriage; sex; literature, particularly colonial poetry; women; public life, with its plethora of officials and professionals; societal and economic phenomena; types, in an endless string from the ingenuous Indian to the lustful avaricious viceroy; and language.

The techniques or stylistic processes comprise some that are broad and many that are specific. Among those of a general nature we could best begin by signaling the overall tone or atmosphere of the *Tradiciones peruanas.* Eastman has explained, "no reputation is more secure, once it is established, than that of the national humorist or comedian."[36] Once he is known and people know what to expect from him, just the mention of his name will predispose them to laugh. The same applies to Palma and his works. Ever since the confirmation of their popularity, a mere allusion to the *tradiciones* has sufficed to stimulate in the initiated reader an anticipation or readiness for the inevitable tickling of Don Ricardo's banter. In this way the general atmosphere of the stories enhances the effectiveness of the mirth therein.

A second overarching facilitator of humor concerns the effect of the unexpected, indirect revelation of often unarticulated truths. Horace speaks of telling the truth with a laugh or with a jest, and satirists have practiced this art for centuries. Indeed, the revelation of truth without fear is a very pleasurable experience constituting "a chief source of the joy motive in popular jokes."[37] Throughout the *tradiciones,* Palma availed himself of these facts, teasing the reader's funny bone while illuminating through irony certainties often hushed in normal social intercourse. Closely aligned with this is another general approach to humor practiced by the *tradicionista,* namely, the use of sudden, surprising deviations or jolts in the logical flow and order of ideas.

In terms of specific techniques for illustrating the comic, in reference to his historical anecdotes, Palma observed that it is "la forma más que el fondo, lo que las torna populares." In order to obtain that style, as noted earlier, the author "took the greatest imaginable care." Consequently, it does not surprise us to learn that a large portion of his humor is rooted in the able maneuvering of the language. Palma is well aware of this relationship between mastery of style and humorous writing, as his own observation indicates: "Precisamente, el escritor humorista, para serlo con algún brillo y llamar sobre sí la atención, tiene que empaparse mucho de la índole del idioma y hacer serio estudio de la estructura de la frase, de la eufonía y ritmo de la palabra, etc., etc." It is true that situational humor exists, but the maximum realization of humor in the *tradiciones* clearly rests on style imbued with irony: "Finally, the style of the *Tradiciones* is the best test of Palma's humor. . . . That extremely rich prose . . . is by itself an invitation to rejoice."[38]

A panoramic overview of Palma's techniques in regard to humor renders patent this assertion. Such a scan places in bold relief comparison, metaphor, circumlocution, wordplay, the modification of set phrases and commonplaces, caricature, the presentation of types, hyperbole, the incongruent joining of words or situational and character elements, dialogue, the insertion of colloquial terms, the colloquialization of sacred things, the softening of truculent, tragic scenes through euphemism, and playing with names. Intimately and inevitably bonded to Palma's humor one also continually discovers irony, satire, and the never-distant subjective presence of the narrator.

Immediately apparent is the fact that the bearers of comicity just listed, rather than revolving in isolated orbits around the aesthetic nucleus of the *Tradiciones peruanas,* complement each other in mutual and in interrelated associations. For instance, inherent in humorous comparisons we often observe puns, caricature, metaphor, hyperbole, irony, satire, and periphrasis. Similarly, humor based on wordplay often crossbreeds with caricature, satire, irony, simile, metaphor, exaggeration, religious allusion, and surprise. The interdependencies are numerous. Like a juggler, Palma manipulates and interweaves them, achieving in the process the renowned weave that typifies what we now envision as a *"tradición peruana."*

This study will examine specific mechanisms in the stories that together so advantageously promote the pervading humor of the collection. First we will examine irony in an effort to dissect with clarity its somewhat labyrinthine intricacies. Another section will address satiric irony and general satire, to which a number of techniques are devoted. The focus of the final section will be on techniques of humor not entirely associated with irony and satire. Given Palma's visible debt to Cervantes and Quevedo, I will call attention to them frequently.

2

The Humor of Irony

"The foremost ironist of the Spanish tongue," Miguel de Unamuno calls Ricardo Palma. The statement is somewhat hyperbolic, perhaps, but it simply confirms what almost every critic of the *Tradiciones peruanas* draws attention to, namely, "the smiling irony that permeates the pages of the *tradiciones*." In much the same manner as the rays of the sun penetrate the earth's atmosphere and warm the surface below, Palma's irony gives off a glow that permeates the air of his stories, teasing and pleasing a multitude of devout readers. Irony constitutes such a distinguishing feature of Palma's works and character that one would have to agree with José Miguel Oviedo when he writes that it is "the ironic accent that makes a *tradición* a *tradición* and Palma, Palma."[1]

Depending on the personality of the writer, irony may serve as a vehicle for satire, humor, or both. In Palma irony fulfills all three missions. As the next chapter demonstrates, a fair portion of the satire of the *tradiciones* comes in the form of satiric irony. This is in connection with such techniques of humor as parody, colloquial phraseology, caricature of types, bonding of eras, exaggeration, *paráfrasis*, litotes, ingenuousness, and surprising turns and is in association with such aspects of reality as religion, politics, social and economic life and customs, literary criticism, and sexuality. In addition to the merriment of these allusions, however, Palma supplies a wealth of irony, the principal purpose of which is the simple creation of humor, "a subtle, penetrating humor" that vivifies his prose throughout. Such subtlety oscillates greatly, though, giving rise to a diversity of opinion among critics. Most stress its somewhat illusive nature—"highly subtle irony," "subtle irony," "irony so subtle that it might easily be missed by the casual reader"—to which García Calderón responds, "He almost doesn't try to be ironic. His jesting is frank."[2] The truth of the matter lies in the wide variation in difficulty of deciphering that Palma's irony presents, which in turn depends on one's awareness of the predominant spirit of the stories and their creator.

In actuality, the initiated reader finds Palma's ironic commentaries quite easy to savor, while one not so forewarned may lose the enjoyment of several observations meant to be taken with a grain of salt. Concerning another aspect of the irony of the *tradiciones*, that is, the spirit or attitude behind it, critics unanimously and correctly concur in highlighting its amiability. Jean Lamore, for instance, speaks of a general impression of "ironic lightness." Feliú Cruz, in turn, underscores "a friendly skepticism." Riva Agüero likewise perceives him as "amiably ironic," bathing his stories in a "caressing irony that . . . , in Cervantine style, augments tenderness, like a sweet lunar ray."[3]

My main point in this study, however, is that the irony of the "abuelo socarrón" is tremendously funny, constituting one of Palma's major techniques of humor.[4] What tactics he endorsed in deploying this very effective instrument of mirth will engage most of our attention. As a preface, however, it would be well to clarify some terms while looking at irony and Palma from an initially broader perspective.

General Definitions and Categories

In the most general sense rhetorical or verbal irony may be defined as "a mode of speech in which the implied attitudes or evaluation are opposed to those literally expressed."[5] D. C. Muecke terms this kind of irony "Simple Irony, in which an apparently or ostensibly true statement, serious question, valid assumption, or legitimate expectation is corrected, invalidated, or frustrated by the ironist's real meaning, by the true state of affairs, or by what actually happens." The ability to express oneself in this manner may be conceived as "an imaginative faculty related to wit, and perhaps a kind of wit in its perceptive, but not its expressive, aspect." The two certainly blend well in Palma, whose highly developed sense of irony was backed, in addition to wit, by "a well-stored memory, a widely and freely ranging mind, and . . . a high degree of sapience in matters relating to life and conduct," all qualities signaled by Muecke as characteristic of such a sense.[6]

During the nineteenth century the increasingly philosophical use of irony closely interrelated in many cases with expansion of European thought concerning skepticism, relativism, liberalism, positivism, the scientific attitude, and romanticism.[7] Curiously, although Palma partook of these currents, especially liberalism and romanticism, and later became a master of irony, the major portion of his irony manifests itself at the familiar, simple verbal level as an expression of his jocose Creole spirit and perspective, rather than in the form of a carefully worked out philosophical orientation. As I noted in Chapter 1, Palma produced no reflective philosophical treatise or collection of thoughts that guided or interpreted his creation of literature. His motivation and perspective were instead historical and aesthetic (stylistic). The jovial irony emerged to a great extent as an adjunct to those purposes and as a result of his own very distinct personality. His retreat from politics in response to some of life's problems apparently encouraged a self-protective stance of ironic humor and satire but, it seems, did not constitute a main factor in the development of that posture.

Among the many endeavors to classify verbal irony, Muecke's analysis by grades and modes has proved most enlightening and most helpful in categorizing Palma's irony. Muecke designates three grades of irony, the first "according to the degree to which the real meaning is concealed," the second "according to the kind of relationship between the ironist and the irony." Of the grades, only overt and covert have any application to the *tradiciones*. Through overt irony the reader is "meant to see the ironist's real meaning at once," which is discerned through the blatancy of the ironic contradiction or incongruity. Covert irony differs from this in that "it is intended not to be seen but rather to be detected." Discernment of the real meaning is achieved, as Quintilian taught, by knowing the character of the writer and the nature of the subject, as well as by perceiving a contradiction between an opinion and the whole text or between our prior knowledge of truth, the author's real opinion, and what is literally expressed.

Irony is characterized as impersonal, as self-disparaging, as ingénue, and as dramatized. The first mode of irony, impersonal, is distinguished by "the absence of the ironist as a person; we have only his words." Through the second mode, self-disparaging, commonly called the irony of manner, comes the character and personality of the writer, which serve as a guide as to his real meaning. We will discuss the third mode of irony, ingénue, in regard to the humor of naïveté and will note that it involves the depiction of an innocent who inadvertently reveals the flaws of those supposedly more intellectual and more cultural than he. Dramatized irony, the fourth mode, involves the presentation of situations and events perceived as ironic.[8]

Naturally, divisions such as these cannot be rigidly maintained when applied to the irony of a particular work. Boundaries often become hazy and much overlapping takes place. In the case of Palma, this is clearly evident. The irony of the *tradicionista* in regard to grades reflects both the overt and the covert. His sarcastic remarks and jocund, but obvious, exaggerations necessitate little effort on the part of the reader for comprehension. Nevertheless, a significant quantity of the *tradicionista*'s ironic style relies heavily on a knowledge of Palma's character and may pass undetected in the absence of familiarity with it. Consider the following examples, the first two of which represent overt and the second set of which represents covert degrees of irony:

> Y a tiempo que Cebada exhalaba el último aliento y que se daba por terminada la fiesta. (895)

> Resuelto, pues, a irse con sus petates a otra parte, dirigióse a la acequia de la cárcel, rompió la escarcha, lavóse cara y brazos con agua helada, pasóse los dedos a guisa de peine por la enmarañada guedeja, lanzó un regüeldo que, por el olor a azufre, se sintió en todo Pasco y veinte leguas a la redonda, y paso entre paso, cogitabundo y maltrecho llegó al sitio denominado Uliachi. (592)

> Y la cosa de ser verdad tiene, porque el libro del señor duque se imprimió en Madrid, en 1764, con permiso de la Inquisición, que a ser embustera la historieta, no la habría dejado correr en letra de molde. (299)

> El cronista que relaciona este suceso lo califica de milagro y de patente castigo del cielo. Por supuesto, que yo también pienso lo mismo. ¡Pues no faltaba más sino que saliese yo ahora descantillándome con negar la autenticidad del milagrito! (146)

In the initial example the obtrusive contrast between Cebada's execution and the word *fiesta* quickly divulges the author's actual disapproval of the scene. In the second example, Don Lesmes Pirindín's extraordinarily far-reaching belch easily alerts the reader to the narrator's skeptical, fun-loving posture. The third excerpt differs strikingly from the first two. Ostensibly frank and candid, it nevertheless seethes with ironic implications. In order to appreciate the irony, however, one must bring to mind Palma's contempt for the Inquisition, his patent awareness that putting something into print in no way guarantees its veracity, and the fact that the author himself was writing irony into a story whose very nature demands a blend of truth and imagination. The fourth example also requires detection, which is accomplished through knowledge of the skeptical character of the writer and through attention to the incongruency of tone suggested by the diminutive *milagrito*.

In regard to mode, Palma's irony comprises a mixture of both the impersonal and the self-disparaging variety. Heavily felt throughout the *tradiciones*, his narrative presence definitely constitutes a major factor in his ironic mirth. Nevertheless, in many instances the flavor of the irony is accessible to the reader without taking into account authorial nearness, although this awareness may facilitate understanding. Impersonal irony, in the first example, and self-disparaging irony, in the second and third, are represented below:

> El 24 de abril de 1814 . . . nos llegó de Cádiz en el navío Asia el batallón Talavera, compuesto de ochocientos angelitos escogidos entre lo más granado de los presidios de Ceuta, Melilla, la Carraca y otras academias de igual lustre. (900)
>
> Dios me hizo feo (y no lo digo por alabarme). (751)
>
> Ahora estoy segurísimo de que en los labios de todos mis lectores retoza esta pregunta: ¡Y bien, señor tradicionista! ¿Quién ganó el pleito? ¿El de Santiago o el de Sierrabella?
> Averígüelo Vargas. (496)

The first quotation evidences no particular narrative presence. We have the narrator's words but not the overt intrusion of his character. The text itself suffices in providing both the irony and the keys to detection. Here the principal clue resides in the internal clash in meaning between *angelitos, academias,* and *lustre* on the one hand and *presidios* on the other hand. The use of the diminutive and the addition of the word *igual* serve as further indexes by intimating a jesting tone and additional contradiction. A note of sarcasm underlies the passage. In the second and third excerpts the irony is intimately related to Palma's narrative-subjective presence and personality. His denial of irony is itself ironic. The irony of the unexpected along with the omniscience of the narrator is the feature of the third extract.

Palma's irony may be relayed through a word, a phrase, or an entire proposition. Rarely does it not afford some degree of humor. The stimulus varies, however, in the force of its impact, as the above examples show. Humorous reactions presuppose, of course, a full understanding of the irony, which, for the most part, presents little difficulty, much of the irony in the *tradiciones* being simple with a single opposition between the level of the ironist and the literal expression. Instances of more complicated irony do occur, however, entailing a more involved reconstruction of meanings.

> Atrapóme el otro día un capitancito de nacionales, muchacho sin oficio ni prebendas, que calza guantes y que es parroquiano de Broggi, y díjome:
> "¡Hombre! ¿Qué me dice usted de Ballén? Todo un doctor metido a cigarrero. ¡Encanallarse así!"
> "¿Y qué hay con eso? Trabajar es mejor que vivir del petardo, y en cuanto a lo de encanallarse, pienso que si no existe tradición profana ni sagrada que nos refiera que el diablo fue alguna vez zapatero, sastre o concejal, hayla, y muy auténtica, de que fue cigarrero en Huacho; lo que prueba, con lógica agustina, que el oficio es aristocrático, cuando el rey de los infiernos nada menos no tuvo pepita para ejercerlo.
> "¡Ah!, ésa no estaba en mi libro," murmuró el mocito. Y tomó el tole. (1443)

Under the irony lie concealed several levels of meaning. First, there is the relationship between Palma as author-narrator and the reader. Since the whole story is ironic in that the narrator is making it up while presenting it to the reader as true, the latter, in failing to apprehend the irony, falls victim to it. Second, within the story the narrator becomes a protagonist who confronts another character with irony. Unable to recognize that he has been ironically addressed, the captain joins the reader (supposing the reader missed the initial irony) as a second victim. If perchance the reader also manages to overlook the ironic tone of the narrator's words to the captain, he then qualifies as a double victim of irony.

In order to decipher the playful skepticism lurking behind the words of the major paragraph other intertwined fibers of irony must be unraveled. Our prior knowledge of the author alerts us to the invalidity of "muy auténtica" and the fallaciousness of his subsequent reasoning. Not only was he a skeptic about religion but also he himself had penned the anecdote on the legend of the cigarette vendor in Huacho. We also know to distrust the intimate historicity of a *tradición*. Furthermore, the Augustinian logic is frustated at two points: the first being that the author really does not have faith in it initially and thus is simply mocking and the second being the illogicality of ascribing regal aristocracy to the devil (in whom he does not believe anyway). The entire example demonstrates both the dispatch with which Palma's irony can be discerned and the potential for omission of possible levels of ironic play.

> En este intervalo el maestro Lucas dio en su prisión tan positivas muestras de arrepentimiento, que le valieron la merced de que se le conmutase la pena.
> Es decir, que en vez de achicharrarlo como a sacrílego, se le ahorcó muy pulcramente como a ladrón. (564)

These concluding words of "Lucas el sacrílego" offer double strands of incongruency for humorous effect. There is an obvious contradiction between *conmutar* and *ahorcar,* and there is blatant disharmony between *ahorcar* and *pulcramente,* which belies the author's true objections and playful attitude. Knowing his tenacious opposition to capital punishment enhances the irony and the humor. Concerning victims of irony, unless one takes into account the varied objects of satiric or situational irony, more often than not the only prey is the reader himself. For that reason the irony of Palma's prose is often classified as "barbless." If one adds the victims of satiric irony, however, the barbs become sharper, as noted in Chapter 1.

With these initial insights in mind, let us now embark on a broader, but still specific, scan of the principal techniques of this famed irony. We shall first consider the irony of pose, including false objectivity and self-conscious literature. Within the latter category we will touch on apparent reader interrogatives, pretended self-defense, self-praise, self-depreciation, pretended uncertainty, and feigned awareness. Second, the very important area of internal contradiction will come under scrutiny, involving stylistically signaled irony, disharmony of facts, logical contradictions, and incongruous names. A third section will deal with conflicts in beliefs. The questions of overstatement, meiosis, pretended defense, feigned praise, and pretended advice will be addressed. Ambiguity, paradox, and irony of situation will round out the analysis.

False Objectivity

Traveling a well-traversed street, a person often encounters traffic signals. In like manner the reader of the more than five hundred *tradiciones* confronts at regular intervals accounts of miracles or other extraordinary events narrated in an outwardly objective or a seemingly naive manner. That they are ebullient with ironic intention is clear to anyone well informed as to Palma's liberal, skeptical orientation. As George Umphrey correctly observes, "the ingenuous candor of many of his stories treating of miracles and superstitions cannot be taken at its face value; the alert reader is well aware of the genial skepticism permeating the apparently candid story and ingenuous comments." Discernment of the irony, however, presents fewer complications in some cases than in others, depending on the degree of authorial presence and stylistic signaling. Thus, Raúl Porras Barrenechea's comment that Palma "uses his most imperceptible irony when, like an ingenuous collector of little flowers, he tells of incredible or childish miracles" holds true more for some stories than for others.[9]

Perhaps the most detached presence of irony occurs in the account entitled "Los mosquitos de Santa Rosa," wherein the *tradicionista* recalls the saint's pact with "los alados musiquines." Except for a brief introduction and a political allusion, nowhere does one find the telltale remarks so common in other anecdotes. The second half of "El alacrán de fray Gómez" manifests a similar tone. In the second half of "El alma de fray Venancio," however, Palma inserts a couple of brief remarks more visibly suspect: "Pero a San Pedro Nolasco no hubo de parecerle bien quedarse sin lucir su gallardía en cuadros al oleo"; "El padre Antolín se quedó como es de presumirse. Cosa muy seria es esto de oír hablar a un difunto" (788). The story deals with Friar Venancio's return from the dead to assure that the money he had deposited with a merchant would be used to paint a mural for San Pedro Nolasco. In "Los ratones de fray Martín" we witness San Martín de Porras taming mice, dogs, and cats; the account is told with apparently believing enthusiasm. "Váyase, hermanito," he counseled the little mouse he had trapped,

> y diga a sus compañeros que no sean molestos ni nocivos en las celdas; que se vayan a vivir en la huerta, y que yo cuidaré de llevarles alimento cada día.
> El embajador cumplió con la embajada, y desde ese momento, la ratonil muchitanga abandonó el claustro y se trasladó a la huerta. Por supuesto que fray Martín los visitó todas las mañanas, llevando una cesta de desperdicios o provisiones, y que los pericotes acudían como llamados con campanilla. (265)

In "El virrey de los milagros" one reads of a Christ statue speaking and extending an index finger, the confirmation of the miracle lying

in the fact that "el dedo no volvió a tomar la posición primitiva."
(249) Elsewhere the narrator verifies that in Father Virrueta's picture
even "la polilla y los ratones le tienen miedo y no le hincan el diente"
(983). Frequently Palma injects such credulous remarks as "Como el
diablo nunca duerme, sucedió que . . ." (123) or "¡Y dirán que no
hay brujas!" (545). Concerning Saint Thomas's visit to Peru, the
reader is assured, given the short distance and manageable road between Calango and Lima, "no es aventurado asegurar que tuvimos
un día de huésped y bebiendo agua del Rimac a uno de los doce
queridos discípulos del Salvador. Y si esto no es para Lima un gran
título de honor, como las recientes visitas del duque de Génova y don
Carlos de Borbón, que no valga" (282).

The failure of the chroniclers to specify whether the saint's right
or left sandal was discovered amid the ash and lava unquestionably
constituted "olvido indispensable en tan sesudos escritores." The
absence of devils, spirits, and miracles in the nineteenth century
sparks the feigned ingenuousness of the concluding paragraph of "La
procesión de ánimas de San Agustín":

> Francamente, no puede ser más prosaico este siglo diecinueve en que
> vivimos. Ya no asoma el diablo por el cerrito de las Ramas, ya los duendes
> no tiran piedras ni toman las casas por asalto, ya no hay milagros ni
> apariciones de santos, y ni las ánimas del purgatorio se acuerdan de
> favorecernos siquiera con una procesioncita vergonzante. Lo dicho; con
> tanta prosa y con el descreimiento que nos han traído los masones, está
> Lima como para correr de ella. (488)

Palma himself was a Mason, having joined just before the 1860
assassination attempt on Castillo. In all of these instances our mind-
fulness of the writer's true perspective and background unlocks the
humor of irony.

Not all such ingenuous irony deals with religious events. Consider,
for instance, Palma's account of the silversmith's quest for an appropriate tree in which to hang himself (his wife having driven him
to it):

> Provisto de cuerda y sin cuidarse de escribir previamente esquelas de
> despedida, como es de moda desde la invención de los nervios y del
> romanticismo, se dirigió nuestro hombre al estanque de Santa Beatriz,
> lugar amenísimo entonces y rodeado de naranjos y otros árboles, que no
> parecía sino que estaban convidando al prójimo para colgarse de ellos y
> dar al traste con el aburrimiento y pesadumbres. Principió Román por
> pasar revista a los árboles, y a todos hallaba algún pero que ponerles. Este
> no era bastante elevado; aquél no ofrecía consistencia para soportar por

fruto el cuerpo de un tagarote como él; el otro era poco frondoso, y el de
más allá un tanto encorvado. Cuando uno se ahorca debe siquiera llevar
el consuelo de haberlo hecho a su regalado gusto.

Concerned that someone might see him at an inappropriate time,
he reasons, "No había forma de que un hombre pudiera matarse en paz."

"¡Pues sería andrómina que a lo mejor de la función, me descolgase un
transeunte importuno! Si ello, al fin, ha de ser, nada se pierde con esperar
un rato, que no llega tarde quien llega." (822-823)

Various incongruities, as well as our general knowledge of life, alert
us to the delightful irony. I refer to contrasts such as *convidar-
colgarse*, "matarse en paz," "lo mejor de la función," fickleness about
the proper tree, and the association of death and "*no llega tarde
quien llega.*" The pretended objectivity is intriguing and inviting.
Later, we learn of a change in the silversmith's wife, "cuyo carácter,
por milagro sin duda de la Divina Providencia, para quien no hay
imposibles, mejoró notablemente" (823).

The *tradición* "Cortar por lo sano" offers a very interesting example of humorous, candid irony. Corvalán has just followed,
though mistakenly, the corregidor's advice and has stabbed Father
Gonzalo seventeen times. "¡Diez y siete puñaladas! Apuñalear es. No
rebaja siquiera una el historiador Córdoba y Urrutia en sus *Tres
épocas*" (415). The unexpected preoccupation with detail startles us
and "upsets our ordinary sense of reality" as it compels "a shift in
our point of view." Employing David Worcester's terminology, we
can say that Palma, by forcing us to accept a grotesque "scale of
values in opposition to our normal scale," creates positive and negative poles between which leaps the spark of irony.[10]

Self-Conscious, Subjective Narrator

Turning to irony backed by a more evidently subjective presence,
we note a number of well-known declarations on the part of the
Peruvian author as to his neutrality or his opined belief in the tales
that he rehearses. Only with a firm understanding of Palma's actual
dubiousness can we full appreciate the irony of the narrator's words.
Consider the following examples:

No es que yo, humilde historietista y creyente a machamartillo, sea de los
que dicen que ya Dios no se ocupa en hacer milagros y que el diablo nunca
los ha hecho. (248)

> Yo, mi señora doña Prisciliana, creo a pies juntillos todo lo que en material de reliquias y de milagros refiere aquel bendito fraile chuquisaqueño. ¡Vaya si creo! (292)
>
> . . . Noé . . . que, cristianamente, debo creer y creo que fue el padre y fundador de la familia. (652)

In the background of these assertions of beliefs lurks skepticism, the knowledge of which predisposes a reader to suspect irony and to smile or to laugh accordingly. Colloquial words contribute to the intimation of the irony. Sometimes Palma ironically parodied a firmness of belief as he indirectly summed up a character's thoughts and arguments. Thus, the Franciscans supported their claim to antiquity in Peru: "Y pues lo dijo el Papa, que no puede engañarse ni engañarnos, punto en boca y san se acabó" (283).

Frequently the narrator adopts a feigned middle-of-the-road attitude concerning his material, which leads the reader to ponder certain statements in light of the jocose atmosphere or context in which they materialize. The narrator usually opts for one of two approaches in these cases: he follows Pilate's example and washes his hands, an allusion that only adds fuel to the irony and the mirth, or he phrases an antithetical expression of noninvolvement.

> Y si éste no es milagro de gran fuste, que no valga y que otro talle; pues lo que soy yo me lavo las manos como Pilatos, y pongo punto final. (250)
>
> Yo no lo niego ni lo afirmo. Puede que sí y puede que no. Tratándose de maravillas, no gasto tinta en defenerlas ni en refutarlas. (210)
>
> Y no se olvide que, por aquellos tiempos, era de pública voz y fama que, en ciertas noches, la plazuela de San Agustín era invadida por una procesión de ánimas del purgatorio con cirio en mano. Yo ni quito ni pongo; pero sospecho que con la República y el gas les hemos metido el resuello a las ánimas benditas, que se están muy mohinas y quietas en el sitio donde a su Divina Majestad plugo ponerlas. (561)

The flame of humor burns brightly on the wick of irony, composed principally of false detachment, which in itself is ironic since the narrator, in purporting objectivity on one level, is actually conveying subjectivity on another level. A classic example of such ironic neutrality occurs in "El mejor amigo . . . un perro." In the tale Errea has just taken a death leap from the bell tower of *la Merced*.

> Los maldicientes de esa época dijeron . . . (yo no lo digo, y dejo la verdad en su sitio), dijeron . . . (y no hay que meterme a mí en la danza ni llamarme cuentero, chismoso y calumniador . . .). Conque decíamos que los maldicientes dijeron . . . (y repito que no vaya alguien a incomodarse

y agarrarla conmigo) que la causa de tal suicidio fue el haber confiado Errea a su hijo político, . . . una gruesa suma perteneciente a la congregación de la O. (861)

This technique of addressing some supposed antagonist or interested party as if he were present highlights Palma's style throughout, contributing significantly to the conversational tone of the *tradiciones*. The addition of this interpersonal dimension widens the humor implicit in the style by introducing the personality of the narrator in a story-telling atmosphere. Known as self-conscious literature, this tradition receives its impetus in *Don Quijote* and culminates in two works of the eighteenth century—*Tristram Shandy* and *Jacques le fataliste*. Unfortunately unaware of the *Tradiciones peruanas*, Muecke affirms that after these two works "there was no further progress in this direction until the more radical anti-literature of the twentieth century."[11]

Self-conscious expressions vary greatly in their humor and length. Short and minimally funny are polite requests by the author for permission from the readers to relate the story—"con venia de ustedes" (629). Still brief, although richer in humor, are excerpts from "El tío Monolito" and "Los ratones de fray Martín": "Ahora, compadre lector, encienda usted un farolito" (745); "¡Ea!, no me hagan reír, que tengo partido un labio" (264). Taking advantage of the friendly ambience he has created, Palma often makes it seem in the narrative as if the reader were interrupting him in his writing.

> Allá en los tiempos en que a las campanas se las mandaba, por vía de castigo, desterradas a América . . .
> "¡Alto el fuego!" me interrumpe el lector. "¿Cómo es eso de la proscripción de campanas?"
> "Va usted a saberlo, señor mío." (1147)

This tactic comes in very handy in altering the course of the narrative and functions prominently as a means of introducing the historical sections of many stories.

> La verdad era que la ejecución se aplazaba porque acababa de morir Grano de Oro, importantísmo personaje cuyo fallecimiento bastaba para entorpecer la marcha de la justicia.
> "Pero, señor, ¿quién es Grano de Oro? ¡Yo exijo que me presente usted a Grano de Oro! ¡Yo quiero conocer a Grano de Oro! ¡Que me traigan a Grano de Oro!
> Calma, lectores míos, que un cronista no es saco de nueces para vaciarse de golpe, y como quien toma aliento, conviene abrir aquí un paréntesis para borronear un par de carillas sobre historia. (748)

This passage is loaded with irony, which is signaled by the contradiction in characterizing the executioner with the epithet *importantísimo;* by the incongruence in the words "marcha de la justicia," revealed through prior knowledge of the author's disagreement with capital punishment; by the intrusion of the *lectores* into the narrative line (highly impolite!); and by the inordinate repetition in the second paragraph. The excerpt also exemplifies a common technique of arousing tension and interest in the *tradiciones,* namely, the suspension of the narrative line. Cervantes, of course, employed it in various interrupted adventures. Palma also employed it throughout many tales, such as "Sabio como Chavarría." There, even in part three, we find him tantalizing the reader:

> "Pero hasta aquí," dirá el lector, "no sabemos quién es Chavarría. Vamos, presénteme usted a Chavarría."
> "Pues con venia de usted. Chavarría es . . . Chavarría."
> "¡Buen achaquito, compadre Cantarranas! Quedo enterado."
> "¡Vaya! Si no sé cómo decirlo. En fin, Chavarría es . . . , que lo diga por mí el *Diario de Lima,* . . . ¡Cataplum! Trátase de un perro pericotero que se exhibió en el teatro de esta ciudad de los reyes. (735)

A variation in these ironic introductions has the narrator pretending to have heard someone ask a question, which constitutes a further exploitation of the conversational posture Palma maintains throughout his prose.

> "¿Y qué virrey gobernaba entonces?"
> Paréceme oír esta pregunta, que es de estilo cuando se escucha contar algo de cuya exactitud dudan los oyentes.
> Pues, lectores míos, gobernaba el excelentísimo señor don Gabriel de Avilés y Fierro. (821)
> "¿Su nombre?"
> ¡Qué! ¿No lo han adivinado ustedes? (759)

In a further modification Palma sometimes seeks to justify a historic digression by proposing it as an appropriate activity to entertain the reader while the action of the main narrative line forges on:

> Dejemos por un rato en reposo al muerto, y mientras el sepulturero abre la zanja, fumemos un cigarrillo, charlando sobre el gobierno y la política de aquellos tiempos. (665)

> Demos tiempo al tiempo y no andemos con lilailas y recancanillas. Es decir, que mientras los amantes apuran la luna de miel para dar entrada a la de hiel, podemos echar, lector carísimo, el consabido parrafillo histórico. (726)

Mientras don Cristóbal va galopando y tragándose leguas por endiablados caminos, echaremos un párrafo de historia. (369)

Of course, irony is introduced when the narrator, with an apparently serious demeanor, suggests a separation between himself and the world he is creating, as if that world enjoys autonomy apart from the stroke of his pen. This is a fertile thought, which brings to mind not only Cervantes' amplification of reality but also works by Unamuno and Pirandello. Palma, however, avails himself of the ploy only as an adjunct to style, tone, and narrative structure and never pursues or exploits it philosophically.

Irony forces the reader to participate in the generation of the literature itself by presenting a new dimension of meaning that must be attained through close examination. Oddly enough, however, as Worcester explains, "our sense of spectatorship is greatly stimulated" and our enjoyment is increased.[12] The narrator enhances this effect of irony by reaching out and drawing the reader into his intimate circle and by ascribing thoughts and questions to the reader. The narrator even thickens the attachment in some instances by pretending to let the reader in on a special secret or some friendly advice—as if no one were present save the reader and the *tradicionista*!

Aunque nadie volvió a tener en Huacho noticias de Eduvigis ni de su amante, yo te diré, lector, en confianza, que el incendio fue un suceso casual; . . . Guárdame, lector, secreto sobre lo que acabo de confiarte, pues no quiero tomas ni damas, dimes ni diretes con mis amigos de Huacho. (696)

Pero háganse ustedes los de vista miope con esos y otros anacronismos, y ahí va *ad pedem litterae* la conseja. (912).

In a further diversification of this basic approach Palma summons the idea of creating a friend or other personage whom he can introduce into the *tradición* as a means of added or varied justification for what he wants to say. Adeodato de la Mentirola and Don Restituto fulfill the role of the Peruvian writer's counterpart exceptionally well. Palma ironically permits them to make him eat humble pie as he confesses his ignorance and meekly announces, "'Soy todo orejas, señor don Restituto. Cuénteme usted la historia de ese Pajarito.' 'Pues páseme usted los fósforos y un trabuquito. Empiezo'" (1149). In "Franciscanos y Jesuitas" the author slyly tells us that after searching everywhere to discover the cause of the sudden friendship be-

tween the two religious orders he spoke one night with Adeodato de
la Mentirola, who had previously "related" to him the story of how
the devil lost his poncho. "¡Hombre, en qué poca agua se ahoga
usted!" The reader is then convincingly informed, "Armé un cigar-
rillo, repantiguéme en la butaca, y fui todo oídos para no perder
sílaba del relato que van ustedes a conocer" (284). In another *tradición* the narrator successfully passes off as authentic an imagined
visit to a dying friend (1203).

Sharing similarities with these examples, as well as with those
previously touched on, is an excerpt from "Los pasquines del bachiller 'Pajalarga.' " There we find the partial recitation of some off-
colored verses greeted with a sudden question from a young girl, as
if she were seated on the narrator's lap: "¿Qué dijo?" His response:
"No sea usted curiosa, niña, que es vicio feo. Dijo . . . lo que dijo, y
lo que a usted no le importa saber" (153). In another story the
narrator responds to the following question from another out-of-
nowhere interlocutor: "'Pero, señor tradicionista, ¿por dónde vino,
desde Galicia a Lima, Santo Tomás?' 'Eso, ¿qué sé yo? Vayan al cielo
a preguntárselo a él. Sería por globo aerostático, a nado o *pedibus
andando*. Lo que yo afirmo, y conmigo escritores de copete, así
sagrados como profanos, es que su merced estuvo por estos trigos y
san se acabó, y no hay que gerundiarme el alma con preguntas im-
pertinentes' " (282). Humor derives in this passage from the irony of
fallacious reasoning and of spurious discussions given as true, from
the irony of pretended praise—"escritores de copete"—and from the
irony of false objectivity.

Another facet of the general irony associated with the narrator's
subjective presence concerns rhetorical questions. In the *Tradiciones
peruanas* rhetorical questions constitute a very visible stylistic technique. Once again the basic irony stems from the implication that
the author is actually interchanging information and feelings with
the reader. The function of the question varies widely. It may, for
instance, shelter "l'impression d'une fausse naiveté":[13] "¿No ha sido
siempre el diablo un tramposo de cuenta? Pues a *fullero, fullero y
medio*, ¡Qué canario!" (591). At other times the question is an atten-
tion-drawing technique like that typically employed by story-tellers.

¡Cómo! ¡Qué cosa! ¿No conoció usted a las Pantojas? ¡Chimbambolo!
¡Pues hombre, si las Pantojas han sido en Lima más conocidas que los
agujeros de los oídos! (733)

¿Qué creen ustedes que hizo Su Majestad? (984)

¿Por qué? Esto es lo que el relato popular va a explicarnos. (1073)

¿Que es filfa? Lean ustedes y se convencerán de que no chilindreo. (641)

Some questions, as Muecke explains, "may be used ironically since, while [they] can have only one answer, [their] form, the form of a question, implies the possiblility of more than one."[14] After citing poetic lines penned by a not-so-talented colonial nun, the narrator asks, "¿Qué tal la monjita?" (502). The answer is rather obvious. Of Gabriel's failure to salute respectfully the governor of Cuzco, the author queries, "Les parece a ustedes que su delito era poca garambaina?" (220). "Naturally!" we would respond. In order to confirm his theory of how a woman eventually falls for "un hombre de sedoso bigote, ojos negros, talante marcial," the author proffers this interrogative analogy: "¿A qué puerta tocan que no contesten *quién es*?" (333).

Palma sometimes used surprise as a source of humor. This may take the form in the *tradiciones* of a posed question to which is attached an unexpected comment. Thus, he wrote in "Rudamente, pulidamente, mañosamente": "Al fin, la cachaza tuvo su límite, y el marido hizo . . . una que fue sonada. ¿Perniquebró a su costilla? ¿Le rompió el bautismo a algún galán? ¡Quia!" (646). Instead, he headed for Chile. We tend to laugh because of both the surprise and the ironic conversational atmosphere that has us on the edge of our seats. As we shall observe in Chapter 3, satire may also be presented in this manner. "¿Habrá en el siglo xix, no digo pelos, sino barba entera, que para un usurero valga medio maravedí?" (102). In analogous manner the *tradicionista* derides the colonial tendency to believe any report of witchcraft. He sums up the thoughts of the people with an inquiry: "¿Bruja dijiste? ¡A la Inquisición con ella! Y la pobre negra, convicta y confesa (con auxilio de la polea) de malas artes, fue sacada a la vergüenza pública" (905).

As evinced in the previous section, Palma enjoyed taking an occasional ironic swipe at opponents of free thinking and freedom of worship. The following excerpt combines false objectivity with an interrogative stance—a fairly common blend in the style of the *tradiciones*. The irony stems from posing a question in such a way as to imply one response (lack of faith and worthiness) while actually stimulating another (belief in the nonexistence of miracles).

Cuando no había en mi tierra la plaga de radicales, masones y librepensadores, cuando todos creíamos con la fe del carbonero, ni pizca de falta hacían los milagros, y los teníamos a granel o a boca que quieres. ¿Por qué será que hoy, en que acaso convendrían para reavivar la fe, no tenemos siquiera un milagrito de pipiripao por semana? Será por algo, que yo no he de perder mi ecuanimidad averiguando lo que no me importa saber. ¿Quién me mete en esas honduras? (365; see also p. 406)

Our awareness of the author's actual support of Masons and free thought and of his skepticism about the multitude of miracles in previous generations, along with the feigned concern over preserving equanimity, aid in the confirmation and the enjoyment of irony. A like blend of deceptive questioning, detachment, and underlying skepticism informs another passage:

Ahora bien, digo yo: ¿no convienen ustedes conmigo en que en este condenado y descreído siglo xix las benditas ánimas del Purgatorio se han vuelto muy pechugonas, tramposas y sin vergüenza? Para delicadeza, las ánima[s] benditas de ha tres siglos. Hemos visto a una de estas infelices en trajines del otro mundo a éste para pagar una miserable deuda de doscientos pesos. ¿Y hoy? Mucha gente se va al otro barrio con trampa por centenares de miles y en el camino se les borra de la memoria hasta el nombre del acreedor. (345)

An interesting technique of impersonal irony concerns a pretended omission of censure. The ironist in this instance lists several negative points and then proceeds to affirm adamantly their inapplicability to the object of his irony. In "El pleito de los pulperos" Palma links this device with a question to the reader: "Eso de que la barraca fue cloaca donde pescaban, sin caña, anchoas y tiburones las sacerdotisas de Venus, zahúrda donde los escolares de Baco estudiaban a sus anchas y zaquizamí donde rodaban de lo lindo las muelas de Santa Apolonia, téngolo por chismografía y calumnia de pulperos. ¿No te parece, lector?" (741).

Several of the above excerpts substantiate the role played by exclamations in Palma's style. They, too, harbor potential for humorous irony that is often fulfilled, as in instances of pretended urging from the narrator himself or from some unseen hearer to proceed with the story: "Basta de introito. ¡Al avío y picar puntos!" (240); "Basta de algórgoras, y a tus fuelles, sacristán" (753). In some cases the reader realizes the irony when presented with a contradiction between the content of the exclamation and a later comment in the story. For example, the reader initially learns, "Gallo hubo reputado por invencible y que contaba por docenas las victorias. ¡Era un diablo el animal!" (624). Afterward we learn the deceit involved, which invalidates the initial adulation. Angel Fernando de Quirós había written more than three thousand sonnets—"¡prodigioso guarismo!" (1135). However, "verdad es que de ese piélago infinito de endecasílabos apenas podría sacarse un centenar dignos de sobrevivir a su autor," thus nullifying the intimated enthusiasm. It is also ironic that Palma assumes the role of a judge over humanity, the foibles of which he himself most likely shares. The proposed marriage between Dávalos y Ribera and the young girl offers a case in point: "Medio Lima patrocinaba a la rebelde, principalmente la gente moza, que no podía ver de buen ojo que tan linda criatura fuera propiedad de un vejestorio. ¡Pura envidia! Estos pícaros hombres son, a veces, de la condición del perro del hortelano" (601).

Besides the above formations, the humorous irony inherent in Palma's self-conscious tone materializes in five additional distinct but closely homologous patterns: pretended self-defense or justification, self-praise, self-depreciation, feigned uncertainty, and pretended unawareness. Three of these approaches are contained in the ensuing passage:

> Cumple a mi honradez de cronista declarar que poco o nada hay de mi cosecha en la conseja que va a leerse, y que ella no es más que un relato popular. Agregaré también que anda muy lejos de mi propósito herir delicadeza alguna, y que si hay prójimo a quien el cuentecillo haga cosquillas, lo dé por no escrito y san se acabó; que yo soy moro de paz y no quiero camorra con nadie, y menos con los que le metieron el resuello al mismo diablo. Ni juego ni doy barato, que no soy más que humilde ropavejero de romances. (589-590)

The self-praise of "mi honradez de cronista" clashes with the task of a *tradicionista,* who, "sobre una pequeña base de verdad" (1475), specializes in the erection of imaginary castles. The necessity of defense of self as a peacemaker is rendered suspect by the skepticism concealed behind his ostensible fear of nonexistent or nonthreatening antagonists.[15] "No soy más que humilde ropavejero de romances" exemplifies the third point—feigned humility or unimportance. Further examples of each category will help us to better envision the abundance of this type of irony in Palma's writings.

Despite widespread awareness of the fictional-historical approach taken in the *tradiciones,* Palma often has fun pretending to address himself to questioning or distrustful spectators. The double-faceted irony of the pretended self-defense technique resides in the absence of such interlocutors and in the concerned attitude of an author whose success springs from not being concerned. Galdós uses this "chronicle" device throughout the *Novelas contemporáneas*.[16]

> Y para que ustedes no digan que por mentir no pagan los cronistas alcabala, y que los obligo a que me crean bajo la fe de mi honrada palabra, copiaré lo que sobre el particular escribe el erudito señor de Mendiburu en su *Diccionario Histórico*. (425)

> Llamábase la chica Nieves Frías, y no me digan que invento nombre y apellido, pues hay mucha gente que conoció a la *individua*, y a su testimonio apelo. (898)

> Ya ven ustedes que busco autoridad en que apoyarme, para que nadie pueda decirme que miento sin temor de Dios. (525)

> Sí señor. ¿Y por qué no he de contar aventuras de un fraile que si pecó, murió arrepentido y como bueno? Vamos a ver, ¿por qué? ¡Vaya! ¡Pues no faltaba más! Cronista soy, y allá donde pesco una agudeza, a plaza la saco; que en mi derecho estoy y no cobro alcabala para ejercerlo. (896)

> ¿Quién fue el padre del infante? ¡Misterio! Nosotros no hemos de repetir los decires de la maledicencia o de la calumnia. (678)

Self-praise becomes ironical, first, when what the narrator commends does not exist or fails to materialize, or second, when it is determined that the narrator is simply putting on a show of ingenuous self-applause for the purpose of arousing delight in the "lector amigo." The latter ploy generally prevails in the *Tradiciones peruanas*, except when Palma depicts his naïveté as a youth.

> Ello es que di en la flor de mirar por encima del hombro a los demás escolares, que, según mis barruntos, no podían ser sino animalitos de orejas largas y puntiagudas, comparados conmigo que sabía tanto como Chavarría. (734)

> Y aquí pongo punto, pues me parece que he dicho algo y que me he lucido en este ramo de la historia cafetuna. (735)

> Parece que me explico, picarillas, y que soy lo que se llama un cronista galante. (1032)

> Según mi leal saber y entender, saco en limpio que . . . (632)

More than one kind of irony often enriches the banter of a passage. In the second example, for instance, the solemnity of *historia* clashes mirthfully with the lightness of the invented term *cafetuna*, while in the third excerpt the suggested wink at the *limeñas* also contributes to our enjoyment.

As a method of blaming by praise, self-depreciation has been around since the days of Socrates, who, according to Quintilian, "was called an ironist because he assumed the role of an ignorant man lost in wonder at the wisdom of others."[17] This approach can be found in Cicero and in Lucian and as early as 1548 in English in association with the term *irony*. Norman Knox explains the several ways in which self-depreciation may function:

> It may be joined to explicit praise of another object and the audience be meant to reverse both judgments, thereby elevating the ironist and depressing his object; or the explicit praise may disappear, the audience being expected to find it implicit in the comparison suggested by the ironist's self-depreciation, both explicit and implicit judgments still to be reversed; or the ironist's self-depreciation may not be reversed to his credit at all, the audience taking his modesty as nothing more than a device of the irony.[18]

Although the narrator's feigned humility is clearly seen as a technique of irony, he definitely means it to be reversed in his favor, at least to some degree, given the transparency of the irony. In cases of satiric irony, though somewhat infrequently, his self-depreciation is accompanied by praise of a group or class of people; the reader is expected to perceive the irony of both. Normally, however, Palma's modesty appears alone, as a further manifestation of his overall ironic personality.

We observed above the manner in which Palma created a character who, while belittling him as narrator, provides the meat of the story. The wealth of knowledge and research evidenced in the *tradiciones* belies responses such as "Confieso mi ignorancia y ruégole que me ilustre" (912) or criticisms such as in the statement "No he cuidado de informarme, que así soy yo de desidioso . . ." (484). In most instances the discredit is conveyed in just a few words, one of which is often modified with a diminutive suffix: "escritorzuelo de poco más o menos" (1201), "humilde historietista" (248), "mi pobrecita tradición histórica" (895), "este articulejo" (1118), "humilde ropavejero de romances" (590), "un papanatas como yo" (637). The mastery of Palma's style totally invalidates the modesty of the reference in "Un Maquiavelo criollo" to "mi lacónico y corriente estilo" (1149). Amusing irony underlies the narrator's inability to remember a girl's name in "De comó desbanqué a un rival," especially in light of several preceding paragraphs of unbridled praise: "¡Vaya una memoria flaca la mía! Después de haberla querido tanto, salgo ahora con que ni del santo de su nombre me acuerdo" (1438).

In a corollary posture of self-depreciation, with which it some-times overlaps, the narrator regularly voices ignorance or uncertainty concerning various matters. If the apparent uncertainty involves a sincere lack of data, the remark may not prove funny. Customarily, however, an element of irony enters in. The story entitled "Quizá quiero, quizá no quiero" closes with a statement of inability or un-certainty that in its exaggerated prudery discloses irony:

> "Lo que sí puedo afirmar con juramento es que . . . andando los tiempos, debió doña Beatriz humanizarse con su marido, porque . . . , porque . . . , no sé cómo decirlo, ¡qué demonche! Sancha, Sancha, si no bebes vino, ¿de qué es esa mancha? Ella dejó prole . . ." conque . . . chocolate que no tiñe . . ." (40)

Also intended for humor and immediate inversion of meaning is this depiction of the citizens of Huacho: "Ellos, por arte de birlibirloque o con ayuda de los polvos de pirlimpimpim, *que no sabemos se vendan en la botica*, transformaban un róbalo en corvina y aprove-chaban la cáscara de la naranja para hacer naranjas hechizas" (789; italics mine).

In "Desdichas de Pirindín" the reader follows the protagonist into a tavern where he calls for "una botella, no sé si de catalán o de Cariñena" (591). The irony is based in the implication that Palma, in re-creating a possibly imaginary scene from 1750, actually had such detailed knowledge as to be able to declare affirmatively that the liquor was of either one brand or the other. The allusion subtly supplies verisimilitude to the tale. A like effect occurs in a statement from "Refranero limeño": "Tenía Nuestro Señor, cuando peregrin-aba por este valle de lágrimas, no sé qué asuntillo por arreglar con el Cabildo de Camaná, y pian piano, montados sobre la cruz de los calzones, . . . él y San Pedro emprendieron la caminata" (1187). Similarly, when it is certified that Venancio's soul "vino del otro mundo, no sé si en coche, navío o *pedibus andando*" (786), the ironic implication is that one of the three choices must be true and that the narrator adheres to that belief.

The rather obvious irony of another declaration, "mis *Anales de la Inquisición de Lima*, librejo que escribí y publiqué no recuerdo cuándo ni cómo" (444), partakes of both ignorance and self-depreciation. In the following excerpts Palma expects the reader to reverse the explicit meaning, ascribing to him breadth and depth of knowledge in the process: "pronunció el siguiente *speech*, maldición, apóstrofe o lo que sea" (592); "en la Constitución reza escrito no sé qué artículo o paparrucha sobre inviolabilidad del hogar doméstico" (548).

In a tactic that might best be called the "absent-minded-author" ploy the Peruvian writer sprinkles his stories with supposedly sudden, unplanned awakenings or realizations. This may take place at the end of an introduction, a digression, or an anecdote.

> Y aquí noto que, habiéndome propuesto sólo hablar de los ratones sujetos a la jurisdicción de fray Martín, el santo se me estaba yendo al cielo. Punto con el introito y al grano, digo, a los ratones. (264)

> ¡Ah! Me olvidaba de decir a ustedes el nombre del capitancito que tan sutilmente protestó contra los despejos. (1041)

> La casa que fabricó en la calle de . . . (¡casi se me escapa!). (803).

In every case the idea expressed is contradicted by the conspicuously well-worked structure of each *tradición*. Other remarks portray the narrator having to contain himself in his exuberance: "Con saya y manto una limeña se parecía a otra como dos gotas de rocío o como dos violetas, y déjome de frasear y pongo punto, que no sé hasta dónde me llevarían las comparaciones poéticas" (165). Feigned unawareness takes on the humor of situational irony in the case of Francisco de Carbajal, who, having hung a lady who would not control her tongue, addressed her cadaver with these words: "¡Cuerpo de tal, comadre cotorrita, que si usted no escarmienta de ésta, yo no sé lo que me haga!" (79).

Internal Contradiction

A contradiction of facts abets the humor in the *Tradiciones peruanas*. A bonanza of irony is due to the evidence of internal contradiction, as noted earlier. The brief discussion that follows exemplifies internal contradictions found in the *Tradiciones peruanas*. Contradiction often takes the form of disharmony between style and content, what Muecke calls a "divergence in fact from the stylistic level appropriate to the ironist's subject or his ostensible meaning."[19] It may also involve a discrepancy of facts within the work or a logical contradiction. For example, a miracle constitutes an extraordinary event manifesting godly power and accompanied by great solemnity; among believers its report would logically be relayed with a tone of soberness tinged in awe, gratitude, reverent exultance, and humility.

Whereas the *tradiciones* recount a number of supernatural occurrences, the style in which they are narrated stands at odds with the contextual material, suggesting some other meaning or feeling than that ostensibly portrayed. We will encounter this phenomenon of humor when we discuss the relationship between satire and the vernacular.

Indeed, the stylistic warning signal that most often tips off the reader is a shift to the colloquial in the form of a diminutive, an augmentative, a lexical play, trade or fashion terminology, or popular words and phrases. A deceptive objectivity or credulity is also often present. Consider, for example, this excerpt concerning Saint Thomas's visit to Peru: "Los peruleros no podíamos quedarnos atrás en lo de la evangélica visita. Pues no faltaba otra cosa sino que, hallándose Santo Tomás de tertulia por la vecindad, no hubiera hecho ascos o andado con melindres para venir a soltar una cana por esta su casa del Perú" (281). In the absence of the everyday phraseology some question might arise as to authorial attitude; with this type of phraseology, the effect is pure comicity. Later, in the same story, the narrator reacts to Saint Thomas's size fourteen sandal: "¡Varajolines! ¡Y qué pata!" (282).

A similar mode of expression pervades "El virrey de los milagros" and the initial portion of "Los ratones de fray Martín." In the first tale the reader discovers to his delight that "apariciones de almas de la otra vida . . . venían a dar su paseíto por estos andurriales" and that "estuvieron de moda las maravillas y prodigios en estos reinos del Perú" (248). Likewise, it is not to be wondered at that "los milagros anduviesen bobos y a mantas" (249). That the widow's petition weighed in at a value of one thousand pesos "era caso de Inquisición o milagro de tomo y lomo" (250). The narrator adds, "Paréceme que el milagro no es anca de rana." In the second story the reader finds fray Martín "optando por la carrera de santo, que en esos tiempos era una profesión como otra cualquiera" (264). Both in life and in death he performed "milagros por mayor" and it is said that "el prior de los dominicos tuvo que prohibirle que siguiera milagreando (dispénsenme el verbo)." After the report of the miracle with the suspended bricklayer, the narrator states, "¿Buenazo el milagrito, eh? Pues donde hay bueno, hay mejor."

Detection of the irony of "El alacrán de fray Gómez" follows a similar pattern. After narrating a pair of wonders, the *tradicionista* quips, "Me parece que estos dos milagritos . . . no son paja picada"

(211). The technique may even filter into a character's words, as in the case of the greedy priest speaking to the candid Indian, " '¿Tanto, taita?' '¿Y te parece poca *mamada* esa de ir al cielo sin chamuscarse ni una pestaña en el purgatorio?' " (1148).

Tonal-contextual discord need not always deal with religious matters, as we have seen in the case of the man who was searching for just the right tree from which to hang himself (see section on false objectivity). The same type of humor derives from such incongruent assertions as "sentando plaza de mendigo" (823) or as receiving a worthless, faded cape "por légitima herencia, pasando de padres a hijos durante tres generaciones" (513). Repetition may serve as a telltale sign of irony: "creo a pies juntillas . . . ¡Vaya si creo!" (292). Repetition also interacts well with exaggeration. Thus, Saint Thomas's sandal "hizo en Lima muchos, muchísimos milagros" (282). Prior to the devil's visit to Ica "los iqueños eran . . . felices, muy felices, archifelices" (914).

Irony belied by the contradiction of facts within a work also supplies substantial mirth in the *tradiciones*. Brevity (often involving one word) typifies most of these allusions, thus alerting the reader not to miss subsurface meanings. Take, for instance, the word *alhaja* when it is used to describe a thief or an antagonist: "era el niño una alhaja de las que el diablo empeñó y no sacó" (1184). "Los endiablados" were "los *héroes* de esta conseja" (1073; italics mine). A jewelry metaphor also characterizes cousins ironically: "Los tales dijes suelen ser una calamidad" (1202). The dishonest *corregidor* of Andahuailas cheated the Indians out of "la *friolera* de veinte mil duros" (638; italics mine). In connection with a gigantic turnip the reader understands, "¡Digo si sería pigricia el rabanito!" (524). Two men beating each other with sticks "se estaban suavizando el cordobán a garrotazos" (914). The residents of Huacho became victims of this type of irony with the announcement that "un fraile de muchas campanillas, y traído al propósito de Lima" (789) was on his way. It was, of course, Father Samamé, who almost always found himself "preso en la cárcel del convento y suspenso en el ejercicio de sus funciones sacerdotales."

A logical contradiction occurs, for example, in "La misa negra," where "la abuelita" relates her miraculous healing at the hands of Ña San Diego: "A mí me sanó de dolor de muelas con sólo ponerse una hora en oración mental y aplicarme a la cara un huesecito, no sé si de San Fausto, San Saturnino, San Teófilo, San Julián, San Acriano o

San Sebastián, que de los huesos de tales santos envió el Papa un cargamento de regalo a la catedral de Lima" (833). Bony saints! A combination of dissembled naïveté and weird logic emerges in Palma's description of a witch at work: "La vieja, que en este momento se ocupaba de clavetear con alfileres un muñequito de trapo, dentro del cual había puesto, a guisa de alba, un trozo de rabo de lagartija, abandonó *tan interesante faena*" (284-285; italics mine). In another *tradición* Laurencio Silva, wounded in battle, asked the doctor if he would die. The doctor responds, "Lo que es morir, me parece que no; pero tiene usted lo preciso para pasar algunos meses bien *divertido*" (998).

Several names and nicknames embody glaring contrasts to surrounding contextual information. Many display largely humorous intent, and frequently irony emerges through authorial commentary that contradicts the connotations of the name—"Valentín Quesada, con agravio de su nombre de pila que lo comprometía a ser valiente, casi murió del susto" (1064). The author may even signal the irony: "hay nombres que parecen una ironía, y uno de ellos era el del vecino Fortunato, que bien podía, en punto a femeniles conquistas, pasar por el más infortunado de los mortales" (729). Similarly, Félix, "lejos de ser feliz, como su nombre auguraba, en la primera escaramuza dio posada en la barriga a una bala vivanquista" (1104).

In these cases we might best speak of paronomastic irony—Valentín and *valiente,* Fortunato and *infortunado,* Félix and *feliz.* Appellative irony also underscores the portrayal of Agustín de Jáuregui, "(apellido que, en vascuence, significa *demasiado señor*)" (686-687). After cruelly executing Tupac-Amaru, Agustín de Jáuregui himself succumbed, victim of a bowl of poisoned cherries. Curiously, a brigantine carried the blustering name *El gran poder de Dios.* The ship, however, "no estuvo a la altura fanfarrónica de su nombre, pues se rindió sin oponer más resistencia que la que opone una pulga a los dedos pulgares" (936).

Physical characteristics may also be intimated in a name by means of ironic contrast wherein, once again, we are forced to reject the immediate implications of the appellative in favor of an opposite or distinct interpretation. Doña Ninfa, for instance, rather than being an attractive young woman, is an old servant who watches over Don Honorio's daughters (807). In "El niño llorón" one discovers that Doña Pulqueria, with a name derived from the word in Latin for beauty—*pulcer*[20]—is presented as "una vieja, . . . con correa de la

Orden Tercera. . . . ¡Mucha plepa era doña Pulqueria!" (451). The executioner's nickname, Grano de Oro, likewise elicits a humorous response, for, along with his career, he is "un negrito casi enano, regordete y patizambo, gran bebedor e insigne guitarrista" (749).

Certain titles or subtitles of the *Tradiciones* adumbrate humor due to textual incongruities. Such disharmony occurs in the tale "Un predicador de lujo," which describes Father Samamé; in "Dos palomitas sin hiel," which depicts the enraged feud between Doña Catalina and Doña Francisca; and in "Mosquita muerta," in which the viceroy starts out seemingly feeble and ends up energetic, honorable, and just.

Conflict in Beliefs

Besides the techniques of irony listed above, and often in combination with these, we are also alerted to ironic intention "whenever we notice an unmistakable conflict between the beliefs expressed and the beliefs we hold and *suspect the author of holding.*"[21] Interrelated sign posts include illogicality, fallacious argument, declaration of known errors, and misrepresentation or false statement, as "when one asserts what is known to be false or denies what is known to be true and relies upon the reader's or listener's prior knowledge for the contradiction." Praise-to-blame and blame-to-praise also may be categorized with this group.[22]

As the reader will recall, many instances of false objectivity and subjective presence succumb to translation by this means. As an example, "convengamos en que hay peligro en cenar queso porque se expone el prójimo a convertirse en trampa para cazar ratones" (526) is offered with a poker face but we laugh, discerning the irony through the fallacious reasoning or, equivalently, through the conflict between the general knowledge of the reader and of the author and what is said. The same holds true when Palma deems *El Comercio,* a Lima daily, an "irrecusable documento" (1118). False reasoning constitutes the irony of a passage from Lope de Aguirre's letter to Phillip II: "*La vida de los frailes es tan áspera, que cada uno tiene, por cilicio y penitencia, media docena de mozas*" (896). Alluding to the interesting custom of housing a girl with her possible mate for three months so she can be tested, the author of "Coronguinos" quips, "¡Vamos! Si cuando yo digo que las buenas costumbres desaparecen sólo por ser buenas" (1143-1144). The irony, comprehended by the reader through knowledge of Palma's support of basic societal constraints, combines with sexual reference for humorous impact.

In one story the narrator cites "los diez mandamientos de la mujer casada" and afterward explains, "Estos diez mandamientos se encierran en la cajita de los polvos de arroz y se leen cada día hasta aprenderlos de memoria" (821). We already know that this is not the case, but it is funny nonetheless. Other statements invalidated by our general understanding or by their illogicality or their obvious falseness include:

> El doctor me aseguró que de un momento a otro las liaba el enfermo, y cuando él fulmina una sentencia, no hay más que, sin pérdida de minuto, comprar mortaja y cajón. (1203)

> En cuanto a obras públicas, parece que ambos virreyes sólo proyectaron una: adoquinar la *vía láctea*. (208)

> Años llevaba ya nuestra *macuita* en pacífica posesión de un trono tan real como el de la reina Pintiquiniestra. (904)

> Pero con las cortinas, ya lo he dicho, no transijo, aunque me aspen como a San Bartolomé o achicharren como a San Lorenzo. (1436)

In the last sentence the *tradicionista* affirms his aversion to the custom of adorning doors and balconies with curtains during processions. The statement harbors irony not only in the misrepresentation (through exaggeration) of the true degree of his feelings but also in the facetious linkage of himself—an avowed satiric ironist of the saints—with religious martyrs. This exerpt, in addition to many others, exemplifies once again the potential role of hyperbole in the interpretation of irony.

To conclude the discussion of this aspect of irony I turn first to an excerpt from "Un virrey y un Arzobispo."

> ¡Pícara sociedad que ha dado en la maldita fiebre de combatir las preocupaciones y errores del pasado! ¡Perversa raza humana, que tiende a la libertad y al progreso, y que en su roja bandera lleva impreso el imperativo de la civilización. ¡Adelante! ¡Adelante! (566-567).

Here the *tradiciones* yield a classic example of the blame-to-praise technique, fortified by burlesque and by sarcasm. Tipped off by the conflict in beliefs, we reconstruct the meaning on the level of the ironist—praise be to progress and to civilization! Sometimes the irony is concealed in the connotation, as when the reader is informed that in 1568, "año en que hubo peste de langostas, nos cayeron como llovidos de las nubes los jesuitas" (283). The phrase "llovidos de las nubes" normally connotes something positive. Here, however, our knowledge of the author's prejudices awakens us to the irony, which is supported by the implied analogy with locusts.

Almost any exaggeration smacks of irony because it means something different than that explicitly expressed. Although hyperbole need not always submit to satire, in Palma it normally does to some degree. Even though we know irony is intended and that the affirmation conveyed is not designed for full digestion, nevertheless an air of light ridicule pervades. Amused reflection is the result. Consider, for instance, Palma's reference to Garcilaso's poetic lines on the desirability of "la fruta del cercado ajeno":

> "Estos dos versecitos han hecho más víctimas que el cólera morbo; porque nosotros los pícaros hombres, a fuerza de oírlos repetir, nos imaginamos que ha de ser verdad evangélica aquello de que el bien ajeno es manjar apetitoso, y del que podemos darnos un atracón sin necesidad de pagar bula." (127)

Though we reject the surface meaning in its inflated state, recognizing and savoring the humorous aim, the moral remains, evoking smiles at the expense of the male population. An analogous pattern prevails in the ensuing examples:

> ¡Cuando yo digo que las mujeres son capaces de sacar polvo debajo del agua y de contarle los pelos al diablo! (166)

> Creo que el que se halla con el crucífero a la cabecera, y ve en el cuarto a la consorte cuchicheando con el primo, se va de patitas al infierno. No hay remedio. Ese infeliz tiene que morir renegando y . . . ¡Abur, salvación! (1203)

> The viceroy to *Ño Veintemil*: ¡Hombre! ¡Para paternidades estamos! ¡Buen zagalón de hijo voy a echarme encima! (668)

In his *Ethics* Aristotle hardened the distinctions between boastful exaggeration, on the one hand, and the avowal of less than one intends, on the other hand. Much later, at the beginning of the English classical period (sixteenth century), the rhetorics regularly discussed understatement by the terms *litotes* and *meiosis* or *diminution*. Toward the end of that century the term *irony* began to be applied to understatement and by the "early eighteenth century [understatement] seems to have been accepted as a standard ironic device"; so is it understood today.[23] As opposed to the abundant irony that implies the opposite of what is said, meiosis means "what it says, but it says only part of what it means." It "leads in the right direction but does not go far along the way." Like other brands of irony, meiosis works by implication, obligating the audience "to keep a sharp eye out for the whole or the hidden meaning."[24]

Palma employed meiosis from time to time, in addition to the related tactic of litotes. A few examples will suffice to illuminate the device. During the colonial era relatives often intermarried, which led to debilitating consequences for descendents. As the narrator notes, "nuestros abuelos andaban atrasaditos en fisiología" (1202). An allusion to his childhood also employs understatement: "Ahora, . . . voy a sacar a luz un cuentecito que oí, muchas veces cuando era muchacho . . . ¡y ya ha llovido de entonces para acá!" (629). In a marvelous example of meiosis Palma has the devil respond to a girl's plea to intervene in a fight in these words: "Yo no soy de esta parroquia" (914). The girl's initial belief that she is speaking to the Savior confers an added layer of irony to the answer.

Pretended defense normally falls into the category of satire and may call on false statements, on fallacious reasoning, and on internal contradiction as needed. Jonathan Swift makes pretended defense a favorite and deadly weapon.[25] Elijah wields it masterfully to the detriment of the priests of Baal. We have encountered ironic defense already in this chapter. Recall, for example, Palma's several justifications of self, his feigned defense of Friar Martín's choice of career, and his support for the miracle in "El virrey de los milagros." In "Fray Juan sin miedo" Palma treats us to another example: "Agrega la *tradición* que *Juan Sin Miedo* cambió este nombre por el de *Juan del Susto;* y si no miente, *que mentir no puede* [italics mine], el ilustre cronista padre Vázquez, . . . alcanzó nuestro lego a morir en olor de santidad" (379). Here, as in several instances of political satire presented in Chapter 3, pretended defense in the *tradiciones* borders on and often spills over into dissembled praise.

During the English Augustan period blame-by-praise was the most common type of irony in literature. Swift is the virtuoso of this type of irony of controversy. As noted earlier, feigned praise often accompanies Socratic self-depreciation.[26] In the *tradiciones* this tactic makes its most frequent appearance in the form of applause for desirable qualities understood to be lacking and in connection with ambiguity. With additional stress feigned praise can be transformed into sarcasm. Usually its detection requires little exertion since the contextual conflicts, the discrepancies with general beliefs and knowledge, or the misrepresentations are obvious.

The irony of the opening paragraph of "Un caballero de hábito" is clear:

> Ello es lo cierto que si me echara a averiguar el origen de muchos de los pergaminos de nobleza que, en este Perú, acordaron los monarcas de Castilla a sus leales vasallos, habría de sacar a plaza inmundicias de tanta magnitud que obligarían al pulcro lector a taparse las narices con el pañuelo. (802)

Ensuing words immediately reveal the irony of the word *leales*. The irony of the term *pulcro* comes into play with our awareness of human beings.

In "Un despejo de Acho" subsequent incongruous reactions betray the real meaning of the adjective—*respetable*—in the phrase "el respetable público" (1041). The same effect occurs in connection with the word *ilustre* (448), applied to Miguel de Santiago, the artist who thrust a spear into his subject so he would better portray the agony of Christ. Our own knowledge plus familiarity with Palma's jocular temperament render suspect the author's ostensible admiration for sacristans and for acolytes who dare to face the foreboding atmosphere of a church at night: "De mí sé decir que nada ha producido en mi espíritu una impresión más sombría y solemne a la vez, y que por ello tengo a los sacristanes y monaguillos en opinión, no diré de santos, sino de ser los hombres de más hígados de la cristiandad. ¡Me río yo de los bravos de la Independencia!" (561).

A highly interesting passage regarding such contradiction comes from "El ombligo de nuestro padre Adán":

> Quépanos, sí, a los católicos hijos de esta tres veces coronada ciudad de los reyes del Perú la satisfacción de decir a boca llena, y en encomio de nuestra religiosidad católica-apostólica-romana que el único limeño a quien la Inquisición tuvo el gusto de achicharrar fue el bachiller Castillo, y aun éste no fue limeño puro, sino retoño de portugueses. (258)

This is pretended pride at its best. First of all, that Lima produced (and then "fried") only one Juan del Castillo, whose witty, joyful personality closely paralleled Ricardo Palma's, and whose "sin" was as weighty as a pin cushion, rather than praiseworthy, casts a very negative shadow on the true religiosity of the citizens of Lima. The parody in "católica-apostólica-romana," the juxtaposition of *gusto* and *achicharrar,* and the inordinate stress on lineage enhance and illuminate the ironic pose.

An extension of the self-conscious tone of the *tradiciones* leads to the irony of pretended advice.

(Alguien me ha contado que como el diablo no puede decir ¡adiós!, es invención suya la palabra ¡abur! con que muchos acostumbran despedirse. Así, tengan ustedes por sospechoso al que diga ¡abur!, y por lo que *potest,* échenle una rociada de agua bendita.) ¡Abur! ¡Abur! (592)

The tongue-in-cheek waggery of this passage is masterful. A combination of feigned detachment, fallacious reasoning, and reader's awareness of the author's character suggests the irony, which is heightened when the narrator himself bids farewell with the suspicious word, thus inverting the credibility of his counsel and making the candid reader even more the victim of irony.

Other instances find the *tradicionista* playing with the reader: "Hasta el nombre del bargantín, armado con seis cañoncitos, era una pura andaluzada, como que se llamaba (agáchate, lector, que viene la bala fría), se llamaba . . . (déjenme tomar resuello), se llamaba ¡¡*El gran poder de Dios!!*" (935). The device of delayed revelation richly moistened in the irony of subjective presence and engaging advice sweeten the reaction of the reader. Palma finalizes the story "Dos millones" by facetiously recommending that the reader embark in search of the treasure buried by Robertson: "Conque así, lectores míos, buen ánimo, fe en Dios y a las Marianas, sin más equipaje" (1034).

Ambiguity

Some of Palma's ironic statements evoke this condition, as, for example, when he speaks of his tale as "auténtica y sencilla" (664). Is it or isn't it? Or is Palma's tale authentic in the sense of being a genuine product of his hand? The involvement delights us. A priest's sly exploitation of ignorant Indians brings this comment: "Convendrá el lector conmigo en que el presbiteroide era hombre que *sabía más que Lepe, Lepijo y su hijo,* y que no era ningún abogado Fernández, de quien dice el refrán que ganaba los pleitos chicos y perdía los grandes" (1148). Yes and no! The priest is sharp as to the ways of the world, but his manner merits only reprimand. Thus, the praise is and isn't warranted.

Paradox

Seemingly contradictory and yet true statements also come under the heading of irony. Palma draws on paradox from time to time, always for humorous effect. Take, for example, Don Restituto's sagacious insights:

> ". . . déjese usted de filosofía palabrera y aténgase a mi regla, que es la de que con sólo pautas torcidas se hacen renglones derechos, y que la línea curva es la más corta. Más seguro se llega rodeando, que por el atajo. Esa es mi matemática social, y tente, perro."
>
> "Pero, señor mío, ¿está usted loco?"
>
> Así hubiera muchos locos como yo y menos cuerdos como usted, y el mundo caminaría mejor." (1149)

Although apparently opposed to common sense, his comments, once understood, take on a viable meaning, namely, to let one who insults others pursue his inclination and sooner or later his action will turn to his detriment, leaving those offended free and avenged. In another paradox one elderly man was "capaz por lo feo de dar un espanto al mismo miedo" (241). An excerpt from a poem concerning the Cayetanas also merits consideration: "No son hombres ni mujeres, / Más pelonas / Que las ranas, / Candidonas / Cayetanas" (513). Cayetanas were girls belonging to a monastery whose members were ridiculed for their absurd dress and hair. Likening bachelors and communists also recommends some contradiction to the reader until placed in context—both like to share in others' "possessions" (123).

Irony of Situation

In order to have an ironic situation there must be both a dupe or victim confidently imperceptive of the circumstances and an observer with a sense of irony. Whether the situation is actual or imagined does not matter since we are now "looking at irony from the observer's not the ironist's point of view." Muecke distinguishes five simple kinds of ironic situations, only three of which concern us here—irony of simple incongruity, irony of events, and dramatic irony.[27]

The first involves only a minimum of irony, with no complication through presentation of action. A good example is the juxtaposition of a hovel and a castle. Irony of simple incongruity surfaces irregularly in the *Tradiciones peruanas* and we will limit ourselves to two examples here. One example is found in "Lope de Aguirre, el traidor," the fiend on whose coat of arms appears the motto "*Piérdase todo, sálvese la honra*" (74). Another instance concerns stormy rows among nuns during elections to chapters: "En los conventos de monjas eran más reñidos, si cabe, los capítulos, y húbolos en que las mansas ovejitas del Señor se arañaron de lo lindo y sin misericordia. En la Encarnación, por ejemplo, vióse una monja, la madre Frías, que mató a otra a puñaladas" (299).

In the category referred to as the irony of events the ironic incongruity lies between the expectation and the event. What we expect and what consequences seem to favor somehow becomes frustrated and reversed. We encounter what we have set out to avoid. The anecdotal nature of the *tradiciones* affords many humorous cases in point. In 1651 Lima found itself accosted by a nocturnal apparition in the form of a shrouded corpse. Feeling his oats, a braggart boasted that he would have a bell attached to the spirit by morning. "Venida la mañana, lo encontraron privado de sentido bajo el nicho de la Virgen, y vuelto en sí, juró y perjuró que el fantasma era alma en pena en toda regla" (395). An ironic reversal befell Juan de Porras as well. While on the way to assassinate Pizarro, he bragged, standing in a puddle: "¡Caracoles! ¡Ahógueme yo en tan poca agua!" (84). As fate would have it, months later, when his horse fell into a puddle, Porras was trapped underneath and drowned. There is also a bit of humor in Don Geripundio's dying one night, having been smothered by a mouse going down his throat, an eventuality he certainly did not entertain as he crawled into his bed.

The tale entitled "Franciscanos y Jesuitas" accommodates both irony of events and dramatic irony, explaining in terms of irony the origin of an attitude. As the tale reads, late one afternoon a sorceress and her four not-so-saintly daughters notice the arrival of three Franciscans, who are on their way to Cuzco. The sorceress entertains the Franciscans with an intoxicating beverage while her daughters dance. When the liquor takes effect one of the friars jumps up, grabs a partner, and begins to dance, exclaiming, "¡Ea, muchachas! También el santo rey David echaba una cana al aire, que en el danzar no hay peligro si la intención no es libidinosa" (285). Another friar soon joins him, shouting: "¡Escobille, padre maestro, escobille como yo!" With a minimum of irony thus already in operation, the plot thickens. Three Jesuits are seen approaching, a twist in the tale that constitutes irony of events. The Franciscans conceal themselves and the scene repeats itself: the Jesuits drink, lose their solemnity, and begin to dance with the girls, shouting "¡Viva Jesús!" At this point dramatic irony intercedes, since the reader foresees what is oblivious to the Jesuits, and in one sense even to the hiding Franciscans. As expected, when the Jesuits reiterate their cry "¡Viva Jesús!" the friars, "abandonando el escondite, se lanzaron en mitad del corro, gritando como poseídos: '¡Y el Seráfico también! ¡Y el Seráfico también!' " Palma dissemblingly would have the reader believe that this brought about the sudden cooperation between the two orders!

Dramatic irony belongs preeminently to the theater and deals as much with tragedy as with comedy. In the *tradiciones,* however, given their predominantly bantering tone, it almost exclusively affords humor. I will bring this chapter to a close with a few final examples. The plot of "El resucitado" is one of the best examples. A humble man, taken ill, presents himself at the San Andrés Hospital. Informed that his ailment presages death, he bequeaths his money to Gil Paz, the administrator of the hospital, requesting only that he purchase for him a fine shroud and pay for some masses in his behalf. After the man's death, however, his trustee decides to renege on his promise and to retain all the money. However, the deceased really isn't dead and while the grave digger is opening his hole, a fresh breeze wakes him from his paroxysm. The grave digger himself, seeing the corpse walking away, collapses, a victim of the irony of events. Gil Paz, meanwhile, busies himself in the hospital "cuando una mano se posó familiarmente en su hombro y oyó una voz cavernosa que le dijo: '¡Avariento! ¿Dónde está mi mortaja?' " (666)— dramatic irony at its most intense and hilarious moment. Paz straightway goes insane.

The same irony befalls a group of royal soldiers in El Callao. Antonio Valero, a ventriloquist, returning to his encampment under cover of darkness hears a patrol approaching. Unavoidably lost, he steps into a threshold and throws his voice out over the soldiers.

> Cada soldado oyó sobre su cabeza, y como si saliera del cañón de su fusil, este grito:
> "¡Viva la patria! ¡Mueran los godos!"
> Los de la ronda, que eran ocho hombres, arrojaron al suelo esos fusiles, en los que se había metido el demonio; fusiles insurgentes, que habían tenido la audacia de prorrumpir en voces subversivas, y echaron a correr poseídos de terror.
> Media hora después el general Valero llegaba a su campamento, riéndose aún de la peligrosa aventura, a la vez que dando gracias a Dios por haberlo hecho ventrílocuo. (1023)

The irony and often the humorous impact are more striking in dramatic irony, since the audience possesses a knowledge superior to that of the victim. We see this principle in effect in "Un predicador de lujo" when the *huachanos* expect to hear a "pico de oro," who, as the reader knows, will be the wayward priest, Samamé. This is also the case in "Dos palomitas sin hiel," where, from a privileged observation post, the reader enjoys a perspective unavailable to the antagonists, who are mutually cutting each other down, unknown to either of them: "en el estrado de doña Francisca se desollaba viva a la *Catuja*, y en el salón de doña Catalina trataban a la *Pancha* como parche de tambor" (290).

In the words of Feliú Cruz, Ricardo Palma was "a man of free spirit and, therefore, his Volterian laughter and penetrating irony hum like a bee through the threads of his brief, substantive prose."[28] I have sought in this chapter to specify the diversity of form and operation of irony in the *Tradiciones peruanas* as it endows his style and his tone with *humorismo* distinctively his own. Chapters 3 and 4 will carry the point further, examining satire and its relationship to Palma's irony.

3

The Humor of Satire and Satiric Irony

Satire has been defined by M. H. Abrams as "the literary art of diminishing a subject by making it ridiculous and evoking towards it attitudes of amusement, contempt, or scorn."[1] Although a summary perusal of the *tradiciones* evinces the bounteous presence of this rhetorical-tonal feature, a careful scrutiny is required to isolate the nature and the dimensions of Palma's satirical manner and the relationship of the satire to his humor and his irony.

There are two main types of satirists and, correspondingly, two basic conceptions of the purpose of satire, with a wide range in between. One group of satirists, as exemplified by Horace, enjoys people but seeks to cure their ignorance, which often leads them to folly and to blindness, by displaying the truth with a smile. The other group, resembling in attitude Swift and Juvenal, hates or despises mankind and proceeds to wound him and to heap scorn on his evils.[2] Palma lies somewhere in between, though surely much closer to Horacian than to Juvenal satire.

Palma was essentially a happy man and although he did not usually seek to evoke harsh contempt and scorn for his protagonists or for institutions, neither was his goal fully restricted to the elicitation of smiles at their foibles or their injustices. From his standpoint as a nineteenth-century free thinker, the Peruvian writer was, on a broad scale, concerned with the inconsistencies and the corruptness of men hindering the progress of his country and adversely affecting his own happiness. In order to convey the truth of his feelings, he employed humor in regard to impairments of integrity and ethics in such a way as to lead the reader, on reflection, to a renewed cognizance of their inequity and undesirability. This understanding, in addition to a varied historical awareness, was the truth Palma sought to instill within his followers.

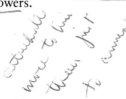

52

Palma was much like Galdós in that he appeared "to have been born with a camera in one eye and a knowing wink in the other." He manifested a particular interest "for the man of flesh and bones, . . . whom he portrays in the vein of a satiric observer." His bantering muse proved always ready to detect "the weak side of man and laugh at the most formal and solemn of human things with a most astute and Aristophanesque smile." True to his cultural heritage, as noted earlier, Palma exemplified the Peruvian "timid, lesser manner of criticizing customs," which permitted him to "censure without losing the smile from his lips nor the sensation of reality."[3] That satire constituted an essential part of his nature seems to be indicated by the fact that he gave vent to such inclinations not only in the *tradiciones* but also, if not more so, in *Verbos y gerundios* and by means of his collaborations in *El Diablo, El Burro* (1852), *El Heraldo de Lima* (1854), *La Campana* (1867) and *La Broma* (1877), all sheets or newspapers of partially or entirely satirical prospectus.

Palma's qualifications as a true satirist, though a satirist of benevolent, ironic bent, are further corroborated by comparing them to the characteristics highlighted as most commonly associated with practitioners of satire throughout the ages. Although Palma certainly does not evidence every characteristic that ever typified a satirist, the list is instructive, both regarding style and technique as well as personality and preparation. In spite of the fact that, as Leonard Feinberg has so comprehensively laid out, satirists and opinions concerning them have differed enormously, often diametrically, Palma clearly embodies the makeup of a light satirist.[4] The following is a list of satirist traits exemplified by Ricardo Palma.

1. Irony informs his expressivity.
2. He possesses a massive vocabulary and employs it in vivid style.
3. He wields effectively witticisms, proverbs, comparisons, and puns.
4. He uses parody and anecdote.
5. Snatches of foreign languages dot his prose.
6. He is given to digression and to interruption.
7. Verse and prose mingle together in his works.
8. He combines and inverts the supernatural and the human.
9. He often has recourse to caricature.
10. He exaggerates while claiming to be realistic.
11. His style is informal, personal, conversational, and colloquial and incorporates up-to-date slang and suggests dirty words.
12. He writes in a tone of improvisation.
13. He alludes to other satirists (Quevedo, Valle y Caviedes, Cervantes, Concolorcorvo) and uses them sometimes as a model.

14. He is topical, i.e., traditional, concrete subjects attract his attention—church, politics, human nature.
15. He relates animals and humans.
16. He writes to have fun as well as to convey truth and to help by enhancing morality.
17. He criticizes life, exposes vice, weakness, and incongruity with a teasing humor that elicits now amusement, now disgust or contempt.
18. A brisk imagination and skepticism impels his pen.
19. His motivation is aesthetic.
20. He is generous, sympathetic, warm, and altruistic.
21. He gives vent through his writing to some degree of frustration with social and political institutions.

Palma's satire is always jocund and often involves irony, though not obligatorily. Depending on the subject, the satire usually encourages amusement and laughter but may leave a residual sense of contempt or scorn. For example, Palma's account of David Gorozabel's encounter with the Inquisition elicits both a chuckle and a vague sense of contempt toward the underlying hypocrisy and treachery of the institution (204). In contrast, the report of the results of Christ's eight-day stay in Ica—no work for physicians, druggists, or notaries, no marital conflicts, and the reconciliation of mothers- and daughters-in-law—creates only an air of levity (912-913). The same holds true for Palma's portrayal of the *lloronas* but with a suggestion born of satire that such artificiality reeks. In that story Palma combined caricature, hilarious invective, satiric irony, and burlesque to entertain the student of colonial customs while conveying a message.

As noted previously, much of Palma's satire involves some moral impetus. We observe this in many instances throughout the *Tradiciones peruanas*. The stimulus is clear in the encounter of Franciscan and Jesuit priests in "Franciscanos y jesuitas," which in essence censures pretense and the perpetuation of social phenomena, in this case religious orders, that contradict genuine human needs and tendencies. The exclamation "¡Gordo pecado es llamar al pan, pan, y al vino, vino!" (469) contains a similar criticism discernible through the obvious irony of sarcasm. In the story entitled "Simonía" the reader discovers a wealth of satiric irony ridiculing benevolently naïveté and gullibility. The *tradición* relates that one night a bell began to ring by itself, "como si una legión de diablos agitara la cuerda que pendía de su badajo." When no one could halt it or discover the source of its activity, the "cura calificó a la campana de posesa del demonio, y al otro día la exorcizó y conjuró con hisopazos de agua bendita." The case eventually goes to court in Madrid, resulting in the bell's subsequent exile to the Indies. Palma then quips with waggish irony apparent through false objectivity and logical contradictions: "Razonable sería presumir que las demás campanas españolas escarmentaron en cabeza ajena. Pues no, señor. La desmoralización cundió, y casi a fines de aquel siglo otra que tal dio idéntico escándalo" (1147).

In true satiric form Palma often displayed his ability to make the reader laugh even at death, although throughout his life he himself decried the unfortunate waste of human life.[5] In the *Tradiciones peruanas* Palma usually merges this perspective with his humor by means of satiric irony. An instance occurs in "La moda en los nombres de pila" wherein we witness that in an argument with a certain gentleman, General Enrique del Castillo, responding to an insult, "echó mano por la charrasca y, también sin ceremonias, le sembró las tripas por el suelo." The narrator then adds, "Me parece que así a cualquiera se le enseñan buena crianza y miramientos" (205). This comment, in addition to the one calling a spade a spade, evinces some sarcasm, often a distinguishable characteristic of Palma's satiric irony.[6] Palma's commentary on the King's methods for extracting confessions is a further example: "¡tan sencillo era el aparato o instrumento que la justicia del rey nuestro señor empleaba para convertir en *canarios* a los reos!" (578).

Gilbert Highet instructs that wounding sarcastic irony such as this, and gentle irony as well, "can be used as weapons in all types of satire," but that they are "most effective in monologue."[7] This has certainly proved true for Palma, a majority of whose sarcasm, satire, and overall humor originates in remarks by the ever-present monologuist-narrator. Of course, some satire originates indirectly through the speech, thoughts, and actions of the characters, who make themselves look ridiculous. However, Palma differs substantially from an author such as Dickens, whose humor, and even satire of institutions, issues from the creation of real characters.[8]

Burlesque-Parody

Highet has termed parody "one of the most delightful forms of satire," one that "springs from the very heart of our sense of comedy, which is the happy perception of incongruity." Parody assumes different forms, each of which necessitates a more refined designation.

A common distinction is to use the term *burlesque* "as the generic term for all literary forms in which people, actions, or other literary works are made ridiculous by an incongruous imitation, and to reserve the other terms as names for various species of burlesque." High burlesque "treats a trivial subject in an elevated manner" while, inversely, low burlesque treats "an elevated subject in a trivial manner."[9]

High burlesque embraces parody and mock-heroic, the distinction between the two being that whereas parody derides through imitation a particular work or style, mock-heroic "employs the conventional attributes and the elaborate style of the epic genre to make a trivial and commonplace subject laughable." Highet finds value in characterizing parody as formal or material. A formal parody derides the external aspects of a work; a material parody, while maintaining the same style as the original, makes the thought within "hideously inappropriate to the form, or inwardly distorted, or comically expanded."[10] Low burlesque is also categorized, travesty mocking "by treating its lofty subject in grotesquely extravagant or lowly terms" and Hudibrastic burlesque dealing with a general type of expression, such as ludicrous colloquial idiom.

The *tradicionista* sought humor through the use of both high and low burlesque of a general nature and by means of satiric mimicry. Rather than parody specific literary works, however, except in the case of the chronicles as a group, Palma imitated styles of speech and terminology common to social, political, and religious institutions. The degree of ridicule varies, depending on the original style being burlesqued, on the subject to which the burlesque is applied, or on those whose actions and speech are reported in the burlesqued style. Consider, for instance, the heretical bell in "Simonía," whose subversive activities were judged guilty by the court in Madrid. The judges "vinieron en mandar y mandaron: primero, que se diera por nulo y de ningún valor el repique; segundo, que se arrancara a la campana la lengua o badajo; y tercero, que se la enviase desterrada a Indias" (1147). In this case Palma satirized through parodic imitation the language of juridical process, the frequent naïveté and incompetence of those on the bench, and, by extension, the cruelty and ferocity born of religious intolerance and fanaticism.

Eleanor Hutchens terms such legalistic parody "the irony of reference," which "consists in the use of words which by implication compare or refer a subject to something else which in its comic dissimilarity points up the real nature of the subject." The device is of ancient vintage, appearing in Rabelais's imitations of "the Bible, the decretals, the jargons of the legal and medical professions, and the stilted speech of scholastic theologians."[11]

A second parody of legalistic jargon arises during Lilit's conveyance of Don Dimas de la Tijereta to hell. "Por el camino gritaba a voz en cuello el escribano que había *festinación* en el procedimiento de Lilit, que todo lo *fecho* y *actuado* era nulo y contra ley, y amenazaba al diablo alguacil con que si encontraba gente de justicia en el otro barrio le entablaría pleito, y por lo menos lo haría condenar en costas" (517). This passage, while tickling the reader's funny bone, also brings under fire the arrogant but tenuous self-sufficiency exemplified by some of the "cuervos de Temis" (281). This might best be termed an indirect parody since the juridical terminology is being used in a summary report of a character's words rather than in a direct comment by the narrator.

Another synthesized parody, this time of legal and ecclesiastical rhetoric, originates in a dispute over Adam's naval. "El domingo probó con muchos latines que Adán no se diferenció de sus descendientes, y que, por tanto, lució la tripita o excrecencia llamada ombligo. El bachiller argüía que, no siendo Adán nacido de hembra, maldito si le hizo falta el cordón umbilical. Contestó aquél con un *distingo* y un *nego majorem*, y replicó el limeño con un entimema, dos sorites y tres pares de silogismos" (257). Reported dialogues of these types are ubiquitous in Palma's narrative and often ridicule indirectly a particular style of expression. I will touch on them again shortly.

Palma also played with royal phraseology, which, in the following excerpt, undermines through irony of contradiction his outwardly unimpeachable stance as an arbitrator and his verdict concerning justice in Peru. "Conque callar y callemos, y que la justicia siga su curso, como en los tiempos del oidor Mansilla. He dicho" (1106). Similar irony casts some doubt on the following brief parody of an invocation: "como todo lo malo encuentra siempre imitadores, . . . abundaron hasta el pasado siglo los curas que por treinta pesos aseguraban a los difuntos la gloria perdurable, que para mis lectores deseo. Amén" (1148). This essentially one-word parody adds to the amusement evoked by the incongruent mixture of deceitful priests, a dubious narrator, and enduring glory. Indeed, there is great irony in a skeptical author wishing for his readers an eternal glory fraudulently guaranteed and exploited by unethical ministers.

Ricardo Palma was exposed to the parliamentary procedures of congress for several years. On occasion in the *tradiciones* he satirically alluded to that mode of expression, evoking visions of bureaucratic ritual combined with little real achievement: "véase, pues, que también en la época colonial se aderezaban pasteles eleccionarios. Pido que conste el hecho (estilo parlamentario) y adelante con la cruz" (546). The *tradicionista* satirized other facets of government by means of a material parody: "hasta los municipales vociferaron sobre la necesidad de imponer al prójimo contribución de diez centavos por cada estornudo" (914). Such satire confirms Palma's critical stance in regard to the administrative inefficiency that hampered the development of his country.

High burlesque may also involve re-creating the archaic style of chronicles and old documents, a technique often employed by Palma when he presented, for example, names of viceroys. More often than not the names are accompanied by titles of nobility, which, while reinforcing an aura of aristocracy and noble birth, present ironic contrast between ostentation of titles and unfruitful reigns. The presence of the elongated titles in a brief genre such as the *tradición* tends to create an incongruency that, whether articulated by the narrator or not, may suggest some question as to the true dignity and integrity of these "grandes de España."

> Don Carmine Nicolás Caracciolo, grande de España, príncipe de Santo Buono, duque de Castel de Sangro, marqués de Buquianico, conde de Esquiabi, de Santobido y de Capracota, barón de Monteferrato, señor de Nalbelti, Frainenefrica, Gradinarca y Castelnovo, recibió el mando del Perú [en] 1716. (527)

Indirect mock encomium perhaps best characterizes this type of burlesque. The ridicule is further brought out in subsequent paragraphs. This appellative burlesque elicits laughter more at the man himself than at the style of the chronicles, thus contradicting charges against Palma that he possessed a spirit subservient to the *colonia* (see Chapter 1, Humor and Palma).

Certain ejaculations in the *tradiciones* preserve the form of devout exclamations while infusing them with highly discordant thought. These also fall under Highet's definition of material parody.

> ¡Por vida de Santa Cebollina, virgen y Mártir, abogada de los callos! (651)
>
> ¡Por vida de Santa Tecla, abogada de los pianos roncos! (914)
>
> ¡Válganos Santa Pereza! (1194)
>
> ¡Válganme los doce pares de orejas de los doce apóstoles! (581)

A different example occurs in "Un predicador de lujo," where Palma gently but laughingly burlesques ecclesiastic discourse. Father Samamé, a drunken priest, is called on as a last resort to speak to church members in Huacho. During his discourse he refers to Christ's promise to the thief on the cross: "A Dimas, el buen ladrón, lo salvó su fe; pero a Gestas, el mal ladrón, lo perdió su falta de fe. Mucho me temo, queridos huachanos y oyentes míos, que os condenéis por malos ladrones." Noting the offense taken at his choice of words, he continues, "Pero Dios es grande, omnipotente y misericordioso, hijos míos, y en él espero que con su ayuda soberana y vuestras felices disposiciones llegaréis a tener fe y a ser todos, sin excepción, buenos, muy buenos ladrones" (789-790). We laugh at the pun not only because it highlights the ingenuousness of both orator and audience but also because of the discord between vehicle—ecclesiastical oration—and content.

Throughout the *tradiciones* Palma interspersed his prose with foreign languages, usually Latin. This proclivity lends itself to humor, frequently of a parodic nature. The parody may ridicule ecclesiastical gravity, the medical profession, or inflated erudition, or it may evoke amusement toward particular modes of thought among contemporary cultures, particularly French and Italian cultures. Foreign words also play a part in ironical or sarcastic remarks. Sometimes they simply supply an added humorous touch.

Beyond these effects, Palma's introduction of foreign terms and phrases into his narrative or dialogue offers several noncomical usages. For example, they can contribute to the characterization of a person who would normally employ a language other than Spanish, including priests and foreigners. In addition, foreign terms easily accompany the report of legalistic transactions. Palma also had recourse on a regular basis to foreign words with commonplace usage in Spanish and in other languages. This applies especially to Italian and French although less to English: *sotto voce* (1127), *pian piano* (283), *prima donna* (1044), *toilette* (1129), *parvenues* (1129), *humbug* (735), *roastbeaf* (461). In "Aceituna, una" Palma even remarks that "hoy se dice *lunch,* en gringo" (171).

Consider the following example. Facetiously alluding to the famous controversy over whether drinking chocolate broke one's fast, a dispute decided in the negative by a Jesuit declaration, the author followed his account of the resolution with the phrase "liquidum non frangit jejunium" (633). Laughter arises from the incongruity between the gravity of Latin and the inconsequentiality of the question. By means of similar imitation Palma grins at other foolish ecclesiastical decrees.

> Entre los primeros actos de eclesiástico gobierno del señor deán, hombre más ceremonioso que el día de Año Nuevo, cuéntase un edicto prohibiendo, con pena de excomunión mayor *ipso facto incurrenda,* que los viejos usasen birrete dentro del templo, y otro reglamentando la indumentaria femenina, reglamentación de la cual resultaban pecaminosos los trajes con cauda en la casa del Señor. (580)

The parodic incongruity again stems from the application of Latin to triviality. The linguistic contrast between the vernacular and the language of Cicero also engenders mirth. In essence, Palma was ridiculing the originators of the foolish decrees by mimicking their mode of speech.

In many instances Latin words, while appropriately harmonizing with the station of the person in question, still produce amusement, owing to certain minor incongruities or humor of situation. The Pope, after eating some Latin American cuisine, "exclamó en latín: '*Beati indiana qui manducant pepiani*'" (628). The bishop of Cuzco, in marrying a couple, was told by the bride, "Quizá quiero, quizá no quiero." Nevertheless, the bishop "los casó en latín *in nomine Patris et Filii et Spiritus Sancto*" (40). When the Latin contrasts with the station of the interlocutor or the character, we also react with amusement: "De puro bueno perdió mi gallo; porque si el contrario no se rebaja a tiempo, le habría clavado la navaja hasta el *sursum corda*" (624).

As can be seen, the Latin terms normally blend right into the flow of the Spanish. Palma enjoyed using them as a means of lightly mocking erudition or as a means of eliciting visions or memories in the reader of clerical, medical, or legal personnel whose mastery of the classical tongue did not fully coincide with their mastery of self or moral principle. At the same time he achieved a further variation in expression, something important in such a large volume of akin anecdotes.

> *Ante omnia* tengo a honra presentar a ustedes al licenciado Benito Suárez de Carvajal. (128)
> Y don Raimundo Pareja cumplió *ad pedem litterae* su juramento. (635)
> *In diebus illis,* digo, cuando yo era muchacho. (209)
> Las muchachas protestaban, *in pecto,* contra la tiranía paternal. (599)
> . . . pero por falta de padrino *nequaquam.* (1441)

Recourse to French and Italian brings similar results. The use of these languages provides an opportunity for the *tradicionista* to mock the philosophy of life commonly linked with those cultures. In one story Palma justified his account on the basis of popular tradition, "y a falta de otra fuente histórica a que atenernos, aceptamos el relato del pueblo, que *se non è vero è bene trovato*" (412). In another story, the reader meets Don Juan de Andueza, who lived, "como dicen los franceses, *au jour le jour,* y tanto se le daba de lo de arriba como de lo de abajo" (573). When Mauro Cordato realized his inescapable predicament, he drew out "un pistolete, lo amartilló y·se voló el cráneo. ¡*Tableau!*, como dicen los franceses" (861).

A significant source of humor in the *tradiciones* lies in the derivation of irony or sarcasm through foreign language terminology. For example, when in "Beba, padre, que le da la vida!" the viceroy's wife summons a group of judges to decide how to proceed concerning the suspected spy, Father Núñez, "opinaron por que, inmediatamente y sin muchas contemplaciones, se echase guante al padre Núñez y se le ahorcase *coram populo*" (425). The irony in this statement arises from the fact that the report of the judges' mistaken condemnation of a priest includes Latin, a language common to both offices and traditionally the conveyor of truth, and from Palma's parody of a supposed conversation among the judges, who, erroneously believing Father Núñez a spurious priest, would confidently ridicule his seemingly false pretention to the dignity of Latin.

A second instance occurs in "Historia de una excomunión." Doña Antonia has come to mass with her daughter, who is dressed contrary to the archdeacon's decree. On sight of the daughter, the archdeacon screams, "¡Fuera esas mujeres que tienen la desvergüenza de venir con traje profano a la casa de Dios! ¡Fuera! ¡Fuera!" Employing an ironic usage of Latin, the narrator then informs the reader that "Doña Antonia no era de las que se muerden la punta de la lengua, sino de las que cuando oyen el *Dominus vobiscum*, no hacen esperar el *et cum spiritu tuo*" (581). The irony of feigned praise becomes sarcasm when the narrator refers to the very best colonial mourner as, "el *non plus ultra* del género" (863).

A number of facetiae in Palma's prose incorporates Latinate phrases. Most frequently these statements inform verbal or written confrontations, leading to great hilarity. For example, to the Dominican epigram, "*Si cum jesuitis itis, nunquam cum Jesu itis,*" Jesuits respond with "*Si cum dominicanis canis, nunquam cum Domino canis*" (283). Likewise, when a Jesuit derisively comments in the presence of red-haired Friar Diego Angulo, "*Rubicundus erat Judas,*" the latter retorts, "*Et de societate Jesu*" (284).

Intermittently the foreign terms function as an adjunct to an already mirthful air created by Palma's ever-visible presence in the *tradiciones.*

> ¿Tener celos del primo de su mujer? Eso sería el *non plus ultra* del ridículo. (1203)

> . . . un empleado del real estanco de salitres, digo, de tabacos. ¡Vaya un *lapsus plumae* condenado! ¡Ejém! ¡Ejém! ¡*Escupe, Guadalupe, escupe!* ¡Bonitos están los tiempos para andarse con equivoquillos! (735)

> Pero eso de hacer la olla gorda a los corregidores *gratis et amore* no le hacía pizca de gracia a su excelencia. (638)

Low burlesque in the *Tradiciones peruanas* assumes the two basic forms of satiric mimicry and the "colloquialization" of elements of sacred history. We will look at satiric mimicry first. Once again, instead of burlesquing specific literary works, the *tradicionista* focused on a particular set of people, eliciting humorous reaction by mimicking their manner of expression. This is one of several techniques that Palma enjoyed in his depictions of types.[12] One of the clearest instances occurs in "La llorona del viernes santo." There, Palma described the style of the colonial mourners.

> Con frecuencia, así habían conocido ellas al difunto como al moro Muza, y mentían que era un contento exaltando entre ayes y congojas las cualidades del muerto.
>
> "¡Ay, ay! ¡Tan generoso y caritativo!" y el que iba en el cajón había sido usurero nada menos.
>
> "¡Ay, ay! ¡Tan valiente y animoso!" y el infeliz había liado los bártulos por consecuencia del mal de espanto que le ocasionaron los duendes y las penas.
>
> "¡Ay, ay! ¡Tan honrado y buen cristiano!" y el difunto había sido, por sus picardías y por lo encallecida que traía la conciencia, digno de morir en alto puesto, es decir, en la horca.
>
> . . . .
>
> Sólo a las lloronas les era lícito sonarse con estrépito y lanzar de rato en rato un ¡*ay Jesus*! o un suspiro cavernoso que parecía del otro mundo. (862-863)

This excerpt could perhaps be termed a socio-literary Hudibrastic imitation since it takes a significant subject of colonial social history and mocks it through grotesque mimicry. Palma's amusing burlesque of a conversation between male and female cousins reveals a like pattern:

Aunque uno sea más cachazudo que Job, tiene que repudrírsele el alma al oír a primo y prima hacer reminiscencias de que cuando eran chiquitines jugaban al pin-pin, y a la gallina papujada, y a la pizpirigaña, y al pellizquito de mano, y a los escondidos, y a los huevos, y a la corregüela, cátalo dentro, cátalos fuera. (1203)

As noted earlier, such indirect reports of exchanges tend to dominate the narrative landscape of Palma's anecdotes, regularly lending themselves to humor, whether through burlesque or some other means. When parody is involved, it is suggested parody, that is, a summarized report of dialogue or action that if reconstructed in the reader's mind would, through exaggerated imitation of style, constitute a parody. Consider some further cases:

... y corrigieron el texto poniendo en serios atrenzos al gallego Gorozabel, que lo menos debía de ser primo segundo de Zorobabel. (204)

Aquello de tener el pelo de un rubio colorado y de hablar el castellano con mucho acento de *gringo* dio al principio motivo para que el pueblo no lo creyera muy católico-apostólico-romano. (868)

Y cata que al ángel caído lo que más le llamó la atención en la fisonomía de los hombres fue el bigote; y suspiró por tenerlo, y se echó a comprar menjurjes y cosméticos de esos que venden los charlatanes, jurando y rejurando que hacen nacer el pelo hasta en la palma de la mano. (1200)

In the first excerpt the narrator facetiously but indirectly reports the thoughts and/or words of the inquisitors, who suspect Gorozabel, owing to the similarity between his name and a biblical one. The second excerpt exemplifies mimicry of plebian speech—"muy católico-apostólico-romano"—that satirizes the ingenuous devotion of the common people. In the third quotation the narrator blends satiric imitation of charlatan vendors and of women who, on learning of a particular product, go wild in their efforts to obtain it.

One of the most comical techniques in the *Tradiciones peruanas* is Hudibrastic low burlesque realized through the colloquialization of beings and circumstances associated with sacred history. This particular shade of burlesque abounds in the humor of spoken Spanish and is not uncommon in western literature.[13] Ventura García Calderón perceives a relationship between Palma and Anatole France in this regard, asserting that Palma initiated in Peru "the amiable genre" of Hudibrastic low burlesque, that is, "the irreverence of putting on stage saints, pious ones, bishops, virgins, martyrs, and confessors, all the characters of the Christian Year and the Gilded Legend, making them speak, laugh, and say naive remarks like men."[14]

This approach to humor has its roots in Palma's skeptical, playful attitude, a manifestation of which is the predisposition to attribute to all beings distinguishably human traits. Its humor arises mainly from the surprise the reader experiences in the face of such novel depictions. The device thrives in stories like "Traslado a Judas," "Los siete pelos del diablo," "Los gobiernos del Perú," "Dónde y cómo el diablo perdió el poncho," "Apocalíptica," "Refranero limeño," "El abogado de los abogados," and "El alcalde de Paucarcolla." Hudibrastic low burlesque realizes its greater efficacy by means of dialogues and the characterizing comments of the *tradicionista*. For instance, as the Lord and his twelve apostles draw near to Ica, Palma relates,

> El Señor se puso la mano sobre los ojos, formando visera para mejor concentrar la visual, y dijo:
> "Allí hay población, Pedro, tú que entiendes de náutica y geografía, ¿me sabrás decir qué ciudad es ésa?"
> San Pedro se relamió con el piropo y contestó:
> "Maestro, esa ciudad es Ica."
> "¡Pues pica, hombre, pica!"
> Y todos los apóstoles hincaron con un huesecito el anca de los rucios, y a galope pollinesco se encaminó la comitiva al poblado." (912)

Before entering the city, Jesus warns his favorite apostle, "Cuidado, Pedro, con tener malas pulgas y cortar orejas. Tus genialidades nos ponen siempre en compromisos." In response, "el apóstol se sonrojó hasta el blanco de los ojos; y nadie habría dicho, al ver su aire bonachón y compungido, que había sido un cortacaras." Later in the story Christ calls his senior apostle apart and says, "Pedro, componte como puedas; pero es preciso que con el alba tomemos el *tole*, sin que nos sienta alma viviente. Circunstancias hay en que tiene uno que despedirse a la francesa" (913).

Peter is prankishly portrayed in various stories as ill-humored and ingenuous. In "El abogado de los abogados," for another example, Palma depicts Peter's error of allowing a lawyer to enter "en la corte celestial" (1193) and, at the urging of the lawyer, of submitting a petition to God requesting an official title on legal paper as keeper of the gate. "'¡Qué es esto, Pedro? ¿Papel sellado tenemos? ¿Qué título ni qué gurrumina! Con mi palabra te basta y te sobra.' Y el Señor hizo añicos el papel, y dijo sonriendo: 'De seguro que te descuidaste con la puerta, y tenemos ya abogado en casa. ¡Pues bonita va a ponerse la gloria!' " (1193).

The same basic technique also occurs in brief allusions such as in

"Don Dimas de la Tijereta," where Palma makes reference to the good thief "a quien don Jesucristo dio pasaporte para entrar en la gloria" (513). Equally amusing to the "lector amigo" are references to Don Angel Malo or to a half foolish gentleman named "don Poncio Pilatos el catalán, sujeto a quien manejaban como un zarandillo un tal Anás y un tal Caifás, que eran dos bribones que se perdían de vista" (1195). Palma characterizes Pilate through one of his favorite techniques—a colloquialized response splashed with humor and satiric allusion.

> Compadritos, la ley me ata las manos para tocar ni un pelo de la túnica del cuidadano Jesús. Mucha andrómina es el latinajo aquel del *habea corpus*. Consigan ustedes del Sanedrín (que así llamaban los judíos al Congreso) que declare la patria en peligro y eche al huesero las garantías individuales, y entonces dense una vueltecita por acá y hablaremos. (1195)

Political satire of this nature abounds in the *Tradiciones peruanas*, as we shall see later.[15]

Judas Iscariot, who must have been the son of "algún bachiche pulpero" proved to be a mischievous child and by eight years of age "ya tenía hecha su reputación como ladrón de gallinas" (1195). The *tradicionista* also renders Satan laughable by endowing him with a Creole mentality and lexicon. When he received (by boat, no less) the announcement of the honors extended to Jesus and his apostles in Ica, "Cachano se mordió de envidia el hocico, ¡pícaro trompudo!, y . . . exclamó: '¡Caracoles! ¡Pues yo no he de ser menos que él! No faltaba más. . . . A mí nadie me echa la pata encima'" (913). Likewise, "recelando que le armasen una zancadilla" (671), the devil never returned to Pusi. A final example pictures a friend counseling one who has been imprisoned for having denied the mystery of the Holy Trinity: "Pues entonces, hombre de Dios, ¿qué le va a usted ni que le viene con que sean tres o sean treinta? ¿A usted qué le importa que engullan como tres o calcen como una? ¿Quién le mete a sudar fiebre ajena? Allá esos cuidados para quien las mantiene y saca provecho de mantenerlas" (964). Such depictions reflect the amiable skepticism and irreverence that characterize the spirit of the *Tradiciones peruanas*.

Religious Satire

Both the religious person and the humorist overcome and resolve the misfortunes and contradictions of life. The first explains and bears them through his faith; the second, by means of his "perspectivism" of mocking resignation. Both are spectators who contemplate the world and interpret it on the basis of the stance they have taken. Each feels at liberty, knowing he is founded on a particular outlook. In this context the humorist often assumes a skeptical position of one or another shade. Whether he slips all the way to nihilism depends on his religious roots.[16]

In Palma we discern a man skeptical toward certain fanaticisms, practices, and beliefs. Through simple, good-natured resignation and/or a degree of essential faith, however, along with disinterest in or lack of aptitude for weightier, Unamuniam-type philosophical ponderings, he was generally able to enjoy life through channels that most fruitfully convey happiness—marriage, children, friends, and success in life's endeavors.

Nevertheless, "everyone knows that humor reflected in the Spanish language is, above all, a humor that concerns spiritual and moral life as well as ecclesiastical institutions," and Palma is in step with a bounteous heritage of writers who confirm that statement.[17] Mocking compassionate skeptic that he was, in the *tradiciones* he wrings from religion every possible opportunity for humor. The stories teem with comparisons founded on satirical or lightly jeering references, along with sexual allusions, metaphors, and ironic exclamations. Caricatures and depictions of priests incongruent due to their licentiousness, gluttony, and love for money, gambling, and the bottle abound. Frequently we laugh at ironic declarations by the narrator concerning his neutral beliefs, or at his ironic colloquial descriptions regarding wonders and miracles. Nor do we overlook the plentiful encounters, rivalries, and clashes between religious orders, which often lend themselves to mirth. In nearly all this, however, Palma works from a perspective of compassionate satire and irony touched with understanding.

The reader finds Palma's portraits and descriptions humorous for several reasons:

1. Because a truth is revealed that we all know or suspect but do not articulate publicly.
2. Due to the incongruence between vocation and fulfillment of responsibilities, which tends to confirm our own humanity.
3. Due to a slackening of tension, that is, because of the liberty or release we experience when supposedly forbidden subjects are mentioned, although indirectly.
4. Due to surprising juxtapositions.

5. In the case of some people, due to some personal hostility or thirst for vengence which receives satisfaction through seeing priests ridiculed.
6. Due to the simple delight we feel in the presence of the comical.

The examples that ensue provide clarification.

Sexual allusions to priestly activities sometimes cause the "lector amigo" to laugh. "*Erase que se era, que en buena hora sea; el bien que se venga a pesar de Menga, y si viene el mal, sea para la manceba del abad; frío y calentura para la moza del cura*" (284). In one tale, after having noted that wonders and marvels were in style "en estos reinos del Perú," Palma proceeded to identify some of the rarest, including the "arrepentimiento de un fraile, cuya barragana dejaba, como las mulas, las huellas del herraje" (248).

Within this category comparisons constitute the most abundant humor. Despite their almost indispensable satire, comparisons embody much sympathy, as the following examples substantiate.

> . . . los haberes del marido se evaporaron *en menos de lo que se persigna un cura loco.* (820)
>
> Por supuesto que el galán se apareció con más oportunidad que fraile llamado a refectorio. (802)
>
> . . . ojos que parecen frailes que predican muchas cosas malas y pocas buenas. (530)
>
> El infeliz ignoraba que el dinero no es monje cartujo que gusta de estar guardado y criar moho. (823)

Palma delighted in caricaturing friars and priests, focusing on and exaggerating one or another of their appetites while excluding many other aspects of their characters. The humor derives principally from portraits of friars in which their various appetites stand out. Such "caricaturesque" satire hails from a lengthy literary heritage—*Il decamerone, El libro de buen amor, Lazarillo de Tormes, El buscón,* and Rabelais, for example. From the *tradiciones* we remember the friars Father Samamé, Father Chuecas, and Father Núñez, among many others. The first led a life "tan licenciosa, que casi siempre estaba preso en la cárcel del convento. . . . Pero si no entendía jota de lugares teológicos ni de oratoria sagrada, era en cambio eximio catador de licores, y váyase lo uno por lo otro" (789). In parallel fashion Father Chuecas was a "jugador impertérrito y libertino como un tenorio" (896). Father Núñez was even subjected to a rigorous test in order to ascertain whether he was indeed a friar. Donã Ana de Borja, his examiner, invited him to eat and on observing that "el padre Núñez no comía, . . . devoraba," she winked at the judges as if to say: "¡Bien engulle! Fraile es." Later, after having consumed several desserts, the good father faced the decisive test—how he would satisfy his thirst:

> El fraile tomó con ambas manos el pesado cántaro de Guadalajara, lo alzó casi a la altura de la cabeza, recostó ésta en el respaldo de la silla, echóse a la cara el porrón y empezó a despacharse a su gusto.
> La virreina, viendo que aquella sed era como la de un arenal y muy fraileuno el modo de apaciguarla, le dijo, sonriendo:
> "¡Beba, padre, beba, que le da la vida!"
> Y el fraile, tomando el consejo como amistoso interés por su salud, no despegó la boca del porrón hasta que lo dejó sin gota. En seguida su paternidad se pasó la mano por la frente para limpiarse el sudor que le corría a chorros, y echó por la boca un regüeldo que imitaba el bufido de una ballena arponada. (426)

A friar's celebrated ability for deep sleep provides entertainment in such passing statements as "donde frailunamente roncaba su paternidad" (841) or "su superior roncaba como diz que sólo los frailes saben hacerlo" (379).

More remains to be illustrated about religious satire in the *tradiciones*. Additonal references to this subject can be found in discussion that follows.

Colloquialisms

Turning now to the general relationship in the *Tradiciones peruanas* between colloquialisms and humor, we should observe along with David Worcester that the "delightful mingling of scholarly niceness with the salty idiom of the common man" has always been the "hallmark of most great satire." He observes the presence of colloquialisms in Erasmus and particularly in Rabelais, who sprinkles his pages with polished classical *sententia*, Greek and Latin, and with the peasant's ancient heritage of folk knowledge. Highet also tags vernacular usage as one of "the typical weapons of satire." In the spoken tongue frequently "this juxtaposition of two heterogeneous elements, the first, popular, almost common, the second, erudite, or a little less, produces that 'clash of two distinct worlds' which engenders hilarity." Anyone familiar with Palma has savored the rich colloquial weave of his narrative fabric. "Creole wit and boldness, words colored with the argot of the common people, . . . short fervent

prayers of zealous church women, spicy remarks of saucy grand-
mothers, terms stolen from experts in tauromachy or gamblers," join
with a wealth of popular sayings and proverbs to constitute in many
instances the *tradicionista*'s most efficacious sources of humor.[18]

Closely linked with his use of the vernacular is "the humor of
familiarity," as Michael Nimetz describes in his study of Galdós. In
the analysis Nimetz pinpoints certain characteristics of Galdós's
style and humor that closely parallel those of Palma. For instance,
each extracts humor from familiarity of narrative tone. Each establishes an intimate relationship with the *lector*. Both, due to a vernacular tone, make what is actually highly polished prose seem easy and
flowing. In the novels of Galdós, as well as the *Tradiciones peruanas*,
one encounters references to previous works, stories, and characters,
thus creating a sense of participation. Both authors employ this
familiar tone in narrative as well as in dialogue or in monologue, the
transition often becoming unnoticeable through the shifting point of
view—direct, indirect, free indirect, for example. Finally, for each
author diminutives, superlatives, proverbs, and popular sayings add
to a rich, racy vernacular that contributes to the elicitation of mirth.
Critics term both styles "oral," "chatty," and "conversational."

In Palma's works these vernacular phrases punctuate innumerable
dialogues and function as vehicles of characterization as well as of
communication. They provoke smiles or laughter depending on the
degree of incongruence, exaggeration, surprise, sexual allusion, religious connotation, or contextual-situational effect. They often reveal the cheerful ironic presence of the narrator, evident in
statements such as "parece que una mañana se levantó Carlos III
con humor de suegra" (672) or exclamations like "¡ vaya un esgrimir
de la sin pelos el de aquellos angelitos!" (544). The reader is amused
by familiar parenthetical remarks—"(la mosca por delante)" (582)—
or by the presence of colloquial phraseology in the mouth of the
king—"¡Oreja, y vengan acá los autos!" (655).

Among the many characters of Peru's past who come alive through
their sprightly, popular expressivity we remember particularly *la Lunareja*, whose diatribes vivify "Una moza de rompe y raja" (970);
Father Pablo Negrón, whose spicy interjections animate "¡¡Buena
laya de fraile!!" (915); the two protagonists of "De gallo a gallo"—
Larriva and Echegaray—whose poetic, satiric repartee stimulates
great humor (1049); Pedro Manzanares and the Andalusian (961);
the wounded Laurencio Silva (998); the magnificently delineated

Doña Pulqueria (451-452); Benedicta Salazar's irascible aunt (725-726); and the ingenuous "alcalde del crimen don Rodrigo de Odria" (455); and a string of *beatas* characterized by ingenious, colorful exchanges.

Caricature

Previously we observed that humor issues from the use of caricature vis-à-vis religious figures. I would like to extend that observation now, since, in truth, the humor of the *tradiciones* originates from a great variety of character sketches of Creole and human types, in addition to protagonists of a religious calling.

Caricature is defined as "a type of portrait which makes a person ludicrous by exaggerating or distorting prominent features without losing the likeness," or, similarly, as "descriptive writing which seizes upon certain individual qualities of a person and through exaggeration or distortion produces a BURLESQUE, ridiculous effect."[19] Caricature inherently blends with satire since both seek to render their subject ridiculous, laughable, or contemptible while conveying a truth, possibly of moral impact. Highet's comments on distorted visions of the world promote understanding of caricature and satire in general and, specifically, their relationship:

> A satirical picture of our world, which shows only human beings as its inhabitants, must pretend to be a photograph, and in fact be a caricature. It must display their more ridiculous and repellant qualities in full flower, minimize their ability for healthy normal living, mock their virtues and exaggerate their vices, disparage their greatest human gifts, the gift for cooperation and the gift for inventive adaptation, treat their religions as hypocrisy, their art as trash, their literature as opium, their love as lust, their virtue as hypocrisy, and their happiness as an absurd illusion. And it must do all this while protesting that it is a truthful, unbiased, as nearly as possible dispassionate witness.[20]

A caricature may consist of a single thumbnail sketch, as are many of Palma's, or of a series of depictions intermingled with other facets of characterization—action and dialogue, for example—to convey a distorted image. Though unnatural, the caricature constitutes an interpretation by the writer of an individual or of a type of individual that suggests, on reflection, a need for change. The *tradicionista* advanced caricatures that oscillate in the degree of underlying seriousness or moral intent. In this regard Palma perpetuated a long-estabished literary and artistic tradition involving Juvenal, Boccaccio, the Archpriest of Talavera, Cervantes, and Quevedo. That he patently benefited from this legacy, particularly from his Golden Age mentors, stands well attested.[21]

In his caricatures the author of the *Tradiciones peruanas* isolated physiological features as well as manias and other weaknesses of personality. Obesity, ugliness, old age, and thinness figure prominently in the physiology of the subjects. Manias and weaknesses of personalities portrayed include avarice, lechery, impertinence, incompetence, excessive rigor, haughtiness, jealousy, cowardliness, gullibility, selfishness, waggishness, drunkenness, and irascibleness. Mayors, magistrates, constables, notaries, lawyers, usurers, mothers-in-law, sisters-in-law, cousins, and women in general, in addition to the bounteous priests, sacristans, and zealous old religious hags, constitute the most prominent bearers of these traits in the *tradiciones*. Many—the avaricious man, the mother-in-law, the gullible, gossipy, ingenuous woman, the cousin, the *escribano*, the old lady, the physician, the *beata*, the widow, and the usurer—are types whose salient characteristics time, tradition, and literary reiteration have sanctioned over the centuries. Palma's resurrection of this tradition provides the reader with continued amusement.

In terms of technique Palma prefered the metaphor in the form of a comparison, often employing animals as the correlative. The use of diminutives, augmentatives, repetition, and puns is also common. Naturally, hyperbole animates nearly all his caricatures. On occasion, following the pattern of Francisco de Quevedo, Palma granted autonomy to certain parts of the body as significant elements of the deformed sketch.

A caricature exaggerates a particular physical or mental trait to the point that other facets of character or physique are overshadowed. Palma seldom restricted his caricature sketches to one single physiological aspect. For example, the exaggeration of a trait such as obesity usually occurs in conjunction with ugliness or generally unpleasant facial features. Priests are often typed in this manner, as in the case of Father Núñez, "un hombrecito regordete, ancho de espaldas, barrigudo, cuellicorto, de ojos abotagados y de nariz roma y rubicunda. Imagínate, lector, un candidato para una apoplejía fulminante, y tendrás cabal retrato del jeronimita" (425). The thick, pudgy neck frequently becomes the focus of passing allusions to friars: "con un furioso berrendo, de esos que tienen más cerviguillo que un fraile" (37). The middle-aged fat woman is also humorously conjured in the *Tradiciones peruanas:* "¿Y a eso llama usted pepita? Pues, a eso en toda tierra de cristianos, se llama doña Josefa" (525). The exaggeration of thinness normally joins old age in the depictions of colonial women. A comparison typically makes the point clearly, as in the case of the professional mourners described in "La llorona del Viernes Santo" as "una asociación de mujeres todas garabateadas de arrugas y más pilongas que piojo de pobre" (862). References such as these illuminate the importance in Palma's humor of the caricature of anatomical unsightliness. The pervading atmosphere of light, warm irony with an absence of vindictiveness enhances the comicity of these drawings, avoiding deterioration into cruel invective.

Homeliness may afflict any person, but traditionally this trait accompanies certain religious and social figures. Judas, for instance, "era colorado como el ají y rubio como la candela. Mellado de un diente, bizco de mirada, narigudo como ave de rapiña y alicaído de orejas, era su merced feo hasta para feo" (1195). Puns and comparisons intensify the unseemliness. Pedro Gutiérrez, a tailor, "era un hombrecillo con una boca que más que boca era bocacalle, y unos ojuelos tan saltones, que amenazaban salirse de la jurisdicción de la cara" (43).[22]

Ricardo Palma wrote over a thousand pages of *tradiciones* with almost every story centering on some aspect of human interaction or motivation. In so doing he essentially covered the whole spectrum of undesirable personality characteristics in his depictions. Not infrequently these portraits highlight a particular trait or a cluster of related features to the exclusion of other points of character, resulting in caricature. Those inclinations that most often caught Palma's eye are avarice and arrogance.

In his scrutiny of colonial history Palma came upon several individuals characterized by an intense desire to accumulate and to retain wealth. Around many of these individuals he constructed highly interesting and often amusing anecdotes. Recall, for example, Don Geripundio in "Una trampa para cazar ratones," Cristóbal Vaca de Castro in "Una carta de Indias," Gil Paz in "El resucitado," Garcí-Gutiérrez de Toledo in "El peje chico," Antonio de Arriaga in "El corregidor de Tinta," and "Don Dimas de la Tijereta." To each Palma dedicated a literary portrait of varying length underscoring his avidity or parsimony and portrayed in intriguing and/or jocose narrative the vital ramifications of these traits in their lives. Each offers a variation of two related characteristics—miserliness and greed.

Don Geripundio, for instance, epitomized niggardliness. His virtues were negative.

> Nunca dio más que los buenos días, y habría dejado morir de hambre al gallo de la pasión por no obsequiarle un grano de arroz. . . . Decía que dar limosna era mantener holgazanes y buscones, y que sembrar beneficios era prepararse coshechas de ingratitudes. (525)

The narrator also informs the reader that Don Geripundio "era de la misma masa de un avaro que murió en Potosí in 1636, el cual dispuso en su testamento que su fortuna se emplease en hacer un excusado de plata maciza para uso del pueblo, y que el resto se enterrase en el corral de su casa, poniendo de guardianes a cuatro perros bravos" and, likewise, that "a su entierro, y lujosamente ataviados a costa suya, concurriesen todos los jumentos de la población" (526).

Palma used similar puns in delineating Don Dimas and Antonio de Arriaga. Whereas Don Dimas "en punto a dar no daba ni las buenas noches" (515), the Corregidor of Tinta proved so avaricious que "si en vez de nacer hombre hubiera nacido reloj, por no dar, no habría dado ni las horas, tal era su señoría" (685). Don Dimas's cupidity undergoes further enhancement through his association with another naturally rapacious type, the notary or *escribano*. Consider the lines "un escribano y un gato / en un pozo se cayeron; / como los dos tenían uñas / por la pared se subieron" (513). Toward the end of the story the narrator explains that Don Dimas suffered a fate similar to that of Judas Iscariot, the archetype of greediness. The latter's soul, excluded from both Purgatory and Hell, eventually found lodging in the body of an usurer: "Desde entonces se dice que los usureros tienen alma de Judas" (518). In Chapter 2 the reader meets Gil Paz, "un avaro más ruin que la encarnación de la avaricia," who gains infamy in the *tradiciones* by hoarding money given him by a dying octogenarian in order to provide a decent burial. Even the name underscores his parsimonious nature, as the narrative humorously points out: "¡¡¡Gil Paz!!! No es posible ser más tacaño de letras ni gastar menos tinta para una firma" (664).

A caricature often revolves around a ruling passion, as in the case of greed. An even more prevalent type in the *Tradiciones Peruanas* is pride or honor, with its accompanying arrogance, conceit, and self-exaltation. Despite the fact that numerous instances of honor in the *tradiciones* involve grave circumstances and occurrences, Palma was often able to infuse in them an element of humor, thus succeeding, as few have, to help man "laugh at himself and at life without causing him to lose his personal dignity."[23] The mirth associated with these accounts may be limited to a passing quip in an otherwise serious story or may emerge from a series of events, as in the case of "Los endiablados," one of whom, Pancho Arellano, put on such a display of elegance in order to win the coveted title of *don* that soon "todo títere empezó a llamarle *don* Francisco" (1073). Regularly a pun or a comparison in the author's remarks concerning pride serves as the primary stimulus to amuse the reader.

Frequent colloquial remarks by the author also yield humor. Often ironic, such remarks are delivered as direct commentary or in a free indirect style reflective of the character's thoughts. An exemplary story in this regard is "Un señor de muchos pergaminos," in which a certain Valdés y Bazán gets into an argument with the Viceroy's nephew over which lineage is greatest.

> Ambos alegaban venir, no del padre Adán, que fue un plebeyo del codo a la mano e inhábil para el uso del Don, sino de reyes, que así pudieron ser los de copas y bastos como dos perdidos. . . .
>   Claro es que nuestros dos hidalgos de sangre azul rechazaban todo parentesco con Cristo Señor Nuestro, porque al fin el Redentor fue hijo de carpintero y plebeyo por todos sus cuatro costados, pues el parentesco con el rey David viene de árbol genealógico un tanto revesado. (433)

Similarly, the citizens of Huánuco "llegaron a imaginarse que Dios los había formado de distinto limo, y casi casi decían como el finchado portugués: 'No descendemos de Noé; que cuando este borracho salvó del diluvio en su arca, nosotros, los Braganzas, salvamos también, pero en bote propio' " (318). "Historia de una excomunión" depicts the aforementioned confrontation in church between the archdean of Cuzco, Dr. Rivadeneira, and Doña Peñaranda. The description of that scene engages the jocund, indirect summation of the archdean's feelings ("caballo del Apocalipsis"); the laugh-provoking dialogue invented by the author; the irony of contradiction in the comment "lo de borrico no era para sulfurarse mucho;" and the use of couplets to elicit further amusement.

The *tradiciones* sport a myriad of dialogues either fully or partially imagined by their author. Many center around a question of honor, pride, or lineage, which is humorously drawn into focus. For example, a young man in rags once took offense at being requested by a friar to hold a stirrup for him.

> "Padre, mida sus expresiones, y sépase que habla con don Fulano de Tal, de Tal y de Tal." Y vomitó hasta media docena de apellidos. A lo que el fraile contestó con mucha flema: "Pues señor don Fulano de Tal, de Tal y de Tal, vuesa merced se vista como se llama o llámese como se viste." (157)

With similar chiasma Antonio López Quirós upbraided a poor *hidalgo* who refused to work in commerce: "Si tan caballero, ¿por qué tan pobre? Y si tan pobre, ¿por qué tan caballero?" (376).

Some anecdotes draw their entire narrative marrow from the competitive haughtiness of the protagonists. In "Un litigio original" Palma satirically depicted the confrontation of two coaches, one belonging to the marquess, the other to the count. Neither individual would retreat to allow the other to pass, and so the quarrel went all the way to the king. Two years later, when the decision returned, "no existía ya un clavo de los coches" (496), passersby and the weather having occasioned their eventual disintegration.

Many figures portrayed are types, embodiments of the almost archetypal *hidalgo* and vulnerable in everything that touches their honor. Palma delighted in portraying them and hardly resisted highlighting their defects. In this, as in many other aspects of style and tone, Palma echoed his Castilian masters of the *Siglo de Oro*. In part 1, chapter 3, of *Don Quijote* Cervantes created a cheerful satire of "the nobility craze," which Helmut Hatzfeld signals as one of numerous examples of the master's own humor.[24]

Below are listed several other overruling passions captured by Palma in his typically succinct, jocular depictions.

Excessive Rigor

> . . . don Crisanto Palomeque y Oyanguren, alcalde del crimen y golilla muy capaz de mandar ahorcar hasta a su sombra si de ella se desprendía humillo que a sospecha de delito trascendiera. (577)

Incompetence

> . . . sus alguaciles *Pituitas* y *Espantaperros*, que eran dos mocetones de los que el diablo empeño y no sacó. (577)

Selfishness

> El lecho del moribundo era rodeado por cuatro o cinco frailes de Ordenes distintas que se disputaban partijas en el testamento. Cada cual *arrimaba*

la brasa a su sardina, o tiraba, como se dice, para su santo; esto es, para el acrecentamiento de los bienes de su comunidad. (299)

Jealousy

El bueno de don Gutierre tenía, entre otros mortalísimos pecados, los de estar enamorado de su mujer hasta más arriba de la coronilla, ser celoso como un musulmán y muy sensible en lo que atañe a la negra honrilla. (396)

Timidity, Fear

Razón tuvo el que dijo que hay hombres que no rebuznan porque ignoran hasta la tonada del rebuzno, y temen desafinar. (1443)

Beyond the two types already isolated—the greedy individual and the individual absorbed in the sanctity of his honor—one discovers in the *tradiciones* several others that Palma very traditionally and comically alluded to or delineated. Physicians, for example, are portrayed in the same satirical vein common to Quevedo, which produces an amusement normally elicited by the depiction of ineptitude in those who profess the opposite.[25] Palma frequently blended into his narrative comments such as "murió de viejo y no de médicos" (435), "la ciencia . . . del matasanos o médico" (678), "leguízamo murió de *médicos* (o de enfermedad, que da lo mismo)" (219), "el doctor Juan de Vega . . . era una de las lumbreras de la ciencia que enseña a matar por medio de un *récipe*" (355), "en Medicina, los galenos, a fuerza de latinajos, más que de recetas, enviaban al prójimo a pudrir tierra" (628), or "el empirismo rutinero que en esos tiempos se llamaba ciencia médica" (471). As in many instances, evident in these remarks is a *Siglo de Oro* influence that reached him both through his reading of the Spanish classicists and through exposure to the works of Juan del Valle y Caviedes, who, like Palma, undoubtedly enjoyed the barbs and comicity of the writer of the Torre de Juan Abad.

In Palma's anecdotes the underhanded, mischievous roguery related to *escribanos* regularly comes to the reader's attention. As Ernest Stowell observes in his study entitled "Ricardo Palma and the Legal Profession," the Peruvian author "makes use of his great cultural heritage, with the resultant social satire, produced in accord with his own cheerful literary personality."[26] These anecdotes may be contained in isolated references in literary portraits, often as part of a pun, or they may constitute a characterizing element of a fuller narrative, as in "Don Dimas de la Tijereta." There, in typical ironic tone, Palma lamented the *escribanos*'s lack of a patron saint: "Los pobrecitos no tienen en el cielo camarada que por ellos intercedan" (514). Such remarks underscore in indirect fashion the author's tendency to debunk unworthy elements of colonial society.

Quips concerning legendarily noisome relatives incite laughter or smiles because they articulate publicly what is often experienced but not personally communicated. Mothers-in-law and sisters-in-law in the *tradiciones* compare nicely to unsavory members of the animal family. For example, due to the Lord's presence in Ica many miracles occurred, even "se les endulzó la ponzoña a las serpientes de cascabel que un naturalista llama suegras y cuñadas" (913). In "Glorias del cigaro" a question arises: "¿Tiene un marido alguna desazón con el boa constrictor llamado suegra? 'La suegra es el eximio divisor, / y la pobreza el aislador mejor' " (1444). Palma ascribed to an anonymous chronicler this added mockery: "La suegra de un amigo mío carga como reliquia dos astillitas; pero no por esas se le dulcifica el carácter a la condenada vieja" (317). A similar reference can be found in his narration "Los primitos." In this case, however, there is an element of understanding, for a Christian can "apechugar con una suegra, que es mal necesario, pues la mujer ha de tener madre que le haya parido, envuelto y doctrinado." Nevertheless, "la ocasión hace al ladrón; pero el ladrón hace a la Policía . . . en hábito de suegra" (1202). When in 1552 the king ordered all eligible bachelors in Lima to change their status within thirty days, the following chant became fashionable: "Si nadie quiere suegra / yo sí la quiero, / para a falta de leña / tirarla al fuego." With feigned uncertainty the narrator then comments ironically: "Y tiene razón que le sobra el cantarcillo. El padre Noé embarcó en el arca todo linaje de alimañas y sabandijas ponzoñosas; pero se cuidó mucho de no embarcar suegra. ¿Tienen ustedes la bondad de decirme de dónde diablos han salido después las suegras?" (131).

Mothers-in-law, however, do not hold a candle to cousins, a relationship that would have been abolished if the narrator had at least been born "para Padre Santo de Roma y sus arrabales" (1201). He goes on to attribute to them in a highly jocular tone the worst qualities imaginable. Rather than dwelling in a vale of tears, we inhabit a world of "primos civilistas y primos demócratas." Furthermore, the narrator says, "desengáñate, lector, no hay bichos más confianzudos y pechugueros, entre los seres que Dios fue servido crear para mortificación y purgatorio de maridos, que los tales primos. Lo que es a mí, me apestan de a legua" (1202).

The presentation of women in their traditional roles in the *Tradiciones peruanas* also serves as a source of humor for the reader. The depiction of this type by Palma perpetuates a long tradition of misogynistic satires dating from the Greeks, descending through Juvenal, Boccaccio (*Il corbaccio*), the Archpriest of Talevera (*El corbacho*), and Quevedo.[27] Although Palma did not intend to be maliciously antifeminist, he seldom shied away from the insertion of a jest at the expense of the daughters of Eve. Women are categorized in the *tradiciones* in several ways, according to age, marital status, religious devotion, or simply by sex in general.

The tendency to gossip, a characteristic attributed to women by misogynous writers, provides a point of departure.

> Y como cuando la mujer da rienda a la sin hueso, echa y echa palabras y no se agotan éstas como si brotaran de un manantial. (549)
>
> Las amigas imitaban a los varones en no mover sus labios, lo cual, bien mirado, debía ser ruda penitencia para las hijas de Eva. (863)

Although the beautiful young *limeña* regularly receives hyperbolic praise in the *tradiciones,* women of other ages fare less well and often serve as the butt of asides or comments by the narrator or protagonists. As Dora Bazán Montenegro points out, Palma seldom sympathizes with older women. Normally they are ugly and evil, as well as old, and merit only terse depiction—"viejas," "mujeres viejas"[28]—or satiric comparisons—"paredes más temblonas que dientes de vieja" (577). In "Asunto concluido" the *tradicionista* supplied a metaphorical categorization of women as he delineated one aspect of Gregorio de Hoyo's character:

> El señor gobernador era de los que dicen que la mujer en aritmética es un multiplicador que no hace operaciones con un quebrado; en álgebra, la x de una ecuación; en geometría, un poliedro de muchas caras; en botánica, flor bella y de grato aroma, pero de jugo venenoso; en zoología, bípedo lindo, pero indomesticable; en literatura, valiente paradoja de poetas chirles; en náutica, abismo que asusta y atrae; en medicina, píldora dorada y de sabor amargo; en ciencia administrativa, un banco hipotecario de la razón y el acierto. (891-892)

The abundance of females in the world leads to the observation "que de hembras está más que poblado este pícaro mundo, y que, como dijo no sé quién, *las mujeres son como las ranas, que por una que zabulle, salen cuatro a flor de agua*" (646). Santa Rosa's unrestraint with the Lord elicits the comment "a la pedigüeña le faltó tacto para conocer que con tanto pedir se iba haciendo empalagosa. Al fin, mujer. Así son todas. Les da usted la mano, y quieren hasta el codo" (233).

The widow, likewise the object of abiding literary satire, provides Palma with a further subtype.

> Esto de casarse con viuda proeza es que requiere más hígados que para habérselas, en pampa abierta y cabalgando en rocín flaco, con un furioso berrendo, de esos [con] . . . puntas como aguja de colchonero.
> Porque amén de que lo sacan a uno de quicio con el eterno *difuntear* (páseme la Academia el verbo), son las viudas hembras que gastan más letras coloradas que misal gregoriano, más *recúchulas* que juez instructor de sumario, y más puntos suspensivos que novela romántica garabateada por el diablo. (37)

Satiric, ironical exaggeration, along with indirect parody, lies at the base of the humor in this example.

Marriage, given the interest that people feel about it, furnishes an ideal subject for humor, whether the reference is to the type of the wife, the widow, or the mother-in-law, or to any other aspect of the relationship. It is, in the words of Max Eastman, "of all human things the most filled full and spouting at the corners with humorous laughter."[29] Throughout the *Tradiciones* Palma satirized women with comments concerning their role in marriage. The allusions involve both the traditional strengths of the woman as the true domineering mistress of the house and her deficiencies. We laugh at each instance because, in some case or another, we have either witnessed the reality of the truths being unveiled or have felt them ourselves.

> El conde de Bornos decía que la mujer de más ciencia sólo es apta para gobernar doce gallinas y un gallo. ¡Disparate! Tal afirmación no puede rezar con doña Ana de Borja y Aragón, que, como ustedes verán, fue una de las infinitas excepciones de la regla. Mujeres conozco y capaces de gobernar veinticuatro gallinas . . . y hasta dos gallos. (424-425)
>
> Bien dijo el que dijo que si el mar se casase, había de perder su braveza y embobalicarse. (821)

Throughout his stories Palma returned to the common metaphor—"media naranja"—to refer to a spouse, particularly a wife. This on occasion proves humorous in itself. A modification of the meaning, however, produces inevitable amusement, as in the case of Isabel, who objected to becoming "no diré la media naranja dulce, pero sí el limón agrio de tal mastuerzo" (1044). Palma also employed brief poetic combinations as effective vehicles for banter in regard to women's role in marriage.

One of Palma's most amusing references to marriage occurs in "El divorcio de la condesita" in the form of a synopsis of divorce proceedings between María Josefa de Salzar and the Marquess of Valdelirios. Her accusation that he was engaged "en relaciones subversivas con las criadas" and that "hacía años que, ocupando el mismo lecho que ella, la *volvía la espalda*" is countered by the following:

> El señor marqués de Valdelirios niega el trapicheo con las domésticas; sostiene que su mujer, si bien antes de casarse rengueaba ligeramente, después de la bendición echó a un lado el disimulo y dio en cojear de un modo horripilante; manifiéstase celoso de un caballero de capa colorada, que siempre se aparecía con oportunidad para dar la mano a la marquesa al bajar o subir al carruaje, y concluye exponiendo que él, aunque la Iglesia lo mande, no puede hacer vida común con mujer que *chupa* cigarro de Cartagena de Indias. (600)

The narrator then suggests that the "lectores maliciosos" imagine the rest for themselves.

Earlier we observed that humor derives from Palma's depiction of religious figures. Regarding women, nuns and *beatas* seem to lend themselves well to his drollery. Whether through complete stories or through miscellaneous portrayals or comments by the narrator, the *tradicionista* maintained for conventual topics the same jocular tone that makes the *Tradiciones peruanas* such a pleasure to read and to reread. For example, there is ample humor in *tía* Catita's mode of expression in "La misa negra": "Entonces declaró la San Diego que hacía diez años vivía (¡Jesús, María y José!) en concubinaje con Pateta. Ustedes no saben lo que es concubinaje, y ojalá nunca lleguen a saberlo. Por mi ligereza en hablar y habérseme escapado esta mala palabra, recen ustedes un credo en cruz" (835). Similarly, we laugh at Palma's delineation of Doña Sebastiana, who turned "beata, y beata de correa, que es otro ítem más; beata de las que leían el librito publicado por un jesuita con el título de *Alfalfa espiritual para los borregos de Jesucristo,* en el cual se llamaba a la hostia consagrada *pan de perro* (pan de pecador)" (242).

Other common ingredients of caricature include speech mannerisms, in the form of repetitions of a verbal identification tag, speech defects, and habitual mispronunciations.[30] Palma evoked amusement through the re-creation of and indirect allusions to dialogues and

muttered soliloquies. At times this type of humor joins with reproduced or explained speech patterns, which caricature in varying
degrees. On other occasions the amusement lies wholly in the situational content of the speech.

Mispronunciations or reproduction of a foreign accent can prove
funny both in real life and in literature.[31] Palma's depiction of Viceroy Manuel Amat y Juniet's Catalan Spanish serves as a case in point.
It was due to his poor pronunciation of *perra chola* that Mica Villegas received the famous nickname *Perricholi* (650). We laugh when
Amat exclaims, "¡Muchi diablus de latrons!" (649), while unknow-
ingly in the presence of the thieves themselves. The repartee between
Pedro Manzanares and the Andalusian barber stimulates amusement
in part because of the caricaturing depiction through dialogue of the
interlocutors, which includes Palma's attempt to capture the Anda-
lusian-Penisular accent by declaring that the barber "exclamó, ce-
ceando '¡María Zantícima!: Hoy me pierdo . . .' " (961).

One particular speech mannerism carries in Spanish the name
muletilla. This "consists of a favorite word or phrase that is the
trademark of a specific individual."[32] Palma's contemporary, Galdós,
used this frequently in his *Novelas contemporáneas*. The brief historical nature of a *tradición* does not often permit its author to stress
a *muletilla*, but once in a while Palma does emphasize its existence
for humorous effect. "No juegues con pólvora" provides an excellent
example of a *muletilla* in the person of Pacorro, an Andalusian youth.
His reiteration of the word *jinojo*, along with his somewhat ingenuous ire, becomes humorous to the reader. A bit of humor also stems
from Palma's reproduction of Ramón Castilla's manner of speech
"con las frases cortadas que eran de su peculiar y característico
lenguaje: '¡Eh! ¿Qué cosa? . . . ¡Muchachos locos! . . . ¡Calaveras!
. . . ¡Cortarles las alas! . . . ¡Faltos de juicio! . . . ¡Que no vuelen! . . .
¡Tunos! . . . ¡Que venga Mendiburu! . . . ¡Sí! . . . , ¡nada de escándalo
. . . , eso es! . . . ¡Romper hilos! . . . ¡Ya, ya!' " (1111).

Another speech identification tag in the *tradiciones* consists of
popular sayings, or *refranes*. Of course, Palma used them relentlessly
as narrator, but certain characters derive a substantial part of their
identity from their mastery of *refranes*. Doña Pulqueria (450-452)
and Gaspar Melchor de Carbajal (529-532) are associated with them
to such an extent that the latter merits designation as "otro Sancho
Panza en la condición refranesca" (530). Other characters take on
life through dialogues spiced with profanity and/or colloquialisms.

Owing to his tendency toward good taste, Palma replaced profanity with less offensive speech but did it in such a way that "la malicia del lector" can guess the intended terms. (This is quite common in the *tradiciones,* as our later study of euphemisms will clarify.) General Lara's harangue to his soldiers constitutes only one of numerous examples in Palma's anecdotes: "'¡Zambos del espantajo!' les gritó. 'Al frente están los godos *puchueleros.* El que manda la batalla es Antonio José de Sucre, que, como ustedes saben, no es ningún *cangrejo.* Con que así, apretarse los *calzones* y . . . ¡a ellos!' " (997). Consider also Friar Pablo Negrón's slightly more colorful advice to Pizí in regard to bullfighting: "bueno será que estés sobre aviso para que no te suceda un percance y vayas al infierno a contarle cuentos a la puerca de tu madre. . . . ¡con que abre el ojo, negrito; porque si te descuidas, te *chinga* el toro, y abur, melones!" (916).

As observed for parody, oftentimes a type is comically portrayed by means of an open dialogue, a monologue, or reported discourse laced with terminology particular to an individual's profession or devotion. In the opinion of Alberto Escobar, such evocative terms "bring out memories that go beyond the communicative function and connect the reader with certain professional environments or that refer him to particular geographical surroundings or levels of society."[33] Palma availed himself of specialized expressions from law, the military, religion, mathematics, and mythology. The humor of the expressions originates either from the abyss between the nature of the profession and a character awkwardly attempting to express himself in technical language foreign for him or from the surprising effectiveness, propriety, and wittiness of the words.

> El escribano llegaba todas las noches a casa de Visitación, y después de *notificarla* un saludo, pasaba a exponerla el *alegato* de lo bien probado de su amor. (515)

> Bien se barrunta que tan luego como llegó el sábado, y resucitó Cristo, y las campanas repicaron gloria, varió de táctica el galán y estrechó el cerco de la fortaleza, sin andarse con curvas ni paralelas. Como el bravo Córdova en la batalla de Ayacucho, el capitancito se dijo: "¡Adelante! ¡Paso de vencedores!"
> Y el ataque fue tan esforzado y decisivo, que Claudia entró en capitulaciones, se declaró vencida y en total derrota. (368)

From time to time Palma structured an animated conversation among several specific types, whom he vivified through word, mannerism, and irony of situation. Contrast between the overly confident, naive manner of the participants, including the terminology they employ, and the reality of the matter or person on which or whom their attention centers proves humorous. The first excerpt below brings together a *beata*, a lay brother from a convent, and a notary; the second, a cobbler, an old woman, a lawyer, a know-it-all adolescent, and a barber, among others.

"Es un escándalo que entierren a ese perro excomulgado en lugar santo," murmuraba una vieja, santiguándose con la punta de la correa que pendía de su hábito de beata.

"Calle usted, comadre," añadía un lego del convento, mozo de cara abotagada, con un costurón de más en el jeme y algunos dientes de menos. "Apuesto un rosario de quince misterios a que su patrón el demonio se ha robado ya de la caja el cuerpo de ese hereje."

"Doy fe y certifico que el dichoso capitán está ya achicharrado en el infierno," declaraba con el estupendo aplomo de la gente de su oficio, un escribano de la Real Audiencia, sorbiendo entre palabra y palabra sendas narigadas del *cucarachero*." (661)

"¿No lo decía yo? ¡Si es hereje!" afirmaba un zapatero remendón.

"La pinta no engaña," añadía una vieja contemporánea del arca de Noé: "es rubio como los judíos."

"Y tiene pico en la nariz," observaba un cartulario.

"Apuesto a que es circunciso," agregaba una mozuela marisabidilla.

"¡No podía ser por menos! Yo sé que ese hombre no reza el rosario," argüía un barbero.

"¡Ni el trisagio!" aumenta otro.

"¡Ni la setena!"

"¡Ni el trecenario!"

"¡Y la Inquisición, que se ha echado a muerta!" murmuraba el vendedor de bulas, que fue probablemente quien en 1807 denunció a don Demetrio O'Higgins ante el Santo Oficio de Lima, como lector de obras prohibidas.

"¡Viva la religión! ¡Muera el judío!" clamaron todos en coro. (868)

We have already witnessed Palma's expertise in colloquializing and contemporizing the speech of characters from sacred history such as Jesus, Peter, Judas, Pilate, and Satan.

Many dialogues offer humor on the basis of content alone. The irony or surprising turn of events portrayed in the exchanges is especially comical. Recall, as examples, the response of the narrator's girlfriend in "De cómo desbanqué a un rival"—"Eres el feo más simpático que ha parido madre" (1438)—or the repartee between Archbishop Barroeta and the lady who went over his head to secure a clerical position for a certain friend:

"Pues, señora mía, si su empeño hubiera sido por canonjía, de balde se la hubiera otorgado; pero dar cura de almas a un molondro . . . *nequaquam*.

El buen párroco necesita cabeza y para ser buen canónigo no se necesita
poseer más que una cosa buena."
"¿Qué cosa?" preguntó la marquesa.
"Buenas posaderas para repantigarse en un sillón del coro." (570)

Repartee constitutes a well-known form of humor, and Palma,
who, as we have seen, continually embroidered reality with imagined
dialogues in his dual effort to portray history and to fantasize, used
it in several *tradiciones*. The exchange between the barber and Pedro
Manzanares (961) exemplifies Palma's use of repartee, as does the
scurrilous flyting between the "dos palomitas sin hiel," Doña Francisca and Doña Catalina (290-291).[34]

Bonding Eras: Political and Social Satire

In the *Tradiciones peruanas* a particularly distinct area of satiric-
ironic humor pertains to contemporary political and social realities.
Over the centuries satirists have tended to be skeptical about associations and programs related to these institutions, and in Peru especially "a political orientation was a distinct feature of satire."[35]
Subject matter presents no barrier to satirists, who have written on
a wide spectrum ranging from the gravest to the most trivial and
from the most austere or sacred to the most licentious or profane
topics. However, the type of subject preferred by satirists has always
proved concrete, topical, and often personal. Politics fulfills these
qualifications well, as we see in the case of Dickens and Parliament
or Galdós and the Restoration period.[36] As discussed briefly, nineteenth-century Republican Peru offered Palma an equally ideal hunting ground with its wealth of "caudillistic," constitutional, and
socioeconomic vicissitudes.

For the most part, however, Palma was writing history and not
contemporary criticism. As a springboard with which to bridge the
gap between the past and the present, he chose the richly humorous
ironic-satirical aside, which came to constitute a significant component of his humorous style. This process of constructing a bridge of
irony between both eras infuses each with added life and vitality.[37]

Satirists tend to be idealistic and to confront reality in light of
their yearning for perfection. This obviously smacks of a romantic
tendency and in this limited regard one might be justified in ascribing
some degree of romantic inclination to all satirists. Palma's propen-

sities along these lines very possibly hearkened back to the days of "La bohemia de mi tiempo," but were heightened by the many difficulties and disappointments he encountered both actively and passively during the second half of the nineteenth century in Peru.

In order to more fully appreciate the politically oriented allusions in the *Tradiciones peruanas,* a reader must become acquainted with the Peruvian political and economic history of which Palma was a part. Born in 1833, nine years after the battle of Ayacucho, Palma lived in the midst of an ongoing series of political maneuvers, intrigues, and confrontations by the caudillos sprung from the war for independence. As he himself observed in one of his tales, "Desde que con la caída del presidente La Mar, después de la batalla del Portete, se fundó por el general Gamarra una era de revoluciones y motines de cuartel, raro fue el año sin dos, tres y cuatro presidentes en Lima, hasta que el general Castilla vino, en 1844, a echar llave y candado al manicomio suelto de los ambiciosos, que no otra cosa que un manicomio era el Perú" (1106).

Principal among these early leaders figured Gamarra, La Fuente, Santa Cruz, Orbegoso, Salaverry, and Vivanco. At age eleven Palma witnessed the assumption of the presidency by Ramón Castilla, a skillful caudillo whose keen ability to placate and to win cooperation from both liberals and conservatives was a major factor in holding a shaky political establishment together during the next twenty years. He served until 1851, enjoying some political success but leaving the economy generally undirected and slowly falling prey to foreign control and debt.

When Palma was eighteen years old José Rufino Echenique was elected president. During Echenique's three-year administration the future *tradicionista* witnessed an impressive display of graft, corruption, and skyrocketing internal debt, concluded by uprisings inspired throughout the country by Castilla. During Castilla's second term, from 1855 to 1862, Palma observed the emergence of two constitutions. The first constitution (1856), heavily liberal in orientation, was supported by Palma; the second constitution (1860), conservative and centralist, was so much to Palma's disliking that he, José Gálvez, and others associated with the Masonic lodges of Lima made an attempt on Castilla's life in 1860, resulting in Palma's exile to Chile for three years. Economically the country continued to founder. During this time expenditures and imports increased, income and exports decreased. The president, pursuing a policy of economic laissez-faire, failed to implement a broad program of taxation that would have helped significantly.

Further scenes of rebellion and military dictatorship occurred against the backdrop of economic decline during the early and middle 1860s. Although saved from bankruptcy by the Dryfus contract of 1869, the country became more firmly entrenched in foreign control. After the contract was ratified, Nicolás de Piérola, José Balta's minister of the treasury, "showed little concern over putting into operation the other announced features of his economic programme."[38] The country continued to rest on windfall capital rather than develop a sound, self-sustaining economy. Ricardo Palma served as Balta's personal secretary and so became intimately acquainted with congressional, ministerial, and presidential weaknesses and proclivities, along with those of the populace and political antagonists. Further economic excesses, including large investments in unprofitable railroad construction, compounded the burden to the treasury. At the age of thirty-nine Palma experienced the horrid events of late July 1872, during which President Balta was shot and three of the conspiring Gutiérrez brothers were gruesomely killed and burned in a huge urn in the Plaza de Armas.

When Manual Pardo assumed the presidency in that year, the economy was in ruins. President Pardo was quickly forced to print paper money unbacked by metallic resources, an inflationary procedure that continued until the end of the century. During Pardo's "república práctica," from 1872 to 1876, Piérola, the minister of the treasury under Balta, seeking to overthrow the government, instigated what uprisings he could. Mariano Prado became president in 1876 but immediately commenced a quarrel with Pardo's *civilista* majority in congress, while Piérola continued to stir up trouble in the south. Pardo was assassinated in 1878 and the war with Chile between 1879 and 1883 accentuated Peru's paucity of political leadership. The next decade, during which Palma, now in his sixties, pursued vigorously his literary career, spanned years of additional military caudillismo—Miguel Iglesias, Andrés Cáceres, Morales Bermúdez. During much of this time Piérola continued his efforts to undermine the Civilist and Constitutional agreement. Finally, in 1895, Piérola's bloody rise against the reelected Cáceres succeeded. Piérola served as president until 1899.

In summary, Ricardo Palma produced his *tradiciones* during a period racked by political greed and intrigue, bitter factional feuds between liberals and conservatives, inept and unfortunate economic policies, self-aggrandizement, uncommitted and unconscientious leadership, and constant attempted or successful revolts, uprisings, and assassinations, as the Republic struggled for political and economic stability.

Not surprisingly, the *tradiciones* reflect this historical ambience with great regularity, despite Palma's withdrawal from politics and his subsequent immersion in the past. References to political unrest, however, although often the product of deeply held opinions, do not bear the form of invective or vituperative satire. Rather, they share the humor and the compassion that consistently distinguish the tone of all the *tradiciones*.

The majority of Palma's contemporary political allusions are directly satirical. A fair number embody highly mirthful satiric irony. A smaller portion of allusions consists of direct criticism devoid of any irony, satire, or humor. Occasionally, the reference is simply a commentary involving little or no faultfinding. Some comments stand out for their sincerity. Other comments are notable for their nostalgic predilection, which occurs more often in social allusions. Some smack of sarcasm. The humor of political and social satire can be traced to principally three areas: first, to the revelation of truth, that is, hearing said what we might hesitate to state or are unable to articulate so well; second, to the contrast, usually based on overstatement, inherent in the irony; and third, to a degree of hostility and a sudden sense of superiority, wherein the reader experiences a modicum of revenge against those whom he blames for the sorry state of the country.[39] An inclination toward comparison and wordplay in these anecdotes is also evident in Palma's political references. Although usually comparisons of inequality, the references sometimes take on a structure of equality. A few examples clarify the nature of political or social references:

Satire

Llámelo usted como quiera; pero ello ha de ser verdad, que mi abuela no supo inventar ni mentir, que no era la bendita señora de la pasta de que se hacen hogaño periodistas y ministros. (284)

Satiric Irony

Desde los barrabasados tiempos del rey nuestro señor don Felipe III, hasta los archifelices de la *república práctica,* no ha tenido el Perú un gobernante mejor que el alcalde de Paucarcolla. (273)

Criticism

. . . si bien es cierto que esta última cualidad empieza a desparecer, para dar posada a los resabios y dobleces que son obligado cortejo de la civilización. (692)

Sarcasm

Cayó sobre él la turba, ya acaso habría tenido lugar un *gutierricidio* o acto de justicia popular, como llamamos nosotros los *republicanos prácticos* a ciertas barbaridades [allusion to the events of 1872]. (521)

Comparisons, Wordplay

. . . don Restituto, vejete con más altos y bajos que la Constitución del 60. (1148)

. . . nuestros gobernantes hacen tanto caso de la prohibición legal como de los mostachos del gigante Culiculiambro. (548)

Imagínense ustedes una limeñita de talle ministerial, por lo flexible; . . . En cuanto a carácter, tenía más veleidades, caprichos y engreimientos que alcalde de municipio, y sus cuentas conyugales andaban siempre más enredadas que hogaño las finanzas de la República. (396)

Haya de la Torre avers that no "institution or man of the colonial era and even of the Republic escaped the so frequently accurate bite of the irony, sarcasm and always the ridicule of Palma's jocose criticism."[40] Though somewhat generalized due to political motivations, the statement captures the impression of an avid reader of the *Tradiciones peruanas* and correlates well with the observations from a study of the humorous political asides.

The substance of the allusions falls within three broad categories—leadership and commitment, individual rights, and fiscal policies. Under the first category the *tradicionista* assailed the president, his ministers, congress, municipal leaders, caudillos, and the *pueblo*. Through satire, irony, or direct criticism Palma censured the leaders' lack of true concern, valor, integrity, energy, and creativity, their failure to fulfill promises and to adhere to the constitution, their predisposition to lie and to seek advancement without merit, and their unwillingness to cooperate for the good of the nation. The political process, electoral system, and governmental red tape were also subject to his jocular reprimands. Expressions within the second category tend to highlight a sense of injustice and a disrespect for guaranteed rights of the individual. With his observations concerning fiscal policies, the third category, Palma chastised his compatriots for detrimental and corrupt management of state funds, harmful economic policies, improper taxation, and the financial hegemony in Peru of foreign investors and corporations.

Although normally general in his remarks, Palma centered from time to time on specific individuals and administrations, such as Manuel Pardo's *república práctica* or Santa Cruz's endeavors. The allusions together constitute a sort of philosophical or ideological stance in regard to morals and ethics of political and social conduct. They establish Palma as covertly antiestablishment in the sense of his opposition to people, policies, and institutional elements that foster ineptness, corruption, and mismanagement. As noted in the introduction, however, his views did not endorse an abandonment of the democratic experiment but rather an abandonment of the selfish or shortsighted tendencies that undermine democracy. The following excerpts are divided into topical categories so as to facilitate fuller appreciation of this style of humor in the *Tradiciones peruanas*.

President
Sospecho que el alcalde de Paucarcolla habría sido un buen presidente constitucional. ¡Qué lástima que no se haya exhibido su candidatura en los días que corremos! El sí que nos habría traído bienandanzas y sacado a esta patria y a los patriotas de atolladeros. (272)

Cabinet Ministers
. . . una legión de espíritus malignos, más reacios para cambiar de domicilio que un ministro para renunciar la cartera. (163)

. . . el escribano era . . . tan pegado al oro de su arca como un ministro a la poltrona. (515)

Oh niña, niña, niña, / la del tonillo / hueco cual la cabeza de los Ministros.[41]

Congress
[Referring to the water of Caylloma, which caused one to become speechless]: Congresante conozco yo que probablemente ha bebido de aquella agua. (524)

Téngase en cuenta que casi siempre el compañero era algún diputado monosilábico, de esos cuya elocuencia parlamentaria se encierra en decir *sí* o *no*, ajustándose a la consigna ministerial. (1108)

Municipal Leaders, Taxation
. . . les caería encima una contribución municipal que los partiera por el eje, en estos tiempos en que hasta los perros pagan su cuota por ejercer el derecho de ladrar. (553)

Caudillos, Military Coups
No se diría sino que acababa de dar fondo en el Callao un galeón con importantísimas nuevas de España, ¡tanta era la agitación palaciega y popular!, o que, como en nuestros democráticos días, se estaba realizando uno de aquellos golpes de teatro a que sabe dar pronto término la justicia de cuerda y hoguera. (354)

El maestre de campo era, políticamente hablando, un hombre que se anticipaba a su época y que presentía aquel evangelio del siglo xix: "A una revolución vencida se la llama motín; a un motín triunfante se le llama revolución. El éxito dicta el nombre." (77)

Justice of the People
Llegada ésta a Lima, en enero de 1744, costó gran trabajo impedir que el pueblo lo hicese añicos. ¡Las justicias populares son cosa rancia por lo visto! (564)

Poor Government in General
[Following Santa Rosa's failure to get God to grant good government to Peru]: Y cata por qué el Perú anda siempre mal gobernado, que otro gallo nos cantara si la santa hubiera comenzado a pedir por donde concluyó. (233)

. . . ni más ni menos que hogaño cuando en los republicanos colegios de provincias se trata de nombrar presidente para el gobierno o desgobierno (que da lo mismo) de la patria. (299)

Ineffectual Leadership
Por dicha para el nombre americano, la sensatez no abandonó a los gobernantes. ¡Cosa rara! (1130)

Verdad es que, entonces como ahora, bandos tales fueron letra muerta. (665)

Cuando Luzbel, que era un ángel muy guapote y engreído, armó en el cielo la primera trifulca revolucionaria de que hace mención la Historia, el Señor, sin andarse con proclamas ni decretos suspendiendo garantías individuales o declarando a la corte celestial y sus alrededores en estado de sitio, le aplicó tan soberano puntapié en salva sea la parte, que, rodando de estrella en estrella y de astro en astro, vino el muy faccioso, insurgente y montonero, a caer en este planeta que astrónomos y geógrafos bautizaron con el nombre de Tierra. (1200)[42]

Absence of True Concern
. . . por tan roñosa suma cometió tan feo delito. ¡Quizá la situación de Judas era idéntica a la que hogaño aflige a los pensionistas del Estado! (693)

Lack of Valor, Integrity, Energy, Creativity
¡Dios de Dios! ¡Y qué falta nos hace en esta era republicana una docena de autoridades fundidas en el molde del corregidor de Ica! (655)

¡Bendita seas, patria de valientes, y que el genio del porvenir te reserve horas más felices que las que forman tu presente! (448)

Failure to fulfill promises and to adhere to laws and the Constitution
En esos tiempos era, como quien dice, artículo constitucional (por supuesto, mejor cumplido que los que hogaño trae, en clarísimo tipo de imprenta, nuestra carta política). (893)

. . . pongo punto por no hacer una lista tan interminable como la de puntapiés que gobiernos y Congresos aplican a esa vieja chocha llamada Constitución. ¡Así anda la pobrecita que no echa luz! (632)

Bien haya el siglo xix, en que es dogma el principio de igualdad ante la ley. Nada de fueros ni privilegios.

Que en la práctica se falsee con frecuencia el dogma, no quita ni pone. Siempre es un consuelo saber que existe siguiera escrito y que estamos en nuestro derecho cuando gritamos recio contra las arbitrariedades de los que mandan. (429)

Por supuesto que el virrey también le sacaba púa al trompo, y hacía política como cualquier presidentillo republicano a quien el Congreso manda leyes a granel, y él les va plantando un *cúmplase* tamañazo, y luego las tira bajo un mueble. . . . Aquello de *acato y no cumplo* es fórmula que hace cavilar . . . a un teólogo casuista. En teoría, nuestros presidentes no hacen uso de la formulilla; pero lo que es en la práctica, la siguen con mucho desparpajo. (637)

Advancement without merit
Parece que en el otro siglo no era moneda tan corriente como hogaño encaramarse sin merecimiento. (303)

Instability, lack of cooperation
. . . don Francisco Pizarro se adelantaba a su época, y pareciá más bien hombre de nuestros tiempos, en que al enemigo no siempre se mata o aprisiona, sino que se le quita por entero o merma la ración de pan. Caídos y levantados, hartos y hambrientos, eso fue la colonia, y eso ha sido y es la república. La ley del yunque y del martillo imperando a cada cambio de tortilla. (54)

Cobraron ánimos los alguaciles, y en breve espacio y atados codo con codo condujeron a los truhanes a la cárcel de la Pescadería, sitio adonde, en nuestros democráticos días, y en amor y compañía con bandidos, suelen pasar muy buenos ratos liberales y conservadores, rojos y ultra-montanos. ¡Ténganos Dios de su santa mano y sálvenos de ser moradores de ese zaquizamí! (332)

Los pueblos son puro espíritu de contradicción. Basta que el Gobierno diga pan y caldo para que los gobernados se emberrenchinen en sostener que las sopas indigestan. Por lo mismo que Gamarra era bermudista, el país tenía que ser orbegosista.
   O hay lógica o no hay lógica. Hable la historia contemporánea. (1057-1058)

Esto fue más serio que batalla de *clubs* en tiempos de elecciones democráticas. (597)

Immature political and electoral process
Una excomunión asustaba en aquellos tiempos como en nuestros días los *meetings* populacheros.
   "¿Qué gritan, hijo?"
   "Padre, que viva la patria y la libertad."
   "Pues echa cerrojo y atranca la puerta." (582)

Los agustinos no se dieron por notificados, y el escándalo se repitió. Diríase que la cosa pasaba en estos asendereados tiempos, y que se trataba de la elección de presidente de la República en los tabladillos de las parroquias. Véase, pues, que también en la época colonial se aderezaban pasteles eleccionarios. (546)

Bureaucratic red tape, delay, and detachment
Afortunadamente para Tijereta, no se había introducido por entonces en el infierno el uso de papel sellado, que acá sobre la tierra hace interminable un proceso. (517)

Si vas, lector, de paseo al Cerro de Pasco, cuando el ferrocarril sea realidad y no proyecto. (592)

Injustice, poorly administered justice
Conque apliquen ustedes el cuento y no me vengan con que estos son mejores o peores que aquellos tiempos, que en el Perú todos los tiempos son uno; pues el ser blandos de carácter y benévolos con el pecador lo traemos en la masa de la sangre. (1106)

. . . de la cual el canónigo C*** de la G*** hizo cera y pabilo en los nefastos días de la ocupación chilena, sin que sepamos que hasta hoy se le haya pedido cuentas por este acto de grosera prestidigitación. Por el contrario, el haber despojado a su patria y a la iglesia de lo que, a la vez que recuerdo histórico, era un primor artístico, le sirvió de recomendación, no para ir a purgar en chirona su sacrílega falta, sino para ascender a la segunda dignidad del coro. ¡Aberraciones de mi tierra! (877)

Disrespect for individual rights
¡Bonita disculpa la de su merced el padre Adán! En nuestros días la disculpa no lo salvaba de ir a presidio, magüer barrunto que para prisión basta y sobra con la vida asaz trabajosa y aporreada que algunos arrastramos en este valle de lágrimas y pellejerías. (514)

Proceso enviado a España era la vida perdurable, era algo así como en nuestros asendereados tiempos un encierro precautorio (de que Dios nos libre, amén) en San Francisco de Paula. (655)

En esos tiempos no estaban de moda las garantías individuales ni otras candideces de la laya que hogaño se estilan, y que así garantizan al prójimo que cae debajo, como una cota de seda de un garrotazo en la espalda. (425-426)

Fiscal mismanagement and corruption
Que las finanzas del Perú han andado siempre dadas al demonio, es punto menos que verdad de Perogrullo. Por fortuna, los peruleros somos gente de tan buena pasta, que maldito si paramos mientes en la cosa.

"Pero, señor, ¿en qué nos hemos gastado tantos miles?" suele preguntar algún homobono.

"En tabaco para el rey," contesta sonriendo, algún vejete—, y punto en boca. (662)

. . . capital tan inagotable para el infeliz judío como para nuestros Bancos de emisión la fábrica de billetes, a pesar de las incineraciones y demás trampantojos fiduciarios. (1131)

Así se puso término entonces a la crisis, y el papel con garantía o sin garantía del Estado, que para el caso da lo mismo, no volvió a parecer hasta que Dios fue servido de enviarnos plétora de billetes de Banco y eclipse total de monedas. Entre los patriotas y los patrioteros hemos dejado a la patria en los huesos y como para el carro de la basura. (969)

Foreign economic intervention
. . . no de esos pesos flacos o soles de menguada luz que valen apenas treinta y tantos peniques, y que en camino van de valer menos el día en que las casas de Graham Rowe, Bates Stockes y demás giradoras, que son quienes hacen la lluvia y el buen tiempo, así lo tengan por conveniente. (872)

These excerpts tend to confirm that Palma generally avoided satiric condemnation of specific political figures of the Republic. A survey of the *tradiciones* reveals that, although Palma mentioned every one of the presidents save Miguel Iglesias at least once, comments usually range between being neutral and being positive in tone. Palma restricted satiric comment to Agustín Gamarra and Manuel Pardo and extracted humor from anecdotes and descriptions only in association with Luis José Orbegoso and Ramón Castilla.

Gamarra, who was president when Palma was born in February 1833, was, in the author's opinion, "el primer caudillo de motín que tuvo la patria nueva y el que fundó cátedra de anarquía y bochinche" (1109). In "Parrafadas de crítica" Palma termed Gamarra "nuestro primer motinista de cuartel," adding, by way of lament and reproof, that "Gamarra tuvo discípulos que le aventajaron" (1492). Palma's references to Manuel Pardo focus primarily on the concept of the *república práctica* and question indirectly the tendency to ascribe full success and wisdom to any particular policy or overall orientation.

This humor derives from underlying irony and from the revelation of a truth by means of lightly satiric contrast. The allusions themselves are important as confirmation of Palma's continuing awareness of and sensitivity to contemporary political issues and orientations and of his later inclination to favor a stronger central leader within the democratic framework.

Pero conste, para cuando nos cansemos de la república, teórica o práctica, y proclamemos, por variar de plato, la monarquía, absoluta o constitucional, que todo puede suceder, Dios mediante y el trotecito trajinero que llevamos. (279)

. . . cuando Castilla y Echenique gobernaban al país por el sistema antiguo (teóricamente); y, ¡qué diablos!, parece que con la teoría no le iba del todo mal a la patria. (733)

> El hombre era voto en la materia, y a haber vivido en tiempo de la *república práctica,* creada por el presidente don Manuel Pardo—y cuyos democráticos frutos saborearán nuestros choznos—, habría figurado dignamente en una de las juntas consultivas que se inventaron; verbigracia, en la de instrucción pública o en la de demarcación territorial. (920)

Palma playfully depicted Orbegoso as the good-natured father of eleven children who could not resist mentioning his family no matter what the situation and who might go down in history as a *mono bravo* "por haber hecho ascos a femeniles carantoñas" (1066). Castilla, on one occasion, derided Orbegoso for this tendency, noting that "mientras otros nos hemos ocupado en *hacer patria,* vuecencia no se ha ocupado sino en fabricar muchachos; pues venga o no a pelo, nos habla de ellos en cartas, y en brindis, y en discusiones serias como la actual" (1066). Castilla is associated with drollery in the *tradiciones,* particularly in "Don por lo mismo," "La conspiración de capitanes," "El godo maroto," and "Historia de un cañoncito." As discussed earlier, Palma, in his characterization of the Peruvian president, focuses on his distinctive manner of speech typified by "frases cortadas" (1111) and "interrupciones que le eran peculiares" (1114).

Stylistically speaking, Palma's satiric-ironic allusions to politics reveal several phenomena worthy of comment. Highly evident, almost to the point of being a motif, is the linkage technique whereby the colonial era is related to the contemporary period or vice versa. Most frequently this is accomplished through the use of the colloquial term *hogaño,* counterbalanced with *antaño, esos tiempos, aquellos tiempos, otro siglo,* or *entonces.* In place of *hogaño* may stand references to the Republic, the *patria, nuestros tiempos, nuestros días, hoy,* or *siglo xix.* This style maintains a bond between the two eras, keeping their interrelationship fresh and forcing a constant awareness of the narrator's presence and perspective. Regular recourse to exclamations and interrogatives fortifies this awareness, both in the contexts we are presently considering and throughout the style of the *tradiciones.* The exclamatory phrase often acts as the principal bearer of irony and/or satire in these allusions, as well as relays simple narrator criticism. This inclination in Palma seems to constitute a partial reflection of his earlier, more dramatically romantic days blended into a predominantly ironic mode of expression. Accompanying these phrases are certain procliticly placed adjectives intended to be read ironically, such as *democráticos, republicano,* or *constitucional*— "nuestros democráticos días" (354). An analysis of the nature of this irony reveals that it rests most heavily on overstatement, logical and factual contradictions, and false objectivity, along with occasional feigned praise and paradox. Substantial repetition serves to tie allusions together as part of a stylistic family rather than isolated excerpts. The references also unite tonally by means of a frequent note of nostalgia often mingled with national pride, along with the satiric irony prevalent in nearly all of them.

Of course, the majority of Palma's narratives incorporate no mention of a nineteenth-century link. Nevertheless, tales of governmental corruption or economic mismanagement narrated in the subjective tone of the *tradicionista* serve the purpose of criticizing contemporary affairs in many instances, although these may not be immediately humorous. Luis Alberto Sánchez illuminates the point: "The personages that file past there do not belong to the sixteenth century but to the nineteenth. This is Ricardo Palma's trick. He speaks to us of the Count de la Vega, and he is describing Juan Pérez; of la Perricholi and, without altering her legendary traits, he describes to us a woman of graceful bearing of his time."[43]

Companion to the bounteous political allusions to the nineteenth century are references with social or socio-religious focus. Though not as plentiful as the political references, they constitute a common landmark in the *Tradiciones peruanas* that further facilitates the unique blending of eras in Palma's historical satire and irony. Due to the visibility of political references, the presence of references centering on social factors is often overlooked. This is the case in Porras Barrenechea's essay on Palma's satire. A few critics, however, do notice this current. Palma's grandaughter, Edith Palma, for instance, underscores his "firm, potent, unremitting vocation as a critic of our institutions and of Peruvian social life in all epochs." Concurring, Luis Avilés Pérez calls attention to Palma's satirizing of "supposed intrinsic values accepted by politicians, society, and religion."[44]

Humor issues from the Peruvian writer's socially or religiously oriented remarks, although some constitute straightforward commentary or denunciation. This nonhumorous commentary occurs more often in regard to social allusions than in regard to political allusions. Mirth most frequently originates in the employment of satiric irony, but statements of direct satire or simple comment also elicit responses of humor. Jocosity normally prevails as the predominant tone. However, sarcasm and nostalgia are not uncommon.

Palma's references to nineteenth-century society can be categorized generally according to several topics: marriage, family life and conduct, women, personal attitudes, standards and interpersonal relationships, quality of products and education, national customs and heritage, and economic relationships. In his comments Palma's underlying attitude ranged from the sincerity of moral concern, on the one hand, to playfulness, on the other hand. While Palma usually lauded a custom or a trend of bygone eras, in some instances he sanctioned the changes that had occurred. Although he voiced his awareness of the natural inclination to eulogize the past at the expense of the present, he pursued that course anyway; and although Palma sought through his comments only humorous effect, it is clear he truly perceived certain deficiencies in contemporary society. On occasion, however, his irony communicates disapproval of the habits of both past and contemporary societies or suggests an ambiguous stance. Furthermore, Palma might compare the practices of the colonial reign with those of the Republic or contrast the customs of his own youth with contemporary tendencies.

In the area of family and marriage Palma's primary interests include what establishes proper preparation for the marriage state and parental discipline and indulgence.

Los chicos de esos tiempos vestíamos pantalón *crecedero,* gorra y chaqueta o mameluco. No fumábamos cigarrillos, no calzábamos guantes, no la dábamos de saberlo todo, ni nos metíamos a politiquear y hacer autos de fe, como hogaño se estila, con el busto de ningún viviente, siquiera fuese ministro caído. ¡Buena felpa nos habría dado señora madre en el territorio del Sur! Dígase lo que se quiera, hace treinta años la juventud no era juventud; vivíamos a mil leguas del progreso. Vean ustedes si los muchachos de entonces seríamos unos bolonios, cuando teníamos la tontuna de aprender la doctrina cristiana en vez del *can-can;* y hoy cualquier zaragatillo que se alza apenas del suelo en dos estacas, prueba por A + B que Dios es artículo de lujo y pura chirinola o *canard* del padre Gual. (544)

Las Pantojas no quisieron alcanzar los días de progreso, en que las muñequitas de trapo serían reemplazadas por *poupées* de marfil, y en que el lujo para vestir una de éstas haría subir su valor a un centenar de duros. ¡Qué tiempos aquellos! ¡Cuánto atraso y miseria! Hoy papas, mamas y padrinos derrochan, por pascua de diciembre, un dineral en juguetes para los nenes, que así *duran en sus manos como mendrugo en boca de hambriento.* La vanidad ha penetrado hasta en los pasatiempos de la infancia. (733)

Palma enjoyed calling attention to traditional feminine foibles, as seen previously in our examination of his treatment of types. This is evident whether Palma singled out minor defects in the females of his own or a past century. His technique is often to suggest either that a woman of the present is not like a woman of the past in a particular respect or that she shares a similar characteristic with the daughters of Eve that went before. Palma's merriment stems from the irony associated with the suggestion that the deficiency in question came into being only with the onset of the nineteenth century and from the light debunking of that tendency, especially in adolescents. "Margarita, que se anticipaba a su siglo, pues era nerviosa como una damisela de hoy, gimoteó, y se arrancó el pelo y tuvo pataleta" (634). Note in this example a common feature in the *tradiciones,* that is, linking a historical figure to contemporary nineteenth century by ascribing to him or her traits typical only of the latter time.

Nervousness and tantrums seem especially to attract Palma's attention, either because each accommodates nicely facetious commentary or due to some unpleasant encounters in his own life. "En esos tiempos era costumbre dejar las sábanas a la hora en que cacarean las gallinas, causa por la que entonces no había tanta muchacha tísica o clorótica como en nuestos días. De nervios no se hable. Todavía no se habían inventado las pataletas, que hoy son la desesperación de padres y novios" (598). The same is true for the inclination to gossip or to defend foolish notions.

> Por entonces estaba aun en limbo, y no se conocía en este cacho de mundo el respetable gremio que hoy se llama de las *madres jóvenes,* asociación compuesta de muy talluditas jamonas, constituidas en confidentes de la coquetería y picardigüelas de sus hijas, y que por cuenta propia saben también dar un cuarto de escándalo al pregonero. (694)

> Pero hoy dicen las niñas que el agua pudre la raíz del pelo, y no estoy de humor para armar gresca con ellas sosteniendo la contraria. También los borrachos dicen que prefieren el licor, porque el *agua cría ranas y sabandijas.* (554)

Interpersonal relationships and personal integrity and ethics offer the satirist a fruitful hunting area not only in politics but in other phases of societal interchange as well. Palma frequently availed himself of this human factor and delighted in employing the technique of century-bonding to convey his comments. His satire or satiric irony, whichever the case may be, evoke smiles while gently deriding such characteristics as deceit, ungratefulness, apathy, low self-respect, unscrupulousness, and superficiality. These allusions apparently have as part of their origin some disagreeable experiences suffered by the author himself.

De fijo que proporcionó tema para conversar un año; que, por entonces, los sucesos no envejecían, como hoy, a las veinticuartro horas. (861; see also 676)

Todo lo había perdido, menos la vergüenza, que es lo primero que ahora acostumbramos perder. (476)

Quien aspire a tener larga cosecha de males, empiece por sembrar beneficios. Esperar gratitud del prójimo favorecido es como pedir hoy milagros a los santos. (476)

. . . ojos de médico, por lo matadores, y de boca de periodista, por el aplomo y gracia en el mentir. (396)

Several facetiae of this type in the Peruvian writer's anecdotes center on the quality of nineteenth-century products and services, as contrasted with the quality of analogous products and services of preceding years. Such humor is light, with little if any implicit moral thrust. Palma's pronounced tendency to return to the same phraseology reveals itself again; food and education constitute principal themes:

¡Aquélla sí era gloria y no la de estos tiempos de cerveza amarga y papelmanteca! (859)

Los banquetes de esos siglos era[n] de cosa sólida y que se pega al riñón, y no de puro soplillo y oropel, como los de los civilizados tiempos que alcanzamos. Verdad es que antaño era más frecuente morir de un hartazgo apoplético. (397)

Ellos no podían soñar que en el siglo xix tendría las mismas y mayores habilidades cualquier mastín de casta cruzada, y que hasta los ratones y las pulgas serían susceptibles de recibir una educación artística. (736)

The initial paragraph of "El divorcio de la condesita" avers that if past generations were to return to Lima in the nineteenth century they would be most amazed at the "completo cambio en las costumbres" (598). Given the *costumbrista* nature of his stories, it is not surprising that Palma perpetuated this theme throughout. *Costumbrismo* supplies the principal stimulus for the nostalgic commentary frequently encountered by the reader of the *Tradiciones*. Nostalgia, however, often diminishes the degree of humor elicited by each allusion. Palma bemoaned the encroachment of European customs that he perceived were diluting, if not entirely extirpating, the practices of national heritage. Of special concern was the disappearance of the enticing, mysterious ambience of Moorish-Christian architecture and alluring *tapadas*.

> Aquella tarde tenía lugar la fiesta de la Porciúncula, y desde las doce de la mañana estaban ocupados los bancos por esas huríes veladas que la imitación de costumbres europeas ha desterrado—hablamos de las tapadas—. ¡Dolorosa observación! La saya y manto han desaparecido, llevándose consigo la sal epigramática, la espiritual travesura de la limeña. ¿Estará condenado nuestro pueblo a perder, de día en día, todo lo que lleva un sello de nacionalismo? (817)

> Lima, con las construcciones modernas, ha perdido por completo su original fisonomía entre cristiana y morisca. Ya el viajero no sospecha una misteriosa beldad tras las rejillas, ni la fantasía encuentra campo para poetizar las citas y aventuras amorosas. Enamorarse hoy en Lima es lo mismo que haberse enamorado en cualquiera de las cuidades de Europa. (599)

> A la inofensiva mazamorra la tenemos relegada al olvido, . . . Lo que hoy triunfa es la cerveza de Bass, marca T, y el *bitter* de los hermanos Broggi. (904)

Turning now to references of religious bent, we find that despite Palma's satiric heyday with religious figures and customs, he had only modest recourse in this area to the device of century-bonding. The main reason for this is that depictions of historical ecclesiastic personages and habits readily transfer on a subconscious level to a similar and pervasive contemporary reality. Thus, portrayal of a gluttonous priest of the 1700s automatically intimates the applicability of like traits to contemporary priests.

Nevertheless, in a few instances the author does use the past as a point of departure for critique of his contemporaries and, apparently, of himself. Some such statements reflect Palma's conflicting ideas concerning an essential, positive, motivating faith in God, which he favors and perhaps retains to a small degree, and foolish superstitions and customs, which he mercilessly but jokingly flagellates. In each case deciphering ironic implications unearths the "truth," or at least draws us as close as we can get to it, since sometimes the intricacies of irony successfully resist interpretation. In "Lucas el sacrílego" the narrator addresses the reader, stating, "el avisado lector . . . no puede creer en duendes ni en demonios coronados, y . . . como es de moda en estos tiempos de civilización, acaso no cree ni en Dios" (561). The first part proves ironic because the "avisado lector" may still believe in demons and spirits. In the second part, the narrator appears to satirize the "civilized" inclination to discard what is enduring and substantive for a fashionable though eventually enervating atheism. The text is clearly more facetious when the narrator announces that he is going to "desenpolvar" some of Mother Monteagudo's prophecies "para solaz de la gente descreída que pulula en la generación a que pertenezco" (435), since he himself cherishes little faith in that regard. A more serious denunciation underlies Palma's derision of the foolishly arrogant youth of the day who "prove" that God is an item of luxury.

Inversely, Palma's indictment of naive superstitions requires no interpretation at all. "Hoy mismo hay gentes que creen en estas paparruchas a pies juntillas," referring to the belief that a certain dead rancher "paseaba por las calles de Lima en un carro inflamado por llamas infernales y arrastrado por una cuadriga diabólica" (567). The narrator announces in "Los panecitos de San Nicolás" that "lo que me trae turulato, y alicaído, y patidifuso es que ya los tales panecitos tengan menos virtud que el pan quimagogo. Tan sin prestigio están hoy los unos que los otros. ¡Fruto de la impiedad que cunde!" (292). This passage seethes with irony founded in style-content contradictions, pretended uncertainty, and false objectivity. The final exclamation literally deluges the reader with a series of ironic contradictions, since the narrator's ascription of the absence of miracles to a contemporary wave of impiety contrasts strongly with the reader's awareness that Palma did not really believe in miracles in the first place.

Palma's irony turned to sarcasm and even to invective when he confronted the church's opposition to freedom of thought and to progress. As is well known, Jesuits particularly merit Palma's scorn.

> Esa orden, tan tenazmente combatida, vuelve en pleno siglo XIX a pretender el dominio de la conciencia humana. Cadáver que, como el fénix mitológico, renace de sus cenizas, se presenta con nuevas y poderosas armas al combate. La lucha está empeñada. ¡Que Dios ayude a los buenos! (661)

Palma held similarly scornful sentiments concerning capital punishment, which he vehemently opposed. Occasionally, the flow of a story provided a logical niche to express those feelings. "Aquí vendrían de perilla cuatro floreos bien parladitos contra la pena de muerte; pero retráeme del propósito el recuerdo de que, en nuestros días, Víctor Hugo y otros ingenios han escrito sobre el particular cosas muy cucas, y que sus catilinarias han sido sermón perdido, pues la sociedad continúa levantando cadalsos en nombre de la justicia y del derecho" (895).

Literary Criticism

As a poet, Ricardo Palma maintained an avid interest in the muses throughout his life. This attention led to the writing of several *tradiciones* composed in great part of literary criticism and collections of verse. These *tradiciones* include "Delirios de un loco," "El poeta de las adivinanzas," "La Argentina," "El Ciego de la Merced," "Los plañideros del siglo pasado," and "El poeta de la Ribera, don Juan del Valle y Caviedes." In many other stories one additionally finds snatches of critical response, normally to poetry. Together the evaluations reveal a wide spectrum of tonal reaction ranging from enthusiastic encomium to absolute denunciation. A majority of critical remarks, however, evidences the same jocular tone that characterizes the *Tradicions peruanas* as a whole.

Palma recognized that his fevered poetic flourishes and those of his youthful friends fell short of meriting a place on Parnassus. "Hilvanadores de palabras bonitas," he called himself and the others, "con las que traíamos a las musas al retortero, haciendo mangas y capirotes de la estética" (1438). Palma manifested a parallel indulgence in some of his criticism of others—"Desgraciadamente, el hijo no *hace,* como poeta, honor al padre" (502); "Quirós no es un poeta muy rico en rimas ni muy fecundo en imágenes" (1136); "Este es, en nuestro concepto, uno de los menos incorrectos sonetos del vate arequipeño" (1137). Many poems, however, particularly those of little-known colonial writers, merited the full brunt of the *tradicionista*'s banter and satire. Palma delighted in ridiculing unskilled, extravagant imitations of *gongorismo* or romanticism by "hijastros de Apolo."

In "Los plañideros del siglo pasado," which proffers several examples of this style, Palma exhibits some of his best humor: "¡Qué tiempo y qué papel tan mal empleados!" (508); "Tantas inepcias son más bien burla que expresión de congoja" (508); "No quedó coplero que no contribuyese con los abortos de su musa en las exequias de

Doña María" (506); "la *limana musa* doña María Manuela Carrillo Andrade y Sotomayor se dirige a la Muerte y en romance indigesto la dice" (508); "Los demás endecasílabos son tan detestables como este soneto de la misma autora" (506). Earlier the author reproduced the sonnet of a bard who was surprised that no precursory comet preceded the death of the king, and he followed the quote with this analysis: "Por supuesto que a esta andanada de preguntas el cometa no responde oxte ni moxte, aunque muy bien pudo contestar que si no salió a pasearse por el cielo fue porque no le dio su real gana. Muchos horrores ha producido la escuela romántica, pero los del gongorismo la aventajan" (502). Elsewhere the narrator reacts to a certain *romancillo:* "Bien chabacana, en verdad, es la mitológica musa que dio vida a estos versos" (621). Worthy of additional mention are the incisive, jolting, yet jocund evaluations; the sarcastic use of *vate* and sobriquets such as *limana musa;* the pervading tone of hilarity at the expense of stupidity; and the sweeping condemnation of entire literary currents.

Denunciation of literary movements shows up with some regularity. Palma, for instance, praised Valle y Caviedes for not becoming contaminated "con las extravagancias y el mal gusto de su época, en que no hubo alumno de Apolo que no pagase tributo al gongorismo" (469). Although basically favorable to Terralla y Landa, Palma nevertheless chided him for paying tribute to the rococo mania of his era (716). He derided romantic tendencies by means of delineating comparisons—consider, for example, the description of Veremunda as "color de sal y pimienta, que no siempre han de ser de azúcar y canela; ojos negros como el abismo y grandes como desventura de poeta romántico" (530). Alluding to Iñigo López de Mendoza, the one responsible for introducing the sonnet into Spanish, the narrator quips, "Tengo para mí que el marqués de Santillana llevó al parnaso una plaga peor que las de Egipto, y que las pudorosas vírgenes del Castalio coro corren peligro de ahogarse en un océano de sonetos infelices. Entre una nube de mosquitos de trompetilla y una andanada de sonetos, elija el diablo, que no yo" (1136).

Stylistically, this facet of Palma's humor relies on a variety of techniques common to the *tradiciones,* namely, minimal aesthetic distance of the narrator-commentator, apt employment of vernacular terminology and irony, and the use of ironic circumlocution ("hijo de Apolo," "abortos de su musa," Castalia imagery). As always, the *tradicionista* is having fun and so is the reader.

Hyperbole and Litotes

As a mode of narrative and conscious humor, hyperbole dates to early western literature. Primitive literature offers many examples. In America in the nineteenth century we see hyperbole come into its own as humor in Mark Twain. Across the Atlantic, the Spanish, along with other southern European nationalities, were famous for their propensity to exaggerate, a tendency that they transmitted to the colonies. Cervantes relied on hyperbole heavily, especially as a means of characterizing Don Quijote. The case was the same for Francisco de Quevedo, who used it constantly, both "in figurative expression as well as in non-metaphoric description."[45]

That Palma incorporated hyperbole regularly in his narrative phraseology soon becomes clear to the observant reader of the *tradiciones.* In his tales exaggeration interrelates with irony and satire— caricature and parody, for example—sometimes taking the shape of a comparison, sometimes not. Actually, one might say hyperbole animates satire, which, while portending truth, inherently exaggerates or distorts. In Palma's works some degree of comicity almost always accompanies the employment of exaggeration. The intersection of tones and arrangements, however, offers different possible combinations for analytical focus. We have touched on this question already in the previous chapter. Under the present heading we will limit our study to non-metaphorical hyperbolic constructions, with few exceptions. The constructions that constitute similes and metaphors, along with other comparisons not of exaggerative design, will be examined carefully under the heading of comparisons.

A vast majority of instances of exaggeration in Palma's style is expressed by the narrator. Nevertheless, a protagonist may avail himself of it, as in the case of the old man who nostalgically extols the virtues of an actress of his younger days: "¡Qué fosfórica es esta juventud! Bien se conoce que no oyeron a la Moreno . . . ¡Oh la Moreno! . . . ¡Cosa mejor, ni en la gloria!" (815). The reader laughs at the incongruent but stimulating association of an actress and heaven, as well as at the naïveté of the speaker. Many of Palma's literary portraits applaud the physical attributes of the *limeña*. There, too, exaggeration often makes its appearance, contributing to the *tradicionista*'s well-known idealization and even "proverbialization" of the women of his native city. Consider in this regard Veremunda, who had an "hoyito en la barba tan mono, que si fuera pilita, más de cuatro tomaran agua bendita" (530). Of course, indisputably, all the "antiguas limeñas parecían fundidas en un mismo molde" (165). The author's enthusiasm frequently carried him to hyperbolic delineations of great plasticity and sensual connotations.

Palma interspersed in his prose exaggertions that originate in his highly visible presence as narrator. Some exaggerations are simply facetious. Others fall more clearly into the categories of burlesque, caricature, and/or ironic satire. Recall the potion "que venden los charlatanes, jurando y rejurando que hacen nacer el pelo hasta en la palma de la mano" (1200). Here, as noted by Beinhauer, Palma again characteristically employed the term *hasta* in order to reinforce intensity in a way common to hyperbole in oral usage. Eastman tells us that if readers are in a state of playful rapport with the author, "a manipulation of the mere quantity or degree of things" will suffice to bring about a humorous reaction.[46]

Caricature, whose essential meaning *is* exaggeration, exemplifies this well. For example, in "El divorcio de la condesita" we find the apprehensive Juan Dávalos y Ribera "encelándose hasta del vuelo de las moscas" (600), an intensification that proves humorous for the "lector amigo." A similar effect is evidenced in the case of Juan Fulgencio, "que era en lo físico un *feo* con *efe de fonda* de chinos" (676). The narrator also reminds the reader of the existence of certain priests "que saben sacar leche con espuma hasta del badajo de la campana de San Pedro" (1412). Instances of the union of ironic satire and overstatement abound in the anecdotes. People are taxed for sneezing, viceroys pave the Milky Way, nerves were invented in the nineteenth century, no one ever expresses gratitude, news always loses its importance within twenty-four hours, a viceroy needs a covered wagon to convey his titles, and even dogs pay for the right to bark. Clearly, Ricardo Palma found hyperbole an effective adjuct to humor, one that he turned to regularly. The conversational tone of the *tradiciones* makes exaggeration, a common element of oral communication, a natural inclusion.

Easily overlooked because of its unobtrusiveness, litotes, or understatement, "in which an affirmative is expressed by the negative of the contrary," nevertheless constitutes a valuable stylistic phenomenon in Palma's prose, one often coupled with humor. In general, the impetus behind the comicity of litotes turns out to be the same satire we have observed throughout the present study. Palma employs litotes regularly, as the following passages confirm.

Cuando llegaban personas amigas de la familia propietaria del nacimiento, se las agasajaba con un vaso de jora, chica morada u otras frescas
horchatas, bautizadas con *el nada limpio nombre* de *orines del Niño.*
(1199; first italics mine)

. . . lienzos que, a decir verdad, no seducen por el mérito artístico de sus
pinceles. (787)

. . . doña Catalina encontraba en el de Andrade olor, no a palillo, que es
perfume de solteros, sino a papel quemado. (290)

Camorrista, jugador y enamoradizo, ni dejaba enmohecer el hierro, ni
desconocía garito, ni era moro de paz con casadas o doncellas. (380)

. . . contábase de él que entre las bellezas mexicanas no había dejado la
reputación austera de monje benedictino. (480-481)

4

More Humor of Satire and Satiric Irony

Comparisons

As Sturgis Leavitt has observed, Palma obviously "has one of the most picturesque styles imaginable." Perhaps the most prominent factor in that achievement is his striking utilization of figurative language, especially simile and metaphor. As Worcester says of *Hudibras*, similes are "thicker than blackberries, and . . . of several sorts."[1] In addition, similes constitute a very significant aspect of the style of humor in the *Tradiciones peruanas*.

In his study of colloquial Spanish Beinhauer discovers that "one of the most beautiful and popular means of expression with which to enhance linguistically the characteristic attributed to a being is to compare it with an object or a person that the speaker's fantasy considers an exponent of the quality alluded to." Beinhauer also states that comparison comprises a "procedure widely used by all of the truly popular writers, including Cervantes himself." The use of figurative writing, as expressed by Maren Elwood, "stresses and sharpens sensory appeal," thus helping "the reader to exercise his own picture-making faculty" and to involve "his own imagination in image building. It helps him, not only to see, but to feel, to hear, to taste. This reaction, in turn, increases his own emotional reaction." Booth explains why comparisons involve the reader in this way, emphasizing that they force construction of "unspoken meanings through inferences about surface statements that for some reason cannot be accepted at face value."[2] Simply put, comparisons make us think more and thus internalize more than a direct description would.

Palma was well aware of the tonal advantages to be gained through wisely situated amplification of his words. As an avid student of the *Siglo de Oro* classicists, Palma was exposed to numerous instances of the use of comparisons for humorous ends. Angel Rosenblat, for example, informs us that while Cervantes extracted numerous comparisons from popular speech and used them appropriately, "that which is truly Cervantine is to play with them or apply them to the most unexpected circumstances." Quevedo displayed tremendous creativity in this regard. Lia Schvartz Lerner explains that discarding the traditional form of the metaphor, "which presupposed the existence of an evident similarity between the compared object and the metaphoric designation," Quevedo went on to generate stunning humorous comparisons emanating from a posture affirming that the pleasure of creation consisted in comparing "two objects from reality very distant from each other."[3]

Palma, knowing its effectiveness in stimulating emotional reponse, turned to comparison to enhance the portrayal of a character, to draw the reader more fully into the realm of his influence through the creation of an intimate, conversational tone, and to serve as a medium for humor, particularly the humor of satire. That the simile constitutes a fundamental facet of mirth-making is further brought out in Eastman's analysis of "poetic humor," one division of which he describes as the "art of incongruous comparison," and in Beinhauer's *El humorismo en el español hablado,* wherein are devoted several pages to the status of comparison in popular humorous phraseology. As far back as 1569, as reported by Rosenblat, Massimo Troiano, in his manual of Spanish for Italians, observed that one of the three principal characteristics of Spanish expression that caught his attention was the "abundance and frequency of comparisons, exclamations, and rhetorical questions."[4]

Nimetz informs us that while satire and irony whittle away at the world, paring it down to its proper size, metaphor performs just the opposite, inflating, distorting, dramatizing, and even poetizing reality. In essence this is true. Often, however, metaphor and simile strengthen the power of satire and irony by extending humorous connotations to the subject of the comparison. Metaphor and simile have long been considered along with the curse and the epithet to be rhetorical constituents of invective satire.[5] Recall their employment in caricature, for instance. Less offensive and virulent than a curse or an epithet, though, metaphor and simile tend to embody a higher degree of comicity. Palma's style in the *tradiciones* exemplifies the use of comparison as a vehicle of humor based on sympathetic, but playful, satire and irony.

As noted, comparisons abound in colloquial language and in literature based on this language. The vernacular, conversational tone of Palma's prose accommodates comparisons easily. As Shirley L. Arora verifies in her analysis of proverbial comparisons in the *Tradiciones peruanas,* much of Palma's figurative language already formed a part of the popular repertoire "current among the folk."[6] In that study, among 883 separate entries, Arora found documentation for 663 figurative expressions in various collections of popular proverbs and comparisons and in certain literary works. A majority of these comparisons are not intended to be humorous. To comparisons that are humorous should be added both similes and metaphors of literary origin and those of Palma's own creation in order to envision his application of this stylistic technique. Also significant is the fact that Palma applied to a number of comparisons not of his own making his masterful touch in the form of variations and extensions, thereby enriching their humor. As with other stylistic phenomena, Palma's utilization of similes and metaphors in his stories underwent diachronic alterations over the many years he wrote. In his first narrative efforts the comparisons reflect the intensity of his romantic leanings. "Emphasized are the plaintive tone, the affected language, and the forced relationships between the object and the correlative of the comparison that often alludes to far-off things." With the passage of time, however, "the relationship between the object and the correlative of the comparison arises spontaneously and sensuality often characterizes the latter,"[7] to quote Bazán Montenegro. Corrections and changes in the style of the earlier *tradiciones* are evident until 1893. Invariably the alterations concern the addition of conceits and jocose figures of speech, as in the description of Miguel de Santiago. Originally this character was depicted as being "de carácter asaz altivo e iracundo." Later editions of the *Tradiciones peruanas,* however, portray him as an artist "de un geniazo más atufado que el mar cuando le duele la barriga y le entran retortijones."[8] Part of this evolution can be attributed to Palma's continued immersion in the Spanish classics, where, as previously noted, Palma encountered a wealth of humor stemming from comparative declarations.

A comparison is composed of two parts connected by a sign. The first part, known as the object, subject, tenor, or *comparante* is enhanced through comparison to the second part, a referent commonly called the term of the comparison, the correlative, or the vehicle. The structure of a comparison may assume one of several forms, all of which Palma uses for comic effect in the *tradiciones*. In a comparison involving equality the subject is equated with its correlative by means of a sign—for example, *tan como, tanto(s) como, como,* or a verb of equivalence. A comparison of inequality may involve either superiority ("más . . . que") or inferiority ("menos . . . que"). Spanish, as opposed to French, for example, prefers comparisons of the "más . . . que" variety, a proclivity that Spitzer traces to the baroque period and "its supernatural and illusionist dimensions."[9] A majority of Palma's humorous comparisons follow this pattern: "Ocupaban la casita del Milagro una vieja con más pliegues y arrugas que camisolín de novia, y su sobrina Jovita" (533). Although scarce, comparisons of inferiority do arise on occasion: "se improvisaban fortunas en *menos tiempo del que gasta en persignarse un cura loco*" (1126). Metaphors abound in Palma's prose, but with less regularity than comparisons employing a sign. "Radegudo . . . aunque papel quemado, no olvidaba sus viejas mañas de soltero" (1067). Conceits, extended metaphorical comparisons, or analogies, can also be substantially humorous in the *tradiciones*.

> . . . avísote que, desde que volviste la espalda, alzó el vuelo la paloma, y está muy guapa en el palomar de Quiñones, que, como sabes, es gavilán corsario. (451)

> La maldita zurcidora de voluntades no creía, como Sancho, que era *mejor sobrina mal casada que bien abarraganada;* y endoctrinando pícaramente con sus tercerías a la muchacha, resultó un día que el pernil dejó de estarse en el garabato por culpa y travesura de un pícaro gato. Desde entonces, si la tía fue el anzuelo, la sobrina, . . . se convirtió en sebo para pescar maravedíses a más de dos y más de tres acaudalados hidalgos de esta tierra. (515)

Along with these familiar comparative structures, a number of variations, which may involve ellipsis, indirect association, different types of connectives, broadened commentary in the correlative, or an unusual use of comparison, appears in Palma's *tradiciones*. Elliptical and associative comparisons rely on the reader's ability to supply connective or missing material in order to participate completely in the humor. Don Geripundio "vestía gabardina color pulga" (525), Don Dimas employed "pluma de ganso u otra ave de rapiña" (513), and a jealous husband entered his wife's bedroom "resuelto a hacer una carnicería que ni la del rastro o matadero" (250). Palma frequently realized simultaneously jocosity and character delineation by means of another associative technique, wherein a character is depicted as belonging to a certain group.

> La muchacha era una de esas limeñitas que, por su belleza, cautivan al mismo diablo y lo hacen persignarse y tirar piedras. (633)

> La hermana demandadera . . . pertenecía a lo más alquitarado del gremio de celestinas. (1045)

In a majority of Palma's simple comparisons the correlative applies directly to an adjective, which in turn reflects on the principal object—"las muchachas, aunque feas como espantajos de maizal, y tontas como charada de periodista ultramontano, podían encontrar marido" (677). In other comparisons the vehicle joins directly to something possessed by the ultimate object of the satire and/or humor: "rechoncho fraile mercedario y con más cerviguillo que un berrendo de Bujama" (471). Some structures engage a verb, either directly or indirectly and either in the tenor or in the vehicle, or in both.

> . . . un pleito . . . trae más desazones que un uñero de dedo gordo. (396)

> Juan Izquieta, que chupaba más que esponja. (590)

> Era un capitan que más mentía que comía, y que si comía era para seguir mintiendo. (1097)

Why do we laugh at these comparisons? In a generalized response one could attribute the humor to two basic factors: the surprise and/or incongruity associated with the juxtaposition of the subject and correlative, and the revelation of truth deriving from the juxtaposition. Also notable is the context. Whereas some comparative statements are self-contained, evoking a humorous response in and of themselves, others lose a degree of their impact when isolated from their original environs. "Fruslerías" offers a case in point. "Y echó la carta en el buzón, retirándose con más seriedad que pleito perdido" (1452). Alone, the sentence might elicit a minor reaction to humor depending on one's fortunes in court. Knowing the context, however, enhances the humor considerably. It describes Ruperto Vomipurga, who, due to a concern about germs, has just tricked a lady into sticking out her tongue so he can moisten his stamp. Congratulating her on her robust health and thanking her for the service rendered, he mails his letter and leaves "con más seriedad que pleito perdido."

More specifically, the humor we enjoy in Ricardo Palma's plethora of comparisons derives from what Eastman calls the humor of quantity, that is, from exaggeration; from irony incorporated in a portion of the hyperbolic comparisons; from wordplay; from satire; and from sexual allusion.

Palma often expressed exaggeration through comparisons. Although such comparisons are sometimes for fun, they usually supplement to some degree a caricatured image. Hyperbolic encomium of the *limeña* constitutes perhaps the only exception. For an example of a simple comparison (although indirect) we turn to the final paragraph of "Los siete pelos del diablo," wherein Palma tells us that he read the story "en un palimpsecto *sic* contemporáneo del estornudo y de las cosquillas" (1201). Several of the most humorous hyperbolic comparisons make fun of old women.

> Llamábase la Ribero, y era una vieja más flaca que gallina de diezmo con moquillo. (834)
>
> . . . una doña Pacomia, vieja tan vieja, que pasar podía por contemporánea de las cosquillas. (284)

Men fare as poorly. While Leonor's husband proved "más manso que todos los carneros juntos de la cristiandad y morería" (646), the man who "de a legua revelaba en cierto tufillo ser hijo de Cataluña" sported a beard "más crecida que deuda pública" (725). Exaggerations of a comparative sort sometimes appear in amplified construction: "cosas leímos contra esa tesis, que hasta a San Pedro, que es calvo, le ponen los pelos de punta, y que, en punto a exageración, corren parejas con la nariz de aquel narigudo que cuando estornudaba, sólo oía el estornudo medio minuto después, por lo largo del trayecto recorrido" (1493).[10]

Exaggeration and irony go hand in hand, Eastman maintains, for "by a little perceptive shift or casuistry any exaggeration may be viewed as irony, and any irony as exaggeration." This is generally so because when we use overstatement, we normally are expressing less than, something different than, or the opposite of the literal meaning of the words. In a number of comparisons Palma joined hyperbole and irony effectively for humor. Surprisingly, Jean Lamore, in his article "Sur Quelques Procédés de l'ironie et de l'Humor dans les

Tradiciones peruanas," only comments briefly on this significant stylistic-humorous technique. He tells us that "irony is served by unexpected and often hyperbolic comparisons," which is certainly true but worthy of expanded consideration.[11]

Palma, as we learned in Chapter 2, regularly employed overt irony, that is, irony wherein the reader is "meant to see the ironist's real meaning at once."[12] What causes irony to be overt is the blatancy of the logical contradiction or the incongruity discerned in the juxtaposition of subject and correlative.

> Su generosidad era larga como pelo de huevo. (525)

Here, as in most comparisons of this type, the reader is baited with a likeness suggesting the possibility that the quality of the tenor may indeed characterize the agent to some degree. This applies even to the unmodified noun of the correlative. The addition of the modifier, however, exposes the irony of the vehicle and belies the trait initially intimated. The following excerpts enhance our appreciation of this technique as it applies to comparisons of equality. Note the use of the adverb *así* in the structure.

> Y así atendía a los requiebros y carantoñas de Tijereta, como la piedra berroqueña a los chirridos del cristal que en ella se rompe. (515)
>
> . . . así se cuidaba de los piratas como de las babuchas de Mahoma. (453)
>
> . . . los cabildantes actuales dan tanta importancia a la prenda como al pañal en que al nacer los envolviera la comadrona. (1130)
>
> Yo . . . creo descender de los Incas por línea recta como el arco iris. (203)

(The final quotation originates with Alonso Carrió de la Vandera). Note the parallel construction of Sancho's declaration: "así sé yo quién es la señora Dulcinea como dar un puño en el cielo" (DQ, II, 599).

Comparative utterances of superiority function in much the same manner, abruptly inverting what at first seems feasible into hilarious exaggeration.

> . . . y luego las tira bajo un mueble, sin hacer más caso de ellas que del zancarrón de Mahoma. (637)
>
> Lo que es ahora, en el siglo xx, más hacedero me parece criar moscas con biberón que hacer milagros. (367)

Very often Palma's lexical and semantic dexterity surfaces in the form of satiric comparisons containing equivoques. Again hyperbole may add to the jocosity of the expression, as it does in the Cervantine and Quevedesque styles that preceded the *tradicionista's* century. Lerner calls the result a decategorization of reality.[13] Consider:

Palma: El tal almirante era hombre de más humos que una chimenea. (280)

Cervantes: ... tenía Rocinante más cuartos que un real. (DQ, I, 39)

Quevedo: ... un sombrero con más falda que un monte y más copa que un nogal.[14]

In comparisons of this type Palma evidences equal preference for nouns and adjectives in the tenor slot. Occasionally the pattern will accommodate a verb. Almost always the correlative centers on a noun.

Tenor = Noun

Decíase de él que tenía *más trastienda que un bodegón,* más camándulas que el rosario de Jerusalén. (513)

... Pacorro era un tarambana, sin más bienes raíces que los pelos de la cara. (459)

Tenor = Adjective

... ella ... es argumentadora y más fina que tela de cebolla. (415)

Pero Pedro Gutiérrez, el sastrecillo, era más templado que sus tijeras. (44)

Tenor = Verb

Este milagro ... fue más sonado que las narices. (366)

Comparisons incorporating double meaning and exaggeration need not adhere to the set pattern of "más ... qué" in all cases. A similar humorous reaction can be obtained through metaphors of freer structures. When Don Lesmes begins to encroach on the Izquieta boys' reputation, the narrator, in a paronomastic play on names, exclaims, "¡Buena lesna era don Lesmes!" (590). The color of Don Dimas's cape is "de color parecido a Dios en lo incomprensible" (513).

Another consideration of humorous satiric comparisons concerns the structural origin of the satire, whether it rests with the subject, the correlative, or both. Significant to our study of the humor of style in the *Tradiciones peruanas* is the fact that, although a majority of the comparisons derive their satire from the subject of the comparison, satire also results from the correlative alone and sometimes from both the subject and the correlative.

For an example of a satiric tenor, we refer to "Creo que hay infierno," in which Pepete has been forced to marry "una hembra de peor carácter que un tabardillo entripado" (738). The reader laughs at the woman but certainly not at the disease. "¡Feliz barbero!" offers a contrary order. " '¡Y estos pelos,' murmuraba el hidalgo, 'que los tengo más crecidos que deuda de pobre en poder de usurero!' " (319). In this instance the image of the avaricious usurer undergoing ridicule is humorous. In order for satire to function on both sides of the comparative sign, the subject must either be a person or an institution susceptible to derision. An excellent example is the case of the friar who, although designated to pronounce mass at one o'clock, had succumbed to the temptation of succulent peruvian dishes at lunch. He confessed, "Sucumbí a la tentación, y *almorcé como canónigo en casa ajena*" (645). Context illuminates the satire associated with the subject and enhances through irony the satire of the correlative. The passage, of course, is humorous by itself, a fact well verified by its use in various proverbial comparisons in Spanish, Portuguese, and French.[15] In most comparisons embodying dual satire, however, the nature of the noun or adjective characterizing the subject immediately alerts the reader to the satire. The following list confirms the abundance of this stylistic technique of humor in Palma's prose.

Satire only in the tenor

Cierto que, por la facha, eres más sucio que un emplasto entre anca y anca. (93)

Al ruido asomó una vieja, más doblada que abanico dominguero. (451)

. . . años de mesa revuelta y anarquía perenne, en que tuvimos más presidentes que cosquillas. (1096)

. . . un granujilla que, por lo espiritado, parecía que estaba haciendo estudios escolares para convertirse en alambre. (1113)

Satire only in the vehicle

Entre tanto, fray Juan Gutiérrez, que andaba más suelto que lengua de beata. (215)

. . . la vida de milicia no es de regalo como la de los frailes. (986)

Cada nacimiento era más visitado y comentado que ministro nuevo. (1199)

. . . y puso como mantel de fonda a fray Tiburcio. (459)

Satire in both tenor and vehicle

... don Alonso González del Valle, ... siguió ... echando más barriga que fraile con manejo de rentas conventuales. (598)

Un vejete, con más lacras que conciencia de escribano. (592)

... Garcilaso ... a veces es más embustero que el telégrafo. (37)

En 1842 la guerra civil traía al Perú *más revuelto que casa de solterón,* ... *y más perdido que conciencia de judío cambista.* (1097)

Generally, comparisons involving satire only in the subject adhere to an *animate-inanimate* pattern since satire innately affects only human beings or animals with human tendencies. In many cases, when the humor resides in the correlative, the pattern reverses itself—*inanimate-animate.* In other cases, an animate subject is retained. Satire on both sides of the comparative sign normally presents an *animate-animate* layout. When synecdochic, however, the correlative becomes human through a step in the thought process (for example, the word *telegraph* would be equated with people sending messages). The above excerpts also demonstrate that comparisons sometimes stray from the set patterns of "más ... que" or "(tan) ... como" and that in many instances of satire in both tenor and in vehicle context is necessary to understand the humor. Although it is not examined in detail, many statements in the *Tradiciones peruanas* originate as proverbial comparisons, which is evidence of Palma's debt to popular phraseology in regard to his humor.

Palma regularly employed throughout the *Tradiciones peruanas* comparisons to enhance or to exaggerate the anatomy of the women of Lima or to comment about them with other instances of sexual allusion. Simile and metaphor are often used in extended series.

Leonorcica Michel era lo que hoy llamaríamos una limeña de *rompe y rasga.* ... Veintisiete años con más mundo que el que descubrió Colón, color sonrosado, ojos de más preguntas y respuestas que el catecismo, nariz de escribano por lo picaresca, labios retozones y una tabla de pecho como para asirse a ella un náufrago: tal era en compendio la muchacha. Añádanse a estas perfecciones, brevísimo pie, torneada pantorrilla, cintura estrecha, aire de taco y sandunguero, de esos que hacen estremecer hasta a los muertos del campo santo. La moza, en fin, no era *boccato di cardenale,* sino *boccato* de concilio ecuménico. (645-646)

Within this stimulating portrait is a variety of figurative humor—comparisons structured on equivoques, hyperbolic similes, exaggerative metaphors, suggestive allusions—incorporating highly visual imagery and corroborated with provocative epithets to render a sound depiction. As has already been discussed, Palma employed such descriptions to ridicule religious, social, and political phenomena while magnifying the delineation. The eyes of the Limean woman constitute one of the subjects most frequently addressed in suggestive humorous comparisons in the *tradiciones*. Little wonder that Bazán Montenegro calls him "one ardently fond of eyes; rarely is there lacking a reference to them in the complete descriptions and often it is the only trait pointed out because it constitutes a woman's principal attraction and a great temptation for men."[16] In his effort to capture the effect of eyes Palma resorted to an array of mostly original likenings, some brief and incisive, others on the order of a conceit.

> . . . unos ojos más incendiarios que el petróleo. ¡Demonche! (1444)

> . . . ojos más negros que noche de trapisonda y velados por rizosas pestañas. (725)

> . . . unos ojos del color del mar, decidores como una tentación. (816)

> Lucía un par de ojos negros que eran como dos torpedos cargados con dinamita y que hacían explosión sobre las entretelas del alma de los galanes limeños. (633)

Palma's jocularity is evident in numerous other metaphorical comments tinted with sensuous overtones. On the whole these references center either on instances of allurement by both men and women or on hints of infidelity, often with some degree of satire or exaggeration. In one story, for example, influenced by the devil, a middle-aged woman gazed with covetous eyes at the groom: "la vieja aquella era petróleo purito, y buscaba en el joven una chispa de fosfórica correspondencia para producir un incendio que no bastasen a apagar la bomba Garibaldi ni todas las compañías de bomberos" (914). Elsewhere the reader is told that a woman "es . . . lo mismo / que leña verde; / resiste, gime y llora, / y al fin se enciende" (368). In "El niño llorón" Doña Pulqueria advises Periquillo not to fret but to do "como tantos que pasean muy orondos una cornamenta más alta que casa de cuatro pisos con entresuelo" (452). On occasion "las mujeres / son como libros, / que por nuevos se compran / y . . . están leídos" (130). Such examples confirm the importance of sexually related comparisons and metaphors in the *tradicionista*'s arsenal of instruments of humor.

Having considered the structure and the humor of his comparisons we must examine the question of correlatives, that is, from what realms of experience Palma drew his material to create his figures of speech. A knowledge of this will further amplify our grasp of his achievement of humor in the *tradiciones.*

Scanning comparisons in the *tradiciones,* it becomes apparent that correlatives focus principally on personal and social matters, literature, history, religion, and nature. Given the extent of Palma's dependence on the animal kingdom for comparative material, the discussion of nature as a subject of comparisons will be treated on a more detailed basis. The use of abstractions in the vehicle also merits brief individual consideration.

One of Palma's primary mentors, Francisco de Quevedo, employed concrete-abstract linkages in both metaphor and comparison—"aquellos gregüescos más rotos que la conciencia."[17] Perhaps inspired by this source, Palma devised several imaginative similes of this type. In over half of the comparisons abstraction stems from religious doctrine and, except for in reference to eyes, is usually of the lightly satirical variety underscoring undesirable anatomical features: "un negro esclavo . . . feo como el pecado mortal" (748). In this absurd bonding of aesthetic and moral values, which is typical in the humor of popular speech, the only link is undesirability. Even though "the conceptual-semantic element is discarded"[18] in these comparisons, the reader reacts to humor precisely because of the absurdity caused by the apparently unbridgeable gap between tenor and vehicle.

[Gil Paz] era un avaro más ruin que la encarnación de la avaricia. (664)

Lo particular es que toda socia era vieja como el pecado, fea como un chisme y con pespuntes de bruja y rufiana. (862)

. . . una tía, vieja como el pecado de gula. (515)

Degollación . . . tenía una cara más fea que el pecado de usura. (813)

Personal correlatives are multiple, eliciting humorous response because of their surprising applicability to the subject. Within this category I include portions, functions, or reactions of the body such as corns, cramps, ingrown nails, heart attacks, ticklishness, and diseases—typhus or *tabardillo,* for example; clothing or anything else covering the body, such as shirts, diapers, shoes, and poultices; domestic articles and foods, including sponges, fuel, paper, wire, tortillas, and wine; articles of personal comfort and enjoyment, such as fans, jewels, money, a child's toy; and miscellaneous items, such as a drum or an organ bellows. This list emphasizes Palma's keen aware-

ness of his surroundings and his capacity to incorporate diverse subjects into figurative expression. The *tradicionista*'s broad utilization
of colloquial humor, also drawing heavily on immediate experience,
again underscores the importance of the vernacular in the mirth of
his style.

> Los primos son en el matrimonio lo que los callos en el pie: excrecencias
> incómodas. (1202)
>
> . . . el oidor Núñez de Rojas, era un viejo más feo que un calambre. (602)
>
> Las revoluciones, como las tortillas, hacerlas sobre caliente o no hacerlas.
> (350)
>
> (Many suitors in pursuit of a beautiful, rich young lady): . . . no eran
> pocos los niños que andaban tras el trompo. (367)

Correlatives extracted from society include the vast assemblage of
governmental, law enforcement, judicial, and monetary entities satirized by Palma and cited in the earlier discussion of political and
social satire. In addition, the author constructed humorous comparisons and metaphors on phenomena drawn from the military and
even from card games. As in the works of Cervantes and Quevedo,[19]
analogies of military heritage dot the style of the *Tradiciones peruanas*. Palma delighted in describing the tactics of love in this way.

> Robertson conoció a Teresa Méndez en la procesión del Corpus, y desde
> ese día el arrogante marino la echó bandera de parlamento, . . . y se
> declaró buena presa de la encantadora limeña. (1032)
>
> . . . hostigando a la muchacha con palabras de almíbar, besos hipotéticos,
> serenatas, billetes y demás embolismos con los que, desde que el mundo
> empezó a civilizarse, sabemos los del sexo feo dar guerra a las novicias y
> hasta a las catedráticas en el *ars amandi*. (367)

The humor in the first example is derived as much from intimate
overtones as from the metaphorical use of military jargon. Terminology from the game table generates such comparisons as "*más empe-
rejilado que rey de baraja fina*" (646) and "ojos . . . más matadores
que espada y basto en el juego de tresillo o rocambor" (514-515).

As a youth Ricardo Palma read widely the works of the great
Spanish writers from the medieval period up to and including romanticism. During the mid-1850s, while serving in the military on
the Chincha Islands, he enthusiastically read "la Biblioteca de clási-
cos españoles de Rivadeneira," which furthered his "devoción por
los grandes prosistas castellanos."[20] Given this exposure, it is not
surprising to discover throughout the *tradiciones* bounteous refer-

ences to certain Spanish authors. A fair number of allusions to writers bear the form of a comparison employing a literary correlative. Such comparisons often prove humorous because the correlative recalls to mind the merriment originally associated with it: "por la pequeñez de su talla, era el campeón un Sancho parodiando a Don Quijote" (297). The majority of the allusions are to these two famous characters and to Quevedo. Also important to comparisons is Don Juan Tenorio, and to a lesser degree, Shakespeare, Espronceda, the *Cid*, and mythology.

One day Lerzundi, goaded by a revolutionary uproar, "se echó a la calle a hacer el papel de Quijote amparador de la desvalida autoridad." He quickly accomodated "una bala de a onza en el pecho" (1094). The hilarious Cirilo Sorogastúa, "una autoridad *sui generis*," was "algo así como Sancho en la ínsula" (639) in his creative judgments. One of Centeno's soldiers, "mellado de un ojo y lisiado de una pierna, parecíase a Sancho Panza en lo ruin de la figura" (93). In another story the crazed Don Pedro Pablo Rosel tears the cup of wine from Father Virrueta during mass and smashes him over the head with it. The blood on the stones so defiles the church that it is not opened for some months, and then only after a celebration of rehabilitation. In order to commemorate the opening a picture is ordered painted. "Pero el padre Virrueta tomó por el susodicho cuadro más ojeriza que Sancho por la manta, y mandó que se le trasladase a la sacristía" (983). Examples involving Quevedo's characters and works include:

> La tradición que va a leerse tiene más padres que el mamón aquel de que habla el romance de Quevedo. (357)
>
> Era el don Diego . . . decidor como un romance de Quevedo. (655)
>
> Y semejante a las brujas de Macbeth, asomó por el ventanillo un escuerzo en enaguas, con un rostro adornado por un par de colmillos de jabalí que servían de muleta a las quijadas, como dijo Quevedo. (695) (Note also the Shakespearean image.)

Numerous characters in the *tradiciones* exude Don Juan tendencies. On occasion, exaggeration, contrast, or contextual information endows descriptions of them with a note of humor.

> Y fue el caso que el gentil joven alcalde y el no menos bizarro comendador, que aunque fraile y con voto solemne de castidad era un Tenorio con birrete, se enamoraron como dos pazguatos de la misma dama. (841)
>
> Hildebrando Béjar era el don Juan Tenorio de Arequipa. Como el burlador de Sevilla, tenía a gala engatusar muchachas y hacerse el orejón cuando

éstas, con buen derecho, le exigían el cumplimiento de sus promesas y juramentos. (1064)

In one of Palma's most famous *tradiciones*, "El alacrán de fray Gómez," the narrator facetiously states that "fray Gómez hizo en mi tierra milagros a mantas, sin darse cuenta de ellos y como quien no quiere la cosa." He then likens this personage to M. Jourdain, a character from Molière's *Le Bourgeois Gentilhomme*, who spoke prose without realizing it. Perhaps through a slip of memory the word *verso* replaces *prosa*. "Era de suyo milagrero, como aquel que hablaba en verso sin sospecharlo" (210).[21]

Sometimes a touch of irony or satire heightens the comedy of the literary correlative and simultaneously expands characterization: "don Fermín García Gorrochano, noble, por supuesto, más que el Cid Campeador y los siete Infantes de Lara" (318-319). Palma was not concerned with consistently explaining the appropriateness of allusions. At times, as in the case of a mythological reference to Father Chuecas, Palma felt impelled to lay it out quite carefully. At other times, as in a later depiction of the same character, he relied on the familiarity of the reader with the correlative text.

La moral era para Chuecas otra tela de Penélope, pues si avanzaba algo en el buen camino, durante los meses de encierro, los desandaba al poner la planta en los barrios alegres de la ciudad. (897)

Tenía algunos puntos de contacto con el célebre cura que pinta Espronceda en su *Diablo Mundo*. (898)

When situations bring to mind parallels in other literary works, the reader's appreciation is further enhanced. This occurs in the familiar anecdote "Las orejas del alcalde," in which the tragicomic aura of an encounter is established by the allusion. Don Cristóbal de Agüero has been checking on Diego de Esquivel's ears regularly, resulting in a growing uneasiness in the mayor. One night the mayor responds to a knock at his door at an inn in Guamanga. "Ni el espectro de Banquo en los festines de Macbeth, ni la estatua del Comendador en la estancia del libertino Don Juan, produjeron más asombro que el que experimentó el alcalde, hallándose de improviso con el flagelado de Potosí. 'Calma, señor licenciado. ¿Esas orejas no sufren deterioro? Pues entonces, hasta más ver'" (126).

Beyond the *tradicionista*'s previously mentioned use of contemporary historical events, entities, institutions, policies, procedures, and customs for humorous effect, the reader of the *Tradiciones* en-

counters many comparisons employing a variety of historical con-
nections, both remote from and coincidental to the author's time.
Some statements overlap with literary correlatives, as in the case of
the *Cid* or Machiavelli: "yo soy de la escuela de Maquiavelo el flo-
rentino y de Pajarito el limeño" (1149). Other statements evince
coincidence of history and religion in certain figures, such as Mu-
hammad. These constructs reveal affinities or identification with
documented proverbial comparisons.

Take, for example, Palma's account of Friar Martín's miracle of
suspending a bricklayer in the air while he went for permission to
save him: "Y el albañil se mantuvo en el aire, patidifuso y pluscuam-
perfecto, como el alma de Garibay, esperando el regreso del lego
dominico" (366). Arora finds this allusion employed in several texts.
José María Sbarbi identifies Garibay as Esteban de Garibay y Za-
malloa, a famous Spanish chronicler of the sixteenth century "whose
ghost was said to haunt his former residence for many years after his
death."[22] Another instance concerns José Joaquín de Larriva, "más
monarquista y godo que el rey Wamba" (1049). This monarch appears in popular tradition in expressions of remote time, but references to him must also have spurred some political inferences for
nineteenth-century Peruvians.[23] Such inferences support the fact
that the humor of some comparisons is a function of the familiarity
of the reader with the historical figure evoked. Everyone has at least
heard of Napoleon and has little difficulty laughing at an old man's
claim to having served as the *padrino* "del general Pata Amarilla, un
militarote que en bravura, dejaría tamañito a Napoleón" (1441).
Fewer, especially with the passage of time, are familiar enough with
the attempted assassination of Napoleon III in 1858 to relate fully
to a quip in "Historia de un cañoncito": "y tales eran los aspavientos
de don Ramón, que los palaciegos llegaron a persuadirse de que el
cañoncito sería algo más peligroso que una bomba Orsini o un tor-
pedo Withead" (1119).[24]

In addition to producing humorous effect, historical correlatives
contribute indirectly to Palma's efforts in the *tradiciones* to increase
the historical awareness of his audience. Each allusion forces the
reader to recollect a person, object, or event from history or even to
engage in inquiry in order to appreciate fully the humor of the comparison. An interesting example occurs in "Desdichas de Pirindín."
Don Lesmes, in cahoots with the devil, goes one night to the home
of a rival's lover. About to cross the threshold, he sees an olive branch

(blessed by a priest, of course). Instantly he jumps "como mordido de víbora. . . . La cosa no era para menos que para dar un salto como el de Alvarado en México" (591), which is a reference to Pedro de Alvarado's celebrated leap over a canal some eighteen feet wide during the "Noche Triste."[25] As with other types of comparisons, some correlatives involve more expanded narrative commentary than others.

In her study of metaphor and comparison in his satiric prose Lerner discovers that Quevedo "shows a special preference for the comic or grotesque use of images taken from the religious ambit and from the liturgy." Rosenblat offers several examples of the same in works by Cervantes.[26] Palma's utilization of religious correlatives touches many facets of the Catholic experience. An analogy common to all three writers, making the sign of the cross betokens physical violence.

Cervantes: . . . apenas puse mano a mi tizona cuando me santiguaron los hombros con sus pinos. (DQ, I, 140)

Quevedo: . . . apenas el hombre me conocía con la cuchillada y no hacía santiguarse de mí *per signum crucis.*[27]

Palma: Transverberación levantaba una mano mona y redondita y santiguaba con ella al insolente. (333)

One of the most amusing comparisons in the *Tradiciones* that draws on the realm of personal religious devotion describes a melee in Ibirijuitanga's tavern: "repartíanse cachetes como en el rosario de la aurora" (332). The antithetical usage of *cachete* in the such diverse spheres elicits the humorous reaction. Palma portrayed shrewd little Carlitos's deception in these words: "El don Carlitos, en presencia de su padre y comensales, adoptaba un airecito de unción y bobería que lo asimilaba a un ángel de retablo" (241)—an allusion of established popular continuance.[28]

Earlier we examined Palma's extensive use of religion, which often appears in the form of comparisons, as a basis for humorous remarks and caricatures. The following serve as examples of these comparisons: "para que no se diga que nos repetimos como bendición de obispo" (874), "porque no digan que me repito como bendición de obispo" (266),[29] "ente más ruin que migaja en capilla de fraile" (577). Aside from satire of the clergy and members of convents, the most frequent correlatives from the realm of religion come from the

Bible. Due to their historical nature, they can rightly be termed
biblical-historical correlatives.

> Y su señoría (¡Dios la tenga entre santos!) pasó un año haciendo méritos;
> es decir, compitiendo con Job en cachaza. (600)
>
> Parece que a don José Luis no le disgustaba el licorcillo aquel que en tan
> mal predicamento puso al padre Noé. (1066)
>
> Los barberos son como el maná de los israelitas: se acomodan a todo
> paladar. (340)
>
> Conocíale el pueblo por tocayo del buen ladrón a quien don Jesucristo
> dio pasaporte para entrar en la gloria, pues nombrábase don Dimas de la
> Tijereta. (513)[30]
>
> Pero ¿lo de zambo, a quien se tenía por más blanco que el caballo del
> Apocalipsis? (581)

It is worth noting Palma's combination of implicit comparison and
satire as a technique of characterization (600, 1066, 513); his use of
the same referent for diverse objectives (1066); his incongruent mixture of colloquial terminology and solemn biblical allusions for humorous impact (1066, 513); and his recourse to satiric irony for
amusement (581).

Methods that enhance the correlative include abstractions (*pecado, avaricia, chisme, pecado de gula, pecado de usura, tentación*);
references to the devil ("un cleriquillo . . . era de la misma piel del
diablo" [154]); and liturgical experiences. On occasion Palma resorted to the image of the Jews' wait for the Messiah to convey the
idea of fruitless expectancy, a technique employed also by Quevedo
with regard to the Christians' anticipation of the Second Coming.

Quevedo:	Nuestras cartas eran como el Mesías, que nunca venían y las aguardábamos siempre.[31]
Palma:	Esperen ustedes a su mentecato Oviedo como esperan los Judíos al Mesías, que ese mamarracho volverá de gobernador el día que lluevan cuernos sobre mi cabeza. (389)

Understanding the humor of such comparisons is dependent on familiarity, and in Palma's culture religion reached into everyone's life.
Consequently, Palma could be assured of a response on the part of
the reader. Being highly attuned to the details of Catholicism's influence and drawing on his own background, Palma enjoyed relative
ease in creating religious comparisons. Ecclesiastic entities offered a

gold mine of opportunities for ridicule, both because people were familiar with mocking these personages, practicing the technique themselves through oral tradition, and because colonial history frequently portrayed members of the clergy as individuals embroiled in laughable pursuits.

Palma viewed nature as a valuable stockpile for creating humorous comparative locutions. Although Palma found animate organisms more useful than inanimate phenomena or plants, he did employ comparisons involving vegetation and nonliving matter. Perhaps as a result of his eight years at sea, several comparisons deal with the ocean and its environs. Normally, these comparisons are made with a light satirical tone. For example, since all beauties have their little defects, "el de doña Catalina era tener dislocada una pierna, lo que al andar le daba el aire de goleta balanceada por mar boba" (289). She is described in general terms from a nautical standpoint as "abismo que asusta y atrae" (892). The insane protagonist of "El Cristo de la agonía" "era de un geniazo más atufado que el mar cuando le duele la barriga y le entran retortijones" (449), while in another anecdote we meet Egas de Venegas, "viejo más seco que un arenal" (526).

Hyperbole can also stress positive traits, as was noted previously in regard to the eyes of the women of Lima. Among the few vegetational correlatives are portrayals of the orange, fig, cherry, raisin, grape, and mushroom, as well as a cork oak and a corn patch. Palma often repeated proverbial, well-known comparisons through vegetational correlatives, as in the case of the raisin, which ordinarily connotes a wrinkled skin condition: "pues más arrugada que una pasa fue la mujer a quien en mi infancia oí el relato" (378). One story begins with the caveat "esta es una tradioncilla que, como ciertas jamonas, tiene la frescura de las uvas conservadas" (753). Certain comparative references involve granite or stonework suggestive of immovability: "pero que tenía el femenil capricho de gastar, para con el doctor del *tibi quoque,* resistencias de piedra berroqueña" (352); "para con él, Mencigüela no fuese de piedra de cantería" (219).

Palma's extensive use of animals, birds, fish, and insects as terms for his comparisons in the *Tradiciones peruanas* perpetuates a stylistic feature common to Cervantes and to Quevedo, one in which images of popular speech are absorbed into the narrative, weaving "a popular veil around all of the novel."[32] Most of these images emanate from the narrator, although a few are disclosed through dialogue. Both sources manifest the array of structural arrangements observed earlier regarding comparisons employing different correlatives, that is, noun-noun, verb-noun and adjective-noun linkages between tenor and vehicle. Normally an *animate-animate* pattern prevails, although *inanimate-animate* is also possible. These comparisons differ from those previously studied in that more are metaphors and conceits, as opposed to similes. Furthermore, one notes a slightly greater tendency toward comparisons of equality (*como, tanto como*) rather than comparisons of the "más . . . que" or "menos . . . que" variety.

Adjective–Noun

Entre los presos hallábase cierto corregidor . . . más voraz que sanguijuela para sacar el quilo a los pueblos cuyo gobierno le estaba encomendado. (673)

Noun–Noun

Era la tal de aquellas que tienen más lengua que trompa un elefante. (451)

Verb–Noun

. . . segurísma de que éste al verla se vendría tras ella como el ratón tras el queso. (447)

Metaphor

Punto a la digresión, que la pluma no ha de ser caballo sin rienda y desbocado. (579)

Conceit

Item, los primos son unos pegotes de la familia de las sanguijuelas. No hay forma de desprenderlos cuando se ponen a cantarle a la oreja a la primita. Un zancudo de trompetilla es menos impertinente. (1203)

In animal comparisons Palma normally employed creatures natural to the Peruvian coast, *sierra,* and jungle in addition to images from literature and traditional expressions. Quadrupeds lead the list, particularly mammals; rodents, reptiles, and amphibians also crop up fairly regularly; also common are allusions to insects; ornithological images occasionally lend themselves to comparative humor. Fish and crustaceans do not often appear in such comparisons.

In a majority of figures of speech satire serves as the main generator of humor while puns and sensual allusions supplement. Being likened to a creature of nature can, of course, prove laudatory; from Palma's pen, however, such a comparison customarily is not complimentary. Ascribing ophidian characterisics to a mother-in-law seldom elicits her pleasure! It is precisely for this reason that animals, insects, birds, and fish occupy such a prominent place in satiric-humorous comparisons and metaphors. Traits associated with a certain animal transfer directly or indirectly to individuals, a style of ridicule that results in amusement at or in scorn toward the object of the comparison. This is the laughter of satire, caricature, and the ridiculous, and Palma was a master of it, enlivening his anecdotes with a myriad of striking original, popular, and/or literary images.

In "San Antonio del fondo" we meet a Franciscan friar "más flaco que esqueleto de sardina" (1092). The humorous flavor of this comment arises not only from the hyperbolic incongruence of the comparison but also from the fact that this friar serves as confessor to "una beata que por vieja y fea era ya de todo punto tabaco infumable." Together the pair cares for the image of Saint Anthony, visited by many devotees. In another reference to *beatas* Palma notified the reader that "diariamente rezan más padrenuestros que pulgas tiene un perro en el verano" (1107). These two excerpts underscore an interesting fact about some comparisons of this type, namely, that rather than always stemming from the immediate passing of the undesirable traits of the correlative to the subject, the humor often arises from a juxtaposition of tenor and vehicle that leads to the caricature of a ludicrous feature or to a more humorous parallel. This is the case in referring to Estúñiga's desire in terms of the propensity of a mosquito, that is, the propensity to drink (307), and when Palma concurs with the Koran "cuando dice que la mujer es el camello que Dios concedió al hombre para atravesar el desierto de la vida" (1444). The attributes of the mentioned animal do not transfer to the subject when the narrator speaks of "los que tienen cura de almas a quienes esquilmar como el pastor a los carneros" (385).

Other comparative locutions parallel a creature's described situation and the protagonist but transfer also the repugnant particularities of the former to the person. For instance, while the statement that a shyster lawyer named Rodrigo Niño was "más tejedor que las arañas" (119) functions mostly to highlight his craftiness, the general loathsomeness of the spider also colors our perception of him. When Satan, on seeing the shape of a cross, attempts to flee "como perro a quien ponen maza" (915) or when Dr. Rivadeneira exhibits "*más orgullo que piojo sobre pobre*" (580) the *lector* reflects mostly on the flight and the arrogance yet recognizes, unconsciously perhaps, the implied kinship between the distastefulness of the mammal and insect and the character of the *comparante*.

In the majority of comparisons an immediate transfer of features occurs, occasioning the typical jocularity of Palma's satire. Thus, the sluggishness of the turtle typifies the leaden delivery of telegraph messages (453), the drawing power of the leech characterizes woman's propensity to siphon off all her husband's possessions and happiness (821),[33] the open display of a female cat on the roof highlights a wife's brazenness (1011), and the cackling of the coop suggests the feminine tendency for excited interchange when a juicy tidbit is discovered (291). The donkey or ass may connote stupidity, stubbornness, or lack of independence; the mule also recalls these traits, but, in addition, characterizes artful resistance.

> . . . *aquí como en Huacho todo borrico es macho.* (530)

> . . . no fue de aquellos mancarrones con más mañas y marraquetas que mula de alquiler, por lo que se ha escrito: "que son como los membrillos: / mientras más viejos, más amarillos." (892)

> Además, era el novio hombre vulgar y prosaico, una especie de asno con herrajes de oro. (1044)

The last excerpt intimates not only the unchastity of the friar but also the empty-headedness of the female, which in turn suggests the friar's beast-like appetite. Fortunately, in this case, he repents—"rareza!" Consider other facets of personality connoted in the examples below.

> Gobernando Amat, virrey que, como hasta las ratas lo afirman, tuvo uñas de gato despensero. (638)

> Uno de mis camaradas . . . era un chico con más trastienda que una botica y más resabioso que un cornúpeta de la Rinconada de Mala [hacienda near Lima]. (1113)

> Pero don Pedro, que era tan vivo como una anguila y que sabía escurrirse por entre los dedos, acertó a esquivar la paliza. (323)[34]

Palma achieved humor when he underscored physical features as well. Recall the thick neck of the friar accentuated through comparison to the neck of a bull (471, 37) and the obesity of a "Santo varón, / más grueso que el marrano de San Antón" (257). Both physical features and character are alluded to in comparisons such as "¡Aguárdate, gallinazo de muladar!" (961), directed at a Negro servant, and "su nariz torcida como el pico de un ave de rapiña"

(525), referring to Don Geripundio's looks and rapacity. Some
expressions provide simple amusement, with no satire involved:

> . . . Juan Enríquez . . . se puso más borracho que un mosquito y salió por
> las calles del Cuzco cargado de cordeles, garrotes y alfanje, para ahorcar
> y cortar pescuezos de los que no siguiesen su bandera. (111)

> Los primeros con quienes tuvieron que romper lanzas fueron los agusti-
> nos; pero ¡con buenos gallos se las habían! (283)

Earlier we noted that comparisons involving creatures of nature
derive their humor not only from satire but also from wordplay and
sexual allusions. Comparisons that embody puns rarely suggest a
transfer of qualities. The fish or animal is there only for the double
meaning it provides. Curiously, there is a higher proportion of pis-
catorial terms in these remarks than in other comparisons.

> . . . el buen viejo . . . gasta más agallas que un ballenato. (848)

> En cuanto a don Alonso de Leyva, tampoco las tenía todas *consigo y
> andaba más escamado que un pez.* (382)

> . . . vivía nuestro don Luis tan pelado como una rata. (633)

Reflecting artful semantic-syntactical dexterity, comparison,
whether ironic, satiric, or simply playful, constitutes a key struc-
tural-tonal element in the humor of style in the *Tradiciones
peruanas.*

Wordplay

Wordplay in literature dates back to the early Greeks. Various
Latin writers practiced this type of humor, and in its multiple forms
wordplay continued to be favored until the *Siglo de Oro,* an age
characterized by its "fondness of witty affected discretion and refined and clever courting . . . [by] a lively exchange of wit, facetious
remarks, humorous sayings, riddles, masked allusions, sparkling
questions and answers, funny witticisms and other games and jokes,"
as Rosenblat has expressed it. In *Don Quijote* "everything . . . is a
game, but a game to enhance a meaning or a double meaning."
Quevedo's proficiency in this area requires no comment. In the nineteenth century one discovers several major writers excelling in
puns—Charles Dickens, Mark Twain, Alphonse Daudet.[35] An
equally brilliant penman in this regard, Palma adopted wordplay to
the extent that it constitutes a significant style in his prose. Before

focusing on wordplay in the *Tradiciones peruanas*, however, let us define and amplify some terms.

Although wordplay can take a variety of shapes, the pun tends to constitute the most common form, offering several possible structures. A pun may involve an ingenious play on two meanings of one homonymic term, as in the case of *alto*, meaning in Spanish *elevated* or *stop*, in which case we have an equivoque or, in Spanish, a *silepsis*. A pun may also occur in the use of homophones, that is, words pronounced alike but different in spelling and in meaning. The words *bastar* and *vastar* provide a good example. When one character employs a term in one sense and another picks it up with a diverse meaning, the rhetorical designation is *diáfora* or *antanaclasis*. These forms of wordplay occur at the level of the signified. Among the possible witticisms at the level of the sign or signifier one encounters *paronomasia*, which consists in the repetition in a sentence of a word with certain phonetic modifications, and *retruécano*, which involves dividing a word to form others or joining several words.[36]

The pun itself is interesting in terms of its effect on the flow of discourse. Lionel Duisit, in his book *Satire, Parodie, Calembour*, calls this figure a *"collision homonymique ou homophonique"* involving a *"déraillement du sens."* Puns may occur by chance, as in everyday conversation, or purposely, which is sometimes the case in literature. When consciously done, "il fonde une activité *ludique* qui détourne l'acte de communication de sa fin première, la clarification du *message*," creating a collision of two or more meanings. The effect or "crime du calembour," on the aesthetic plane, is to create maximum expressive potential while realizing minimal semantic investment. It is the impact of revelation during the semantic game that stimulates the humorous reaction. Rosenblat comments, "the frequency of puns reveals a mental attitude prone to cultivate form at the expense of content."[37] Actually, that depends on the writer, since content may in fact be enhanced by the intimations—often satiric in nature—of the pun.

Wordplay contributes vitally to the bantering tone of the *tradiciones*. The source of the humor, aside from the obvious pleasure associated with the discovery of witty double meanings, resides in the genial satire typical of the *tradicionista*. Palma relied on wordplay in the characterization of his colonial and nineteenth-century *dramatis personae*, apparently well aware of the fact that using a pun, when pointing out a feature of physique or personality, accentuates the meanings forced into play by the author's manipulation of terms.[38]

Palma manifested for the signified an overwhelming preference for the equivoque, both in comparative and noncomparative statements. Comparative statements have already been examined: "más humos que una chimenea," *"más trastienda que un bodegón,"* "más camándulas que el rosario de Jerusalén," "más gracia andando que un obispo confirmando," "más tieso que su almidonada gorguera," "más hígados que un frasco de bacalao," "más campanillas que mula madrina." Equivoques not encased in a comparative mold furnish equal amusement.

> Refieren que un arzobispo vio de una manera casual bailar la mozamala, y volviéndose al familiar que lo acompañaba, preguntó:
> "¿Cómo se llama este bailecito?"
> "La zamacueca, ilustrísimo señor."
> "Mal puesto nombre. Esto debe llamarse *la resurrección de la carne*. (573)

The play is on the words underlined by Palma. In one sense, the words refer to the body at resurrection; in another sense, the words refer to stimulation of carnal feelings and actions.

> Las picarescas limeñas, . . . no vieron nunca de buen ojo a la condesa de Lemos, y la bautizaron con el apodo de la *Patona*. Presumo que la virreina sería mujer de mucha base. (425)

Two meanings for *base* are foundation and big feet. As Beinhauer notes, "a big foot always displeases," giving rise to humorous word-play in popular speech.[39]

> . . . el excelentísimo señor virrey don Manuel Amat y Juniet, . . . condecorado con un *cementerio de cruces*, había sido un dechado de moralidad y honradez administrativas. (651)

The humor lies in the play on *cruces*, which is engendered by the highly connotative noun *cementerio*.

> La causa, . . . gracias a la aplicación del tormento a los reos, que es el medio más expedito para *hacer cantar hasta a los mudos*, quedó terminada el 20 de julio. (584)

The double play on words here increases the delight in the use of *cantar*, meaning either to sing or to confess, and in the use of *mudos*, meaning either dumb or silent.

In some instances of double meaning the narrator creates a pun by remarking on a word or phrase that otherwise might have gone unnoticed or proved ambiguous.

> Lo que yo tengo que hacer es casarte, y te casaré como hay viñas en Jerez, y entre tú y la Teresa *multiplicaréis hasta que se gaste la pizarra.* (83)

The final clause invokes humor by investing *multiplicar* with a meaning otherwise not discernible from the semantic context and by proferring a metaphorical analogy through the expression "gastar la pizarra," meaning "to wear out the body."

> Llamábase Consuelo la niña, y los maldicientes decían que sabía hacer honor al nombre de pila. (395)

The humor in this instance stems from sensual suggestion originating in play on the girl's name. Such name play is common in the *tradiciones*.

In *diáfora* a word or phrase used by one individual is understood with diverse significance by another individual.

> Cuentan de don Geripundio que una tarde llegó un mendigo a la puerta de su tienda y le dijo:
> "Hermano, una limosna, que Dios y la Virgen Santísima se lo pagarán."
> "¡Hombre!" contestó el avaro, "no me parece mal negocio. Tráeme *un pagaré* con esas dos firmas, y nos entenderemos." (526)

Pagar in this passage should be read as both *to bless* and *to pay.*

> Constituyóse un día el provisor en el locutorio del monasterio, y entre él, que aconsejaba a la rebelde volviese al domicilio conyugal, y la traviesa limeña se entabló este diálogo:
> "Dígame con franqueza, señor provisor, ¿tengo yo cara de papilla?"
> "No, hijita, que tienes cara de ángel."
> "Pues si no soy papilla, no soy plato para viejo, y si soy ángel no puedo unirme al demonio." (601)

The humor and the meaning of the pun come to life through additional metaphorical play, a common occurrence in Palma's style, which, incidentally, favors culinary metaphors in the depiction of male-female relationships.

> "¡Lástima de pícaro!" decía al pie del patíbulo don Rodrigo a su alguacil.
> "¿No es verdad, Guerequeque, que siempre sostuve que este bellaco había de *acabar muy alto?*"
> "Con perdón de usiría," contestó el interpelado, "que ese palo es de poca altura para el merecimiento del bribón." (458)

Palma regularly returned to the same pun two or three times throughout the *tradiciones*. Given the number of years and pages involved, however, it is amazing that Palma is able to display as much versatility as he does. The play on *alto* differs from the example from page 862 of the *Tradiciones peruanas* in that one character, to the amusement of the reader, grasps the pun offered by another character and elaborates on it.

A variation of this technique transpires when the narrator or the protagonist uses the same word two or more times in close proximity with different meaning. Good-natured satire underlies the employment of this device by Palma. For example, Don Dimas is depicted as a man who, "a fuerza de *dar fe*, se había quedado sin pizca de fe, porque en el oficio gastó en breve la poca que trajo al mundo" (513). *Dar fe* could be a verb meaning *to attest* or *to certify,* or *fe* could be a noun (separate from the verb) meaning *faith.* Palma's reaction to a ballad provides another instance: "un músico hace una pepitoria de los tecnicismos de arte, y ensarta un romance que él llama heroico, acaso por la heroicidad del prójimo que acomete la empresa de leerlo íntegro" (508). Here the wordplay involves the application of a related but different meaning: heroic poetry/heroism. The narrator interrupts an introductory digression by telling the story of a judge who intruded on a lawyer's long-winded allegation concerning a boy's paternal relationship by saying, "¡basta de preámbulo, y al hecho!", to which the lawyer responded, "el hecho es un muchacho hecho; el que lo ha hecho niega el hecho; he aquí el hecho" (1035). Consider the following examples:

> . . . el escribano era un abejorro recatado de bolsillo . . . que *en punto a dar no daba ni las buenas noches.* (515)
>
> Entréme fraile, pero la frailería no entró en mí." (460)
>
> . . . decía muy espiritualmente que era preciso guardarla de los muchos que la guardaban, y defenderla de los muchos que la defendían. (472)

Many of Palma's depictions involving satire operate on a "shift-in-focus" principle wherein an initial feasible meaning is shifted to refer to an aspect of character or to a broader facet of anatomy by a subsequent clarifying phrase. Many of these have already been examined under different headings: "nariz de escribano por lo picaresca" (645), "ojos de médico, por lo matadores" (396), "boca de periodista, por el aplomo y gracia en el mentir" (396), "inclinación a escribano en no dejar botella en la que no se empeñe en dar fe" (307). A common device in humor that Palma occasionally employed is termed by Leacock as the "face value" technique; it deals with "the contrast between the face value of the words or phrases as usually used and the logical significance of it."[40] In the following selection from the *tradiciones* Palma unexpectedly shifted the point of emphasis from *traicionado* to *mejor*.

> "¡Canalla! Me has traicionado con mi mejor amigo."
> "¡Mal agradecido!" le contestó ella, . . . "¿No sería peor que te hubiera engañado con un extraño?" (1011)

The satiric humor emanating from a dialogue found in "Montalbán" stems from a similar shift.

> "¿Qué se vende en esta tienda?"
> "Cabezas de borrico," contestó amostazado el mercader.
> "Si la de usted es la de muestra, no compro, y sigo mi camino." (676)

On the level of the signifier we most often encounter a play on words in the form of *paronomasia*. The technique is simple but humorous, ingeniously blending meaning and form. Additional humor may come from context, from metaphor, from the creation of neologisms, or from the rhythmic or alliterative effect of similarly written words. Rhyming devices lend themselves well to popular sayings and poetry, frequently surfacing in humorous verse. "El obispo de los retruécanos" offers a fine case in point. An envious and arrogant priest, who had enjoyed favoritism with the previous bishop, Las Heras, denounced a certain clergyman to the present bishop, Pérez y Armendáriz, when the clergyman was nominated to a particular parish. The bishop, reacting with surprise, sent for his secretary, and to the shock of the *chismoso*, gave the best of the vacant parishes to the clergyman. When the chagrined priest protested, Pérez y Armendáriz retorted, "¿Cómo ha de ser, hijito? ¡Paciencia! En tiempos de Heras / todo eras. / En tiempo de Pérez / nada esperes" (890).

Playing on words in a similar manner, the people of colonial Lima trivialized the devout viceroy, Gabriel de Avilés, through a homophonous and paronomastic play on his name: "en la oracón *hábil es*, y en el gobierno *inhábil es*" (822). Another case of wordplay from the *tradiciones* involves Bishop Romaní's stammered pronunciation of "vacante." Supposing the bishop dead, the canons and relatives make haste to expropriate his possessions. When one of them kneels on his stomach to reach for a picture above his bed, he awakens. Later, in response to the hypocritical rejoicing that the Church had not gone into "sede vacante," the bishop remarks, "¡Gracias! ¡Gracias! Se han escapado ustedes de entrar en sede *rapante*" (631), a possible allusion to the evident lack of concern and the every-man-for-himself philosophy. Consider the ensuing excerpts:

> Las musas y las mozas fueron mi diablo y mi flaco. (897)
>
> Cállese usted, cojete; / cojo y recojo, cojo con bonete; / cojo con muletilla; / cojo y cojín con sudadero y silla. (1050)
>
> Alborotar merindades para luego salir con paro medio es proceder como el galán que presumía de robusto, *de noche chichirimoche y de madrugada chichirinada.* (452)

Wordplay often engages etymological relationships. An observation by Rosenblat concerning *Don Quijote* might also be appropriately applied to the *tradiciones,* although not to the same degree: "etymological or pseudo-etymological play with the form of the word is constant."[41] This predisposition in Palma is further evidenced in the examples below:

> No somos de esos librepensadores que no quieren que los demás piensen libremente. (1086)
>
> . . . para escarmiento de poetas vergonzantes y desvergonzados. (656)
>
> . . . el platonicismo es manjar de poetas melenudos y de muchachas desmelenadas. (791)

Palma seldom broke a word in the middle for the sake of humor. A statement by the protagonist in "Los escrúpulos de Halicarnaso" contains one of the few instances of *retruécanos* in the *tradiciones.* After having been asked to aid in an amorous encounter in the back of his shop, Halicarnaso responds, "Con mi lesna y mi persona soy amigo del colegial y de usted, señorita. Zapatero soy, y no conde de *Alca* ni marqués de *Huete.* Ocúpeme usted en cosas de mi profesión y ver que la sirvo al pespunte y sin andar con *tiquis miquis*" (802). The words used in the titles, *Alca* and *Huete,* together form the word *alcahuete,* meaning a go-between. An interesting play on the word *Guatemala* in "Los caballeros de la capa" falls within this same range, while evidencing points of contact with the previously mentioned "face value" technique: "salimos de Guate-mala / y entramos en Guate-peor/ cambia el pandero de manos, / pero de sonidos, no" (54). The word *Granada* offers an opportunity for similar wordplay: "San Juan de Dios en Gra-nada, / y este Pedro en Guate-mala, / realizaron, Dios mediante, / una cosa nada-mala" (439). A bit of irony enlivens the humor of a passage from "Una moza de rompe y raja": "¡Canario! El cantarcito no podía ser más subversivo en aquellos días en que la palabra *rey* quedó tan proscrito del lenguaje, que se desbautizó al peje-rey para llamarlo *peje-patria,* y al pavo real se le confirmó con el nombre de *pavo nacional*" (970). This type of wordplay can involve an exchange of parts between two words for humorous effect as well as intensified meaning: "lo más llano era la excomunión, que al más ternejal le ponía la carne de gallina y lo dejaba *cabiztivo* y *pensabajo*" (582). The bewildering and devastating impact of excommunication is paralleled and reflected by the structural-semantic interchange between the terms.

Like Quevedo before him and like other contemporary romantic writers, Palma approved a variety of new words for the Spanish tongue, nearly all emanating from natural roots. As Emilio Carilla wisely observes, "in Ricardo Palma . . . neologisms naturally identify with a spirit of satire and play." Carilla then cites as examples of this tendency "*cascabelear, escarabajear, escopetear, suegreaba, manducable, majadereo, cuequeaba* (es decir, bailaba la cueca), *architurulato, desmondongaron* (por mataron), [y] *enfarolarse*", to which I add *barullópolis* (29) and *canallocracia* (877).[42] The novel term *cornitradicional* refers to Palma's tale entitled "El primer toro." Frequently the narrator ironically asks for forgiveness for using a particular word, as in this reference to allowing women to smoke cigars: "se hiciera usted cómplice del (páseme la palabra) *desmujerización* de la mujer" (1446).

Ricardo Palma, as one of the foremost masters of the Castilian tongue, demonstrated in his prose works a special sense of euphonious articulation, often with humorous effect. The plethora of internally alliterative words are particularly significant to the sonorous, or "musical" aspect of Palma's prose. The *tradicionista* instrumented such terms as *barrumbada* (146), *paparrucha* (786), *dingolodangos* (455), *barrabasada* (318), and *birlibirloque* (789), the latter two appearing throughout the *tradiciones.* Nouns include *pirlimpimpim* (789), *recancanillas* (310), *rifirafe* (318), *chichisbeo* (610), *rimbombancias* (637), *pampiroladas* (965), *zurriagazos* (124), *ringorrangos* (695), *ñiquiñaque* (1445), *triquitraque* (383), *desparapajo* (590), and *plepa* (695). Verbs, adjectives, and adverbs of this nature are scarce—*cascabeleábamos* (246) and *opíparo* (689) or *opíparamente* constitute significant exceptions. Internally assonant words also contribute an air of merriment to his highly fluid, pleasant sounding prose. The following is a sample of words used by Palma: *Perendengues* (590), *gurrumina* (1193), *colombroño* (89), *michimo-*

rongo (1439), *morrocutudo* (590), *garambainas* (794), *faralares* (820), and *chilindrina* (373). Again, one finds few verbs and adjectives in this style—*escarabajeaba* (787) and *rabisalsera* (590) are two examples. Polysyllabic terms that lack real assonance include *apergaminado* (815) and *empingorotado* (651), some of his most preferred epithets, and several lengthy verb forms: "se engolosinarían" (904), "se la desencapotaron" (382) and "se había empestillado" (242).

In connection with the euphony of these terms and with Palma's paronomastic, etymological wordplay are repetitions of otherwise identical terms that have undergone modification by means of suffixes or prefixes: "Feo, feísmo defecto," (1089), "¡Borrachito! . . . ¡Borracho! . . . " (1089), "era bellísima, pluscuambellísima" (858), "más mirada y remirada que estampa de devocionario" (314). Somewhat similar is a tendency to graduated accumulations, evident in prose by both Cervantes and Quevedo. Palma uses it to a minimal extent.

Cervantes:	Yo he hecho mal en leerlos y peor en creerlos y más mal en imitarlos.[43]
Quevedo:	Redondo de cara, malas barbas y peores hechos.[44]
Palma:	. . . tuvieron que conformarse con mala cena y peor lecho. (570)
	Esto, un mucho de repetir de coro trisagios y novenas, un poco de codimentar dulces y ensaladas, y un nada de trato de gentes, y pare usted de contar, fue la educación de la millonaria y bella damisela. (241)

Modification of Expressions

The love of the Spanish people for freedom and independence and the latent protest within them against any conventional human coercion has been identified by Beinhauer as an imporant factor in the sublime disrespect that the Spanish speaker tends to manifest "in the face of the set, grammaticalized forms of his language." Rather than originating in unbridled individualism, this inclination stems from a keen awareness of the present moment "with an extraordinary sensitivity able to capture and scrutinize the peculiarities of a given situation and for whose expression the set formulas, consecrated by use, sometimes turn out to be insufficient." A principal manifestation of this tendency, both in everyday speech and in literature, concerns the humorous modification of set expressions, idioms, popular sayings, or traditionally expected linguistic sequences. This technique, known as *paráfrasis*, finds favor as a comic device in the works of Cervantes and Quevedo. Benefiting once again from his *Siglo de Oro* mentors, Palma enlivened his narrative style with the use of *paráfrasis*, usually in connection with satire.[45]

The effect of *paráfrasis* is to renew overworked expressions of language in order to revitalize their metaphorical vigor. According to Lerner, "in this manner there is produced a type of ironical destruction of the traditional formula of the popular saying when one of its terms is interpreted with a generally colloquial or direct meaning that annuls the aphoristic value of the phrase." The humorous impact of this phenomenon is generally in the surprise occasioned by the contrast between the original terms of the expression and their modified version or between an altered word of the idiom and its remaining components. As Bergson has pointed out, surprise constitutes an important factor in comicity and occurs very effectively when a reader or listener is suddenly made aware of the laughable aspects of a rigid form whose continuity has been taken for granted. Leacock explains further that the words or phrases undergoing *paráfrasis* "are forced into a meaning never given to them, but which on examination seems perfectly logical, as a meaning they ought to bear. The sudden verbal novelty brings a pleasant shock of surprise" similar somewhat to the effect of the "face value" technique.[46]

In the *tradiciones paráfrasis* takes on an array of forms. Sometimes Palma played with a proverb or an adage, as in the case of "El hombre propone y Dios dispone." Monsieur de Saillard had prepared himself for a duel with Ramón Castilla and was about to embark for Peru, "pero el hombre propone, y la fiebre amarilla dispone" (1090). He died in the port of Guaira. Satire underlies a more extended play on the same maxim: "pero un hombre propone, un juez dispone y un escribano descompone, y gracias si no toma también carta en este tresillo un abogado" (1447). An idea associated with "El bien se nos venga, el mal se nos vaya" appears, "*el bien que se venga a pesar de Menga, y si viene el mal, sea para la manceba del abad*" (284). Exaggeration frequently plays a part in these modifications. The alteration or replacement of one word often suffices to engender the humor. A prisoner, when requested to compose a brief poem, snidely replies, "no tengo el menor *conveniente*" (959). The expression in

Spanish for "every other day" is "un día sí y otro no;" Doña Quirina, however, replenishes the oil in a night light "un día sí y otro tambíen" (1091). Similarly, the *tradicionista* changed the phrase "golpe de estado" into "uno de aquellos golpes de teatro" (354), while analogically explaining elsewhere that Gamarra "fundó cátedra de anarquía y bochinche" (1109).

Humor emerges when, as noted above, the literal meaning of a set expression experiences revitalization due to the modification joltingly imposed upon it. For example, in assuaging a judge's conscience concerning a proposed execution, the Count of Santiesteban admonishes, "firme usía de una vez y quédele horra la conciencia, que esto es cortar por lo gangrenado y no por lo sano" (416), "cortar por lo sano" meaning to use drastic measures. In a letter a brother writes to his unkempt sister, "Besa a V. las manos, si por casualidad se las ha lavado" (490). Doña Pulqueria mocks her neighbor, telling him that if he is going to wait for his wife to open the door "tarea te doy hasta el día del juicio por la noche" (451). The addition of "por la noche" draws the ephemeral down to earth while further expanding the hyperbole.

Introducing contemporary allusions into traditional locutions proffers an additional variation of this technique. The biblical idea of mortality phrased in terms of being a vale of tears and a "valley of the shadow of death" is transformed to read, "valle de lágrimas y pellejería" (1148) and "valle de primos civilistas y primos demócratas" (1202). These examples again reveal Palma's use of this device for making light of individuals and institutions. In "De gallo a gallo" Larriva counters his rival, Echegaray, whose nickname is *tinaja* because of his obesity, with the quatrain, "Cuando Dios hizo esta alhaja, / tan ancha de viento y lomo, / no dijo: 'Faciamus homo,' / sino: 'Faciamus tinaja' " (1051).

Context often holds the key to the humor of the modification. In "El chocolate de los jesuitas" Palma recorded his sentiments on hearing a delegate in congress refer to another man, in seemingly offensive tones, who suffered from partial deafness: "achaque que lo obligaba a nunca separarse de su trompetilla acústica." As it turns out, the statement contained no affront. If it had, the reader is assured, "habría sido antiparlamentario y grosero y dado motivo justo para que el agraviado le rompiese, por lo menos, *la trompetilla*" (632; italics mine), as opposed to the expected nose, face, or head.

Paráfrasis also occurs when a literary formula or traditional metaphor undergoes alteration. For instance, instead of the customary opening for fairy tales—"érase que se era"—Palma initiated "La misa negra" with "erase lo que era" (833). In a further example, Palma renewed the overworked metaphor for wife, *media naranja,* by way of comments such as "muchas medias naranjas que estaban en camino de pudrirse y servir de almuerzo al diablo" (1118).

Surprise

Aristotle originally identified a joke with deceived expectation. Pascal perpetuated the notion, observing that "nothing produces laughter more than a surprising disproportion between that which one expects and that which one sees." The opinion attained a position of authority when it appeared in the aesthetics of Immanuel Kant. "Laughter," he wrote, "is an affection arising from the sudden transformation of a strained expectation into nothing." Eastman phrases the same sentiment, "Indeed anything that drops pleasantly and well ripened into the lap, . . . being sufficiently unexpected to possess an eventful character, will usually be greeted laughingly by people not sitting under the incubus of some dull ideal of decorum."[47]

The truth of the "disappointment theory" is well attested in many examples cited in this book. In truth, the cause of most of our laughter in the *tradiciones* is pleasant surprise at the novelty and ingenuity of the author's stylistic expression and agreeably startling twists of thought. In some instances, however, the unexpected constitutes the main cause of amusement, whether it concerns a modification of a common expression or not. "¿Has entendido, lector?" the narrator queries after citing an eight-line stanza. "Pues yo tampoco" (814). After a suggestive quatrain he asks, "¿No la conociste, lector?" Again the reader reacts with surprise to the narrator's response, "Yo tampoco" (650). "Historia de un cañoncito" yields this interesting explanation: "en palacio había lo que en tiempo de los virreyes se llamó *besamano,* y que en los días de la República, y para diferenciar, se llama lo mismo" (1119). In another *tradición,* certain cock fighters, whose bird has lost, withdraw from the arena, "llevando el dueño, bajo la capa se entiende, el cuerpo del difunto, que con arroz y pimientos hallaba al otro día sepultura digna en el estómago del zapatero y de sus camaradas" (624). The word *digna,* ironic in its usage here, misleads the reader by preparing him psychologically for something else. Later in the same story a judge promises to look into some possible illegalities in connection with another cockfight, and the narrator satirically comments, "Lo que resulte lo sabremos . . . el día del juicio" (627). An unexpected response adds humor to the portrayal of Gutierre de Ursán in "El encapuchado."

> "No era don Gutierre de la pasta de aquel marido cuyo sueño interrumpió un oficioso para darle esta nueva: 'A tu mujer se la ha llevado Fulano.' '¡Pues buena plepa se lleva!' contestó el paciente, se volvió al otro lado del lecho y siguió roncando como un bendito." (396)

Sexual Allusion

This section constitutes a summation of a point to which much attention has already been directed. Samples of sexually oriented humor in the *Tradiciones peruanas* materialized in our discussion of Latin inserts, religion, types, dialogue, hyperbole, comparisons, wordplay, *paráfrasis,* and litotes. Sexual allusion usually accompanies satire and irony, but alone it is sometimes the source of amusement. I emphasize the relevance of this tonal feature to our overriding theme with a few more examples.

Among the bounteous stanzas of verse fused into the narrative style of Palma's tales are many that harbor sensual overtones.

> Si yo me viera contigo / la llave a la puerta echada, / y el herrero se muriera, / y la llave se quebrara . . . (650)

> El viejo que se case / con mujer niña, / él mantiene la cepa / y otro vendimia. (600)

The latter quatrain has reference to a count, an ugly sixty-year-old man, who married thirteen-year-old Marianita Belzunce. When, after a year of denying him, she hid in a convent, licentious couplets began to circulate around Lima accusing him of impotence. Among the couplets Palma cited the following:

> Con una espada mohosa / y ya sin punta ni filo, / estáte, conde, tranquilo: / no pienses en otra cosa.
> Toda tu arrogancia aborta / cuando la ponen a prueba: / tu espada, como no es nueva, / conde, ni pincha ni corta.
> Lo mejor que te aconsejo / es que te hagas ermitaño; / que el buen manjar hace daño /al estómago de un viejo.
> Para que acate Mariana / de tus privilegios parte, / necesitabas armarte/ de una espada toledaña. (601)

One discovers the combination of eroticism and satire throughout the *tradiciones,* particularly in connection with libertine priests.

Fun, spicy exchanges between lovers are sometimes condensed into popular verse songs or epigrams: "Porque un beso me has dado / gruñe tu madre; / toma, niña, tu beso, / dila que calle" (98); "Mis ojos fueron testigos / que te vieron persignar. / ¡Quién te pudiera besar / donde dices *enemigos!*" (380). Everyone knows that "cuando dos que se quieren / se ven solitos, / se hacen unos cariños / muy rebonitos" (207). Of a somewhat different tone and very unpoetic structure is the uncouth compliment of a boorish soldier to an aristocratic widow: "¡Abur, brigadiera! ¡Que no te comiera un lobo y te vomitara en mi tarina!" A complaint to the commander elicits the response, "No sea gazmoña, señora; que el requiebro es de lo lindo, y prueba que mis muchachos son decidores a su manera y no bañan con almizcle las palabras; agradezca la intención y perdone la rudeza" (901). All this closely parallels the humor derived from jests concerning marriage, which, as has been noted, Palma resorted to frequently.

Of course, humor from sensuous intimation need not always take poetic form. The *tradiciones* offer many instances of this brand of humor resulting, for example, from the intrusion of the mischievous narrator, as when he affirms that "los comunistas y los solterones son bípedos que se asimilan" because they present such a threat "contra la propiedad del prójimo" (123). In another instance, the narrator refuses to describe Paca Rodríguez's shapely legs: "si hemos de hablar, lector, en puridad de amigos, creemos que mejor es no meneallo y que, pasándolas por alto, te libertemos de un pecado venial" (816).

Palma wrote principally to his fellow citizens in a tone and in regard to matters that harmonized with their interests. Waggish, often satirical allusions of a suggestive nature were assured of garnering their attention while amusing and teaching them.

Ingenuousness

Hearing a naive absurdity related in a mood of serious belief is amusing. In literature the depiction of ingenuousness combined with irony provides a treasure chest of humor. Palma's historical anecdotes are no exception. In them he depicts a number of characters whose words and actions exemplify the "confident unawareness" necessary to ignite irony. Satire normally attends the portrayals, since the process of highlighting someone's naïveté almost assuredly involves some element of ridicule. Only in the face of inevitable stupidity, as in the case of an uneducated Indian or one who has gone mad, or when there exists an underlying current of admiration, as with *tía* Catita, does the element of satire in Palma dwindle, leaving only the pure humor of innocence.

Muecke proposes three formal requirements of irony, that there be two levels, that of the victim and that of the ironist or observer; that there exist opposition between the two levels in the form of a contradiction, incongruity, or incompatibility; and that an element of innocence be present, that is, there must be a victim who is confidently unaware.[48] These three points are evident in the humor of ingenuousness throughout the *tradiciones*.

In "El judío errante, en el Cuzco" Palma related the tale of the 1856 epidemic of typhus in Cuzco that coincided with the popularity throughout Peru of a novel by Eugene Sue entitled *El judío errante*. Sue's story tells of an errant Jew who wanders the earth accompanied by a devastating plague. When, during the same year, an unfortunate Spaniard who fit the description of the wandering Jew happened into the town of Zurite, the inhabitants immediately identified him as the protagonist of the novel. To his explanations they "confidently" retorted, "'¿A nosotros con ésas? . . . ¡No somos tan bobos! Maldita la falta que nos hacía su visita. Ya quedará usted escarmentado, compadre; y pagará por junto las que ha hecho en el mundo'" (1131). Having burned him at the stake, these "tan cristianos vecinos" held a great celebration. The people of Zurite manifest a confident impercipience of the truth. Prior knowledge causes the reader to perceive from their graphic depiction of simplicity their naïve deductions. Palma's ability to get a laugh out of capital punishment is again demonstrated.

In another instance, when the viceroy is beaten in a card game, the news spreads like wildfire, each person eager to be the first to make the announcement to those yet uninformed. Between two who meet on the street we overhear the following dialogue:

"¡Hombre! ¿No sabe usted lo que hay de nuevo?"

"¿Noticia de los piratas? Hasta los pelos estoy de mentiras, buenas y gordas," contestaba el otro.

"¡Qué piratas ni qué niños envueltos! Guárdeme usted secreto. Lo que hay es que al virrey le han cortado anoche el revesino."

"¡Hombre! ¿Qué me cuenta usted? No puede ser."

"Pues sí, señor, sí puede ser; y por más señas que el de la hazaña ha sido el marqués de Villafuerte. A mí me lo ha contado todo, en confianza, la mujer del sobrino del compadre del repostero de palacio. Ya ve usted que no atestiguo con muertos.

"¡Caramba! La cosa es de mucho bulto; pero hay que creerla, porque quien se lo ha dicho a usted tiene por qué estar bien informado. (467)

From our level we perceive each interlocutor as artless, both in connection with his belief in the notableness of the news itself and in regard to his confidence in the source of the information. The discordance with logic contained in the source—the wife of the nephew of the friend of the palace pastry cook—suggests the irony while intensifying our enjoyment of the provinciality of the speakers.

The above examples of naïveté involve the humor of satire. Implicit is that the people in question really have no valid excuse for their impercipience. If not through secular education, at least by means of their church activity they should have absorbed sufficient illumination to avoid such muddled thinking. The case of two Indians sent down to the coast with a load of melons, however, is different; no possibility for enlightenment exists. Consequently, although we are amused by their innocence, we experience no sense of ridicule, contempt, or scorn. As related by Palma, the two Indians become hungry and mistakenly think that by hiding a written message accompanying the shipment they can eat one or two melons without detection. "Escondamos la carta detrás de la tapia, que no viéndonos ella comer no podrá denunciarnos" (148). Of course, on arrival they are soundly thrashed.

Naïveté bordering on or turning into full-fledged insanity operates in like fashion. The well-known story of "No Veintemil" supplies one case in point. Another centers on a teacher, Bonifacio, a strict disciplinarian who uses the whip daily in his school. His students suspect he is touched in the head and their intuition is confirmed when he takes them to see a man executed. So they do not forget the lesson, he pulls out his whip and cracks it. His enthusiasm gets the best of him and he begins to whip everyone in the crowd. Everyone scatters. Some knaves cry, "¡toro!, ¡toro!" One busybody runs to tell the viceroy that Chilean insurgents are screaming for his head. When troops arrive, they find Bonifacio "descargando furiosos chicotazos sobre los leones de bronce que adornaban la soberbia pila de la plaza" (896). He is escorted to the insane asylum. This tale once again emphasizes Palma's facility in extracting mirth from the portrayal of ingenuousness, even in the absence of satiric intent. It also highlights the importance of the omnipresent jocose tone in the *Tradiciones peruanas* that is amusing to the reader no matter what seriousness a topic would normally connote in everyday life.

A variation of the humor of ingenuousness takes the form of what Worcester has called "ingénu satire" and Muecke, "ingénu irony." This form involves a "simple soul" whose innocence or ignorance suffices "to see through the woven complexities of hypocrisy and rationalization or pierce the protective tissues of convention and *idées reçues*."[49] The guileless Indian sometimes fulfills this role in Palma's *tradiciones*. During a period of simony and other excess on the part of the clergy, an Indian is told that he must officially relinquish his bachelorhood and marry the female he is cohabiting with. "'*Taita*,' contestó el infeliz, 'amancebamiento no puede ser malo; porque corregidor tiene manceba, alcabalero tiene manceba y cura tiene también manceba' " (546).

5

Other Modes of Humor

Throughout previous chapters I have attempted to point out where applicable that techniques of humor presented as being ironic or satirical also evoke mirth in the absence of these moods, and in some instances I have offered examples to that effect. In this final section I shall attempt to synthesize the nonsatiric, nonironic areas in order to round out our perception of the style of humor in the *Tradiciones peruanas.*

Exclamations

The vernacular style of Palma's anecdotes seems to have dictated a healthy usage of exclamatory phrases, echoes of the famous Cervantine and Quevedesque styles. Exclamations are expressed by characters as well as by the narrator himself. Through these phrases Palma characterized, reaffirmed his subjective presence, and gave vent to a spectrum of humorous, ironic, and satirical hues. Palma's style differs from the styles of his antecedent masters in that his narrator articulates a large number of the exclamations in his prose: "¡Y qué demonche!" (166), "¡Qué diantre!" (128), "¡Quia!" (991), "¡Canario!" (970), "¡Qué!" (759), "¡Eh!" (446), "¡Vamos!" (887), "¡Cómo! ¡Qué cosa! . . . ¡Chimabambolo!" (733), "¡Cataplum!" (735).

Palma's exclamations often convey satirical humor and frequently cater to expressions of irony. However, many provide amusement without the involvement of satire or irony. Several exclamatory remarks enrich *tía* Catita's stories: "¡Dios nos libre y nos defienda!" (834), "¡Jesús me ampare!," "¡Jesús, María y José!," "¡Jesucristo sea conmigo!" As in Cervantes and Quevedo, certain characters are depicted in terms of their propensity for exclamatory declaration: Sancho, in *Don Quijote;* the soldier, in *El buscón;* and Francisco de Carbajal, in the *Tradiciones peruanas.*

Ricardo Palma's style reveals a decided preference for apposition, and frequently his appositional epiphonemas reflect a marked predisposition for exclamations: "alzó ella los ojos, sus mejillas se tiñeron de carmín y . . . ¡Dios la haya perdonado!, se olvidó de hacer la cruz y santiguarse. ¡Cosas del demonio!" (368); "pasó su alma a experimentar el sentimiento opuesto al odio. ¡Misterios de corazón!" (382). Many times, rather than use a true epiphonema, the narrator sums up in a humorous manner the overriding feelings of a passage or even of a complete story: "¡O somos o no somos!" (546).

Palma's dependence on exclamations illustrates well the interdependence of humor and style in the *tradiciones.* Although some amusement stems from situational humor and from jokes, the majority of merriment in Palma's prose is verbal and is tied directly to a particular facet of the author's mode of expressivity.

Suffixes

In his analysis of the changes that Palma made in his second version of "Mauro Cordato" Alberto Escobar remarks, "Now it seems that we are hearing Don Ricardo talk."[1] Among other reasons, Escobar highlights the addition of diminutives as the cause of this ability to speak. The use of diminutives signals the difference in the tone of the reworked version. In effect, augmentative, diminutive, and superlative endings contribute significantly to the tone that characterizes the *tradiciones* in general. Palma's mastery of the language is evident in his use of suffixes for humorous, ironic, satiric, or merely communicative effect. The presence of suffixes in his prose constitutes one of several key factors that combine in the realization of Palma's personal style.

As is customary in Spanish, Palma's use of the diminutive suffix *-ito* is most frequent—"beatita" (459), "bien cargadito" (285), "maestrito" (801), "personita" (1203), "secretitos" (1203), "subiditos de color" (600), "orejita" (803), "cualquierita" (1069), "diablitos" (266). Along with humor and satire, diminutives may express sarcasm, as is the case with "comerciantito" (668) and "doctorcito" (1149), the latter term being in reference to a doctor whose promotion has fallen through. Another common diminutive in the *tradiciones* is the suffix *-illo:* "olorcillo" (526), "calorcillo" (285), "pelillos" (286), "Gonzalvillo" (426), "chicotillo" (474), "peca-dillos" (695), "durilla" (568), "granujilla" (1106), "celillos" (1203), "pueblecillo" (1147). Though usually devoid of malice or affection in Spanish, in Palma's *tradiciones* diminutives often purvey humorous connotations, as when a brazen leech suggests to a viceroy's face that even he, the viceroy, is not above stooping to under-the-counter "negocillos" (668).

By means of diminutives of lesser recurrence, such as *-ete, -ejo,* and *-uelo,* the author continued intermittently to reaffirm his jestive presence while he conveyed impressions of self-depreciation, satiric amusement, and light contempt. For example, when Viceroy Don Baltazar de la Cueva imposes careful audits on the royal coffers, he catches many red-handed, thus restoring to the treasury "algunos realejos" (456). The suffix amuses in its twofold intimation of insignificant quantity and the propinquity of a blithesome narrator.

Like diminutives, augmentative suffixes, such as *-ete, -ejo,* and *-uelo,* contribute to the chatty air of the stories while suggesting extravagance in a satiric manner. Although in the terms "formalote" (273), "amigote" (286), and "guapote" (1200) the suffix tends mostly to infuse a sense of playful exaggeration, in "seriotes oídores" (637) and "cobardote" (84) the augmentative shades the signified with a visible degree of contempt that never fully escapes the ever-present, albeit toned-down jauntiness so characteristic of Palma.

Words bearing a suffix may be amusing in and of themselves, or they may, as is frequently the case, join forces with other purveyors of humor. Ño Veintemil, in a tale emphasizing situational humor, for instance, relies on a series of superlatives in an effort to win the viceroy's favor: "Sí, señor. He renunciado a mi apellido para adoptar el de vuecencia, primero, por la mucha admiración y cariño que me inspira la ilustre persona del libérrimo prócer, del integérrimo gobernante, del . . ." (668). A diminutive and a superlative add to the colloquialized reaction of the Lord to Satan's quest for a beard: "'¡Hola!; exclamó el Señor, . . . ¿Esas tenemos, envidiosillo y soberbio? Pues tendrás lo que mereces, grandísimo bellaco" (1200).

The presence of a suffix often enables the reader to envision more clearly both scene and character and to participate more fully in the humor as a result. We perceive physique, as well as emotion, through the use of suffixes, while being drawn into the tonal atmosphere set by the narrator. An examination of suffixes demonstrates again that humor derives from a salient stylistic phenomenon.

Jokes

Occasionally during the course of a story Palma interrupted narrative to tell a joke. Though employed relatively infrequently, jokes comprise another stimulant of humor in the *Tradiciones peruanas.* Palma's jokes qualify well. According to Max Eastman's standards for jokes, they engage our interest, arouse balanced feelings naturally induced, and are easily understood but not obvious from the beginning.[2] Such play harmonizes with the atmosphere of the stories.

Circumlocution and Euphemism

Expressivity, dynamism, liveliness, singular impression—these constitute the reactions generally evoked by Palma's style. Thus, Guillermo Feliú Cruz calls Palma "the chisler of beautiful phrases, the incomparable speaker who made of the Castilian tongue an admirable instrument of beauty and charm."[3] The salient points of style that normally attract critics include the blend of archaic and colloquial terms, the liberal interpolation of *refranes,* proverbs, and verse, the constant presence of a warm irony and self-conscious narrator, and the *tradicionista*'s dazzling feel for the language. Usually overlooked is a fundamental stylistic factor that perpetuates both the vitality and the humor of the *tradiciones.* I refer to circumlocution and, closely associated with this style, euphemism.[4]

Throughout his prose Palma consciously and repeatedly altered the manner in which certain lexical-syntactic phenomena experienced articulation. These variations obey a decidedly festive orientation and have been cited regularly during the course of this book, particularly in connection with irony, the vernacular, popular sayings, poetry, exaggeration, figurative language, wordplay, modifications, litotes, and sexual allusion.

Palma was attracted to the anecdotal life of the viceroyalty. Perhaps as a consequence, alternative expressions related to basic aspects of life abound in the *tradiciones*—birth, living, sleeping, eating, dying, believing, thinking, forgetting, understanding. Given the bloody confrontations in many stories, periphrastic language naturally arises in connection with fighting, hanging, jailing, and killing. Other acts whose descriptions Palma skillfully alters include gossiping, hurrying, falling, and robbing. Circumlocutions proliferate as Palma identifies jobs, parts of bodies, doctors, women, men, children, years, dates, ages, nationalities, religions, and cities; this tendency is similar in allusions to the process of writing, researching, and publishing.

In his book on humor in spoken Spanish, Werner Beinhauer devotes several pages to "perífrasis" and emphasizes "the highly Spanish fondness of more or less veiled allusions." Hatzfeld, in *El 'Quijote' como obra de arte del lenguaje*, illuminates at length the use of circumlocution by Cervantes, including litotes, meiosis, and euphemisms.[5] Palma's mastery of the tongue, in part a heritage imparted by Cervantes, permits him to call on the resources of language in his exploitation of the unlimited possibilities offered by humorous periphrases.

According to Dámaso Alonso, periphrasis as a stylistic medium seeks to "communicate to the representation of the object a plasticity, a tinted relief, a dynamism that a concrete word cannot give."[6] Alonso's statement seconds my affirmation concerning the importance of circumlocution in the Limean author's style. Furthermore, with the alternative expressions frequently bringing into play an appropriately inappropriate incongruence, humor is enhanced. *Tradiciones peruanas completas* is a case in point. In connection with *fray* Martín de Porres, for example, Palma notifies the reader, "Bástele al lector saber que como el viejo Porres no le dejó a su retoño otra herencia que los siete días de la semana y una uña en cada dedo para rascarse las pulgas, tuvo éste que optar por meterse lego dominico y hacer milagros" (365). Irony of logical contradiction and irony of feigned objectivity stoke the humor in a lengthy substitution for the word *nada*. In order to say that a door does not close, the author strings together these words: ". . . esa puerta no sirve para lo que han querido todas las puertas desde la del arca de Noé, la más antigua de que hacen mención las historias, hasta la de la jaula de mi loro" (328). The reader reacts humorously to the incongruous association of Noah's Ark and the cage of the narrator's parrot, as well as to the author's seeming obliviousness to the inordinate length of his statement.

Aversion and anger occasion various periphrastic remarks in the *tradiciones*, often with colloquial underpinnings.

Pero a quien supo todo aquello a chicharrones de sebo fue a la Inesilla. (619)

A Ruiz Alcedo le supo el desaire a rejalgar con vitriolo. (746)

Al cabo se le subió la pimienta a la nariz de pico de loro. (1196)

Al oírse apostrofar así, se le avinagró al andaluz la mostaza. (961)

Designations for thievery or dishonesty reflect similar inventiveness in analogy and irony.

> Los apóstoles practicaban el comunismo, no sólo en la población, sino en los caminos. (406)
>
> La afición a las ninfas del toma y daca lo perdió al fin. (1048)
>
> . . . los devotos de la hacienda ajena. (561)

The use of a whip originates such alternative phrases as "repartir más cáscara de novillo" (894) or "uso y abuso del jarabe de cuero" (895). In order to state that women were not permitted to learn to write, Palma went to amusing lengths: "no se le permitía hacer sobre el papel patitas de mosca o garrapatos anárquicos" (598). He took equal pains to avoid saying "women": "las descendientes de los golosos desterrados del paraíso" (999).

In *El español coloquial* Beinhauer finds the language to be exceedingly rich in euphemisms. That Palma's style supports this observation is obvious to the careful reader of the *tradiciones*. Like Cervantes, though, Palma was not "a finicky person, one who uses euphemisms to hide any frivolity or even to hush the spicy." True, Palma did take the edges off the risqué—"he even tended to evaporate the salaciousness of the people into literary clouds"—in order to assure widest possible diffusion of his stories.[7] Nevertheless, his moderation itself became a striking stylistic achievement, the two principal results of his euphemistic posture being a highly enriched expressivity and a deluge of humor. Despite the veiled language of many passages, this style remains suggestive and stimulating to the imagination.

Palma resorts to euphemisms particularly in order to soften allusions to sex, improper language, and the unpleasantness of death and killing.

> Al primer barrunto que éste tuvo de que un cirineo le ayudaba a cargar la cruz, encerró a su mujer en casita. (383).
>
> . . . ella no gastó muchos melindres para inscribir en el abultado registro de San Cornelio al que iba por esos mares rumbo a Cádiz. (396)
>
> Había en el lugar una señora viuda de un cabildante, jamón apetitoso todavía, . . . la cual gozaba fama de ser cumplidora del precepto evangélico que manda ejercer la caridad dando de beber al sediento. (445)

Analogy, irony, and ingenuity of phrase combine for humorous reading. Nudity or intimate parts of the body also are often conveyed on the wings of euphemistic circumlocution.

. . . las mujeres que, llamándose honestas, se presentan en público luciendo cosas que no siempre son para lucidas. (547)

. . . las protuberancias de oriente y occidente. (801)

. . . al niño y al mulo al . . . digo, adonde suene mucho y dañe poco. (894)

. . . para que en ella dejasen al prójimo más liviano de ropa que lo anduvo Adán antes que se le indigestase la manzana. (676)

As noted in the section on caricature, Palma normally avoided crude or profane words in his prose. He achieved this either by substituting an inoffensive term sharing initial letters with the disagreeable word or by naming unpleasant animals.

¡La perra que lo parió al muy pu . . . chuelero! (970)

"¡La pim . . . pinela! contestó el Libertador. (1007)

. . . echando sapos y culebras por la boca. (591)

The humor derives in these instances from the intimation of the forbidden, combined with the humor of the situation.

Henry James suggests in *The Future of the Novel* that humor may be used to deodorize subject matter. Nimetz discusses this effect in regard to Galdós, observing that humor may act as a balm against reality while at the same time, "with its weight of truth," achieving a sense of reality.[8] Of course, as will be recalled from the chapter on satire, Palma's humor often abets transmission of the author's true feelings. More often than not, however, his euphemisms concerning repellent bodily functions or death elicit only amusement. Consider Palma's description of a soldier's urgent need: "en cierta marcha separóse un soldado de filas y escondióse por breve rato tras de una roca, urgido por la violencia de un dolor de tripas. Violó don Francisco, . . . y esperó con toda pachorra a que el soldado, libre ya de su fatiga, volviese a ocupar su puesto" (90). Death is often amusingly colloquialized: "en 1604 lió el petate" (481), "lo había sorprendido la Flaca" (665), "pasó a la tierra de los calvos" (486). Those already dead are "los que están pudriendo tierra y criando malvas con el cogote" (911). To be in danger of death is to run the risk "de que lo convirtiesen en chicharrón" (404) or "en tostón" (269), while to be killed comes out as "lo *desmondongaron* de un balazo" (1096). Several allusions to hanging also embody a euphemistic structure:

. . . menudeaban las ordenanzas que les ponían la gorja en peligro de intimar relaciones con la cuerda de cáñamo. (89)

. . . Francisco de Carbajal, . . . quiso medirle con una cuerda la anchura del pescuezo. (202)

. . . había condenado a hacer zapatetas en el aire al desdichado barbero. (336)

As Osvaldo Crispo Acosta has noted, there is "in Ricardo Palma such a deeply rooted tendency to joke that he even seasons the toasted flesh of the Inquisitorial fires with the salt of his wit."[9] These few excerpts represent a multitude of circumlocutions and euphemisms that inform the style of the famous anecdotes, confirming again the key interrelationship of style and humor.

Poetry and Epigrams

The numerous snatches of poetry, both popular and literary, that add texture to the *tradiciones* comprise a significant feature of Palma's stylistic humor. Palma himself was, in his estimation, a "mediano versificador" and during his lifetime published several collections of his own poetry, plus some translations.[10] Into the weave of the *tradiciones* Palma threaded many of his own creations, in addition to ones by other poets, some of which he modified, when necessary. At times it becomes difficult to discern which lines belong to the *tradicionista* and which do not. Palma was evidently sensitive to verse and skillfully took advantage of "the mischievous musicality of couplets" on many occasions. As with *refranes,* verse is interpolated throughout the *tradiciones* "in the manner of finely enameled miniatures."[11] And as with other characteristics of style, the degree of usage of popular verse in the tales evolved with the passage of time. Verse was added to early works when reworked at a later date. Wilder explains that "although in later tradiciones Palma greatly increased the quantity of popular verses, usually of a comical or satirical nature, he had already interpolated a number of them in the *Edición princeps.*"[12]

The stylistic pattern of prose mingled with portions of verse goes back at least to the time of the Cynic Menippus (circa 340 to circa 270 B.C.), who employed it for satiric purpose. In works by Cervantes this style takes the form of abundant allusions to the romances, most of which "are in the service of humor." Poetry in Palma's narrations assumes a variety of shapes and styles ranging from one line to entire pages and operates in several ways. It may on occasion synthesize the moral of a story. In another setting "poetic lines may serve to initiate a tradition, like a musical chord that prepares the spirit":[13] "Principio principiando; / principiar quiero, / por ver si principiando / principiar puedo" (209). Often the poetry characterizes or describes. Most important for our present purpose, however, is the fact that the *tradicionista* frequently employed poetry for humorous effect.

In terms of size, many verse excerpts of the *tradiciones* constitute epigrams: "si el fósforo da canela [*sic*], / ¡qué dará la fosforera!" (1009). Humorous quatrains are also common. Several stories involve brief pasquinades, often in a kind of repartee or flyting. Some anecdotes begin with a jocular stanza, which sometimes takes the form of an epigraph. Palma occasionally expanded the humor of a narrative by concluding with some humorous lines, as in "Los barbones" and "No juegues con pólvora."

An analysis of the poetic insertions in Palma's *Tradiciones peruanas* suggests the following divisions in terms of origin of humor. Some verse is humorous due to a surprising but pleasant thought. Some verse alludes to sex. Still other verse gains force from irony, satire, and wordplay. Finally, much of the verse in the *tradiciones* derives comicity from situational setting and involvement.

In "Aceituna, una" the narrator draws out the question, " '¿Y por qué, . . . llamaban los antiguos las once al acto de echar, después del mediodía, un remiendo al estómago? ¿Por qué?' Once las letras son del aguardiente. / Ya lo sabe el curioso impertinente" (171). Here Palma created a digression around a humorous epigram with which he was already acquainted and with which he hoped to sweeten one of his stories.

As noted in Chapter 3, a number of verses in the *tradiciones* cause amusement because of sensual intimations contained therein. As Martinengo has correctly observed, "they often accompany the entire narrative, like a discreet, sardonic comment on the part of the people (or the author himself) on the course of events."[14] Thus, the Count of Monclova's licentious behavior elicits the pasquinade, "Al conde de la Monclova / le dicen *Mano de Plata;* / pero tiene mano de oro / cuando corteja mulatas" (475).

Leacock maintains that "in the world of humor, poetry plays a very subordinate part. Its range is very limited. Practically all the great masterpieces of humor are written in prose. The effects to be obtained from poetry lie rather in the domain of the 'comic' than of the larger humor; they are for the most part the mere cracklings of verbal wit, water running over pebbles in the sunlight, not the deep moving current of humorous thought."[15] This statement describes well the function of humorous verse in Palma's prose and is particularly true inasmuch as a number of interpolated poems incorporate puns. Recall, for example, the elderly olive vender, Ño Cerezo, whose wife became pregnant: "Dicen por ahí que Cerezo / tiene encinta a su mujer. / Digo que no puede ser, / porque no puede ser eso" (171). Evident in this example is the sensual orientation that accompanies the play on words, thus supplying a double dose of humor. Of course, puns contained in verse touch on other subjects also. In response to an impecunious fellow seeking the post of standard-bearer was the verse: "pretendes una bandera / y es cosa que me da risa, / pues quien no tiene camisa / no ha menester la . . . vandera" (606). As discussed earlier in our study of satiric wordplay, and as these examples further demonstrate, both homonyms and homophones blend well with the banter of the *tradicionista*.

Poems of a satiric nature sometimes sound harsh. For the most part, however, the prevailing geniality of the anecdotes renders them amusing. In regard to the manner in which they are incorporated into the story, some poems merge with the narrative line, some initiate the tale, heralding a certain focus or establishing a particular atmosphere, and some are used, as Martinengo explains, "to express, in a stylized manner, his own opinion or judgment."[16]

El signo del escribano
dice un astrólogo inglés,
que el signo de Cáncer es,
pues come a todo cristiano. (739)

Marqués mío, no se asombre,
ría o llore, cuando veo
tantos hombres sin empleo,
tantos empleos sin hombre. (746)

The humor of irony also thrives in stanzas that significantly enliven the *tradiciones*.

Cuentan de un hombre aburrido
y de genio furibundo,
que exclamaba enfurecido:
Si es como éste el otro mundo,
en llegando . . . me suicido. (741)

Another aspect to the humor of poetry in the *Tradiciones peruanas* relates to its use by participants in situations. The couplet, epigram, or longer stanza usually makes obvious the humor. In "Una causa por perjuicio" the narrator relates the story of a German drunkard who promised his wife that the end of the year would see him take his last drink of beer. A little before midnight on New Year's Eve the man approached his wife and said, "Permita Dios que reviente / antes que cerveza beba. / Año nuevo, vida nueva . . . / Desde mañana . . . , ¡aguardiente!" (256).

Poetry, then, comprises another point of style that, while embellishing the expressivity of Palma's prose, concurrently adds to the range of his humor. In addition, the poetic medium enhances humor with its innate musicality and blends especially well with wit and wordplay, which also demand careful selection and manipulation of terms.

Humor of Situation

A few remarks on situational humor will bring this study to a close. Throughout this book I have alluded to the anecdotal nature of the *tradiciones*. Indeed, as Luis Alberto Sánchez observes in *Don Ricardo Palma y Lima*, all characters are "unmistakable and tied to the anecdotal life of the city."[17] It is little surprise, then, that a portion (though relatively small) of the overall humorous content of the stories stems from a felicitous coalescence of circumstances. Since this subject has been analysed under specific categories already examined, two final accounts will suffice here to illustrate the point.

In "De cómo desbanqué a un rival" the narrator shares the tale of his personal courtship with a certain lady. This is an account that involves several humorous events. The lady in question owns a beautiful black cat, about which is related, "Lo confieso, llegó a inspirarme celos, fue mi pesadilla. Su ama lo acariciaba y lo mimaba demasiado, y maldita la gracia que me hacía eso de un beso al gato y otro a mí." More than once, when he trys to shoo the animal from her lap, it lands him "un arañazo de padre y muy señor mío." One day he kicks the animal. "¡ Nunca tal hiciera! Aquel día se nubló el cielo de mis amores, y en vez de caricias hubo tormenta deshecha. Llanto, amago de pataleta, y en vez de llamarme ¡bruto! me llamó ¡masón!, palabra que, en su boquita de repicapunto, era el *summum* de la cólera y del insulto." To calm her, instead of arsenic, he has to give the cat some sponge cake, stroke its back, and "¡Apolo me perdone el pecado gordo!, escribirle un soneto con estrambote" (1438).

In another example, *La Lunareja,* owner of a miserable little shoe store, openly refused to receive paper money and in so doing voiced many insolent and obscene statements. Eventually the viceroy, Torretagle, sends the magistrate to warn her. When she receives him "con un aluvión de dicterios tales, . . . al buen alcalde se le subió la mostaza a las narices, y llamando a cuatro soldados hizo conducir, amarrada y casi arrastrando, a la procaz zapatera a un calabozo de la cárcel de la Pescadería." The next day she is tied to a post and shaved bald. "Durante esta operación lloraba y se retorcía la infeliz, gritando: '¡Perdone mi amo Torretagle, que no lo haré más!' " (970). A group of youngsters enjoying the proceedings shout back in unison, "Dele, maestro, dele, / hasta que cante el *miserere.*" Although she tries to praise the Republic and denounce the followers of the King (of which she still is one of the most avid), "la granujada era implacable, y comenzó a gritar con especial sonsonete: '¡Boca dura y pies de lana! / Dele, maestro, hasta mañana' " (971). With the shearing complete, the executioner ties a bone to her as a muzzle and leaves her to endure public shame until late afternoon—a very humorous scene, given her flighty, insolent character and Palma's depiction of her with the *refrán* "Mujer lunareja, / mala hasta vieja."

6

Conclusion

A leading factor in the enduring popularity of the *Tradiciones peruanas* is the masterful fusion of humor, rooted principally in irony and satire, and style into an irresistably alluring rhetorical whole. The harmonious interdependence of these four elements provides the key to understanding the impossible task facing would-be imitators, for Palma was both a stylist of humor and a humorist of style. In his manner of storytelling Palma bequeathed nineteenth-century Peru with a literary creation that ensuing generations of readers and critics have sanctioned as a stylistic masterpiece of humor.

My objective in the present undertaking has been to elucidate through the presentation and interpretation of concrete examples the numerous facets of Palma's humor and their vital link to the carefully wrought expressivity of the anecdotes. The study proves valuable in its illumination of the wide range of stylistic options available to and exploited by the author and in its revelation of the rich, multifaceted texture of Palma's famed irony. The analysis of irony and satiric irony firmly establishes the *tradicionista* as an independent spirit who, throughout the pages of the *Tradiciones peruanas* continually, albeit amiably, takes to task the various social, clerical, and governmental elites of Lima for defects in character and in wisdom that have injured both the country and the individual, including the author himself. The preponderance of verbal humor over situational humor stands well attested. I have also sought to specify the elements of reality from which the humor draws its life, an endeavor that underscores Palma's immersion in his contemporary environment as well as his bond with the antecedent and coetaneous world of literature and scholarship. Despite certain flaws of style, such as reiterated usage of phrases, and despite the obvious debt to previous authors in terms of tone and stylistic patterns, I am confident that this analysis highlights and explicitly affirms Palma's creation of a unique, very original and apparently inimitable work of stylistic humor and irony, the coalescence of personality, anecdotal substance, and language.

A few comments about the longstanding question of Palma's ideological stance seem in order at this point. As noted, Palma was keenly aware of his society, especially in relation to political and economic questions and societal innovations. His intimate familiarity with history furnished him with an unusually vivid historical perspective, which, coupled with his own personal experiences, greatly influenced his ideas. Palma understood well the foibles of human beings. He lauded human strength, while he incessantly satirized and made irony from weaknesses, which he viewed as unavoidably predominant, whatever the political system. Despite the many flaws of the republican experiment, however, Palma clearly championed it, a few facetious remarks to the contrary notwithstanding. He was, nevertheless, painfully cognizant of the lack of true leadership and cooperation, which he maintained were qualities essential for a successful democracy. His satiric irony, though relentless concerning disappointments that the republic originated, never seriously suggests support for socialistic policies. In fact, Palma did not have much at all to say about such ills of society as latifundium and the oppression of the lower classes. What did concern him was the loss of tradition and links to the past occasioned by the influx of foreign ideas, fashions, and merchandise. He frequently decried this loss of heritage, apparently sensing that, as a result, future generations would be isolated from the vital, although marred, past in whose roots lay the key to historical consciousness and thus self-understanding.

Finally, I would add that although several of the points examined in this study have been grazed in considerations by such critics as Martinengo, Escobar, Riva Agüero, Sánchez, Tamayo Vargas, Oviedo, and others, nowhere has the fuller spectrum been laid out so as to supply a more finished perspective and appreciation concerning Palma's irony and the stylistic roots nurturing the comicity of his phraseology. Ahead remains the task of pursuing all aspects of style in detail and interrelating them in a solely stylistic analysis of this famed prose. Whether that materializes or not, however, the present study has already united most aspects of style, the vast majority inevitably communing with mirth as they flowed from the pen of the master.

Notes

Notes to Chapter 1: Introduction

1. Enrique de Gandía, *Orígenes del romanticismo y otros ensayos* (Buenos Aires: Atalaya, 1946), 211.

2. José Toribio Medina, "Prólogo," in Aurelio Díaz Meza, *Leyendas y episodios chilenos* (Buenos Aires: 1968), I, 1-2, as cited in Merlin D. Compton, *Ricardo Palma* (Boston: Twayne, 1982), 151, trans. by Compton.

3. Respectively, Raúl Porras Barrenechea, *Tres ensayos sobre Ricardo Palma*, 56; José de la Riva Agüero, "Elogio de don Ricardo Palma," in *Ricardo Palma: 1833-1933*, 35; Merlin D. Compton, "Spanish Honor in Ricardo Palma's *Tradiciones peruanas*," 60; Jean Lamore, "Sur quelque procédés de l'ironie et de l'humor dans les *Tradiciones peruanas*," 106; Tomás Acosta, "Palma y la historia," 211.

4. Ventura García Calderón, *Del romanticismo al modernismo*, 325; Edith Palma, "Ricardo Palma y sus *Tradiciones peruanas*," in *Tradiciones peruanas completas*, xxviii. (Hereinafter referred to as TPC. All references to the *tradiciones* themselves will be to this edition and will appear in the text.)

5. See César Miró, *Don Ricardo Palma: el patriarca de las tradiciones*, 148.

6. Riva Agüero, "Elogio," 36.

7. See Edith Palma, xxxii.

8. Santiago Vilas, *El humor y la novela española contemporánea*, 46.

9. Ibid., 52. Although Max Eastman terms the sense of humor "a distinct hereditary emotional endowment," "the humorous attitude" is really more along the lines of "a rare and precious gift," to quote Jacob Levine and Fredrick C. Redlich. See Eastman, *The Sense of Humor*, 236; and Vilas, *Humor y la novela*, 44-45, respectively.

10. Phyllis Rodríguez-Peralta, "Liberal Undercurrents in Palma's *Tradiciones peruanas*," 287, and José Miguel Oviedo, *Genio y figura de Ricardo Palma*, 150.

11. See Werner Beinhauer, *El humorismo en el español hablado*, 65.

12. Stephen Leacock, *Humor: Its Theory and Technique*, 202.

13. Porras Barrenechea, *Tres ensayos*, 9.

14. Alfonso Noriega Cantú, *El humorismo en la obra de Lope de Vega*, 30, citing Fernández Flores and Robert Escarpit, respectively.

15. See Vilas, *Humor y la novela*, 66.

16. Frederico de Onís, "El humorismo de Galdós," 293; Vilas, *Humor y la novela*, 101, notes that humor "is often the authentic essential synthesis of its time, of each historical moment."

17. Vilas, *Humor y la novela*, 64.

18. Lamore, "Sur quelque procédés," 112.

19. See Vilas, *Humor y la novela*, 90-97.

20. Leacock, *Humor*, 107; Noriega Cantú, *El humorismo*, 29.

21. Michael Nimetz, *Humor in Galdós*, 36, citing Julio Casares, *El humorismo y otros ensayos* (Madrid, 1961), 79; see Esmeralda Gijón Zapata, *El humor en Tirso de Molina*, 14, 16, 18, 24;

Noriega Cantú, *El humorismo,* 27-28; Eastman, *Sense of Humor,* 7, 169.

22. Respectively, Helmut Hatzfeld, *El "Quijote" como obra de arte del lenguaje,* 153; Eastman, *Sense of Humor,* 169.

23. Respectively, David Worcester, *The Art of Satire,* 34, 81; D. C. Muecke, *The Compass of Irony,* 5; Wayne C. Booth, *A Rhetoric of Irony,* 30; George Meredith, "An Essay on Comedy," 470; Nimetz, *Humor in Galdós,* 10, alluding to Mary A. Grant, *The Ancient Rhetorical Theories of the Laughable* (Madison, 1924), 47; See Vilas, *Humor y la novela,* 95-96; see Leonard Feinberg, *The Satirist,* 177-78.

24. Rosa Arciniega, "El 'volterianismo' de Ricardo Palma," 28, 27; Gijón Zapata, *Tirso de Molina,* 40; Juan J. Remos, "El alma del Perú en las *Tradiciones* de Palma," 84.

25. Luis Fabio Xammar, "Elementos románticos y antirrománticos de Ricardo Palma," 105.

26. Carlos Miró Quesada Laos, *Rumbo literario del Perú,* 51.

27. José de la Riva Agüero, ed., *Ricardo Palma: 1833-1933,* 254.

28. See Oviedo, *Genio y figura,* 103-104, and Rodríguez-Peralta, "Liberal Undercurrents," 292.

29. See José Carlos Mariátegui, *Siete ensayos de interpretación de la realidad peruana,* 267, and Luis Alberto Sánchez, "Reactualización de don Ricardo Palma," 63.

30. See Luis Alberto Sánchez, *La literatura peruana,* VI, 63-64.

31. Walter J. Peñaloza, "Significado de don Ricardo Palma en nuestra cultura," 88; José Miguel Oviedo, ed., *Cien tradiciones peruanas* by Ricardo Palma, xxxvi.

32. *Diccionario de la lengua española,* 725; Luis Alberto Sánchez, *Don Ricardo Palma y Lima,* xvii; Luis Alberto Sánchez, *Nueva historia de la literatura americana,* 279; Osvaldo Crispo Acosta, *Motivos de crítica hispanoamericanos* (1965), I, 47. This reminds one of Worcester's words concerning Swift on p. 104 of *The Art of Satire:* "Gulliver's Travels is tragic and comic at the same time, as ironical works are apt to be."

33. Miró Quesada Laos, *Rumbo literario,* 41; see Luis Avilés, "La Indisciplina de Ricardo Palma," 49, 50, 51, 53.

34. Manuel Beltroy, "La poesía de Palma," 282, cited in Kenneth William Webb, "Ricardo Palma's Techniques in Re-creating Colonial Lima," 90-91. Porras Barrenechea, *Tres ensayos,* 12, concurs: "In his *Traditions* Palma reveals himself as an authentic creole, undisciplined, an enemy of authority, irreverent in religious matters, oppositionist by temperament, evil, and witty."

35. Benjamin Jarnes, cited in Vilas, *Humor y la novela,* 51; see Alberto Escobar, "Tensión, lenguaje y estructura: las *Tradiciones peruanas,*" for a comparative study of "Mauro Cordato" and "El mejor amigo . . ., un perro." See also William Russell Wilder, "The Romantic Elements in the First Edition of the First Series of the *Tradiciones peruanas* by Ricardo Palma," 93.

36. Eastman, *Sense of Humor,* 230.

37. Ibid., 42-43; see Gilbert Highet, *The Anatomy of Satire,* 19, 47, 191, 234.

38. Ricardo Palma, in a letter to Vicente Barrantes, cited in Oviedo, *Genio y figura,* 153; Ricardo Palma, in a letter to Barles, cited in *Genio y figura,* 165; Porras Barrenechea, *Tres ensayos,* 15.

Notes to Chapter 2: The Humor of Irony

1. Respectively, cited in Pedro Rumichaca, "Ricardo Palma 'tradicionista pero no tradicionalista,' " 194; Alberto Escobar, "Tensión, lenguaje y estructura: las *Tradiciones peruanas,*" 55; José Miguel Oviedo, *Genio y figura de Ricardo Palma,* 172.

2. Respectively, Juan J. Remos, "El alma del Perú en las *Tradiciones* de Palma," 84; Rosa Arciniega, "El 'volte-

rianismo' de Ricardo Palma," 28; Pamela Francis, ed., *Ricardo Palma: Tradiciones peruanas*, by Ricardo Palma, viii; George W. Humphrey, ed., *Tradiciones peruanas*, by Ricardo Palma (Chicago: Benj. H. Sanborn, 1936), xxvi; Ventura García Calderón, *Del romanticismo al modernismo*, 327.

3. Respectively, Jean Lamore, "Sur quelque procédés de l'ironie et de l'humor dans les *Tradiciones peruanas*," 106; Guillermo Feliú Cruz, *En torno de Ricardo Palma*, II, 347; José de la Riva Agüero, *Carácter de la literatura del Perú independiente*, 200; José de la Riva Agüero, "Elogio de don Ricardo Palma," 41.

4. Carlos Miró Quesada Laos, *Rumbo literario del Perú*, 47.

5. M. H. Abrams, *A Glossary of Literary Terms*, 44.

6. D. C. Muecke, *The Compass of Irony*, 23, 94, 96.

7. See ibid., ix.

8. Ibid., 53, 54-57, 64-98.

9. George W. Umphrey, ed. *Tradiciones peruanas*, by Ricardo Palma, xxvi; Raúl Porras Barrenechea, *Tres ensayos sobre Ricardo Palma*, 57-58.

10. See David Worcester, *The Art of Satire*, 67-68.

11. See Muecke, *Compass of Irony*, 172-77, for a consideration of this tactic.

12. Worcester, *Art of Satire*, 74.

13. Lamore, "Sur quelque procédés," 108.

14. Muecke, *Compass of Irony*, 69.

15. However, on occasion Palma did encounter repercussions from angry descendants. Thus, some ambivalence may be evident, since, although he is speaking with tongue in cheek, an attempt to ward off possible attacks may have some validity.

16. See Michael Nimetz, *Humor in Galdós*, 94.

17. Cited in Norman Knox, *The Word "Irony" and its Context, 1500-1755*, 5.

18. Ibid., 100.

19. Muecke, *Compass of Irony*, 76.

20. See Dora Bazán Montenegro, *Los nombres en Palma*, 61.

21. Wayne C. Booth, *A Rhetoric of Irony*, 73.

22. See Muecke, *Compass of Irony*, 73, and Booth, *Rhetoric of Irony*, 57, 75.

23. See Knox, *The Word "Irony,"* 4, 15, 79, and Max Eastman, *The Sense of Humor*, 52.

24. Knox, *The Word "Irony,"* 78-79.

25. See Muecke, *Compass of Irony*, 73; see Knox, *The Word "Irony,"* 119.

26. See Knox, *The Word "Irony,"* 13, 90, 99.

27. Muecke, *Compass of Irony*, 99-115.

28. Feliú Cruz, *Ricardo Palma*, II, 347.

Notes to Chapter 3: The Humor of Satire and Satiric Irony

1. M. H. Abrams, *A Glossary of Literary Terms*, 82.

2. Gilbert Highet, *The Anatomy of Satire*, 235.

3. Michael Nimetz, *Humor of Galdós*, 39; Enrique Díez-Canedo, *Letras de América: Estudios sobre las literaturas continentales*, 156; Rosa Arciniega, "El 'volterianismo' de Ricardo Palma," 27; José Miguel Oviedo, *Genio y figura de Ricardo Palma*, 176.

4. These characteristics were amassed from David Worcester, Gilbert Highet, Michael Nimetz, M. H. Abrams, and Leonard Feinberg.

5. See Chapter 4, Circumlocutions.

6. Orlando Gómez-Gil, *Historia crítica de la literatura hispanoamericana*, differs, but generalizes: "his humor is wholesome, not mordacious, bitter or sarcastic," 347.

7. Highet, *Anatomy of Satire*, 57.

8. See Stephen Leacock, *Humor: Its Theory and Technique*, 108.

9. Respectively, Highet, *Anatomy of Satire*, 67; Abrams, *Literary Terms*, 9; David Worcester, *The Art of Satire*, 47.

10. Abrams, *Literary Terms*, 10; Ibid; see Worcester, *Art of Satire*, 48; Highet, *Anatomy of Satire*, 70.

11. Eleanor N. Hutchens, "Verbal Irony in *Tom Jones*," 49; Worcester, *Art of Satire*, 59.

12. See section on caricature and types for a fuller examination.

13. See Beinhauer, *El humorismo en el español hablado*, 183, 102, and Highet, *Anatomy of Satire*, 105.

14. Ventura García Calderón, *Del romanticismo al modernismo*, 325.

15. See also the exchange between Santa Rosa and God, *TPC*, 233.

16. See Santiago Vilas, *El humor y la novela española contemporánea*, 56-57, Max Eastman, *The Sense of Humor*, 24, and Esmeralda Gijón Zapata, *El humor en Tirso de Molina*, 20, for discussions in this regard.

17. Helmut Hatzfeld, *El "Quijote" como obra de arte del lenguaje*, 153.

18. Respectively, Worcester, *Art of Satire*, 50, 157; Highet, *Anatomy of Satire*, 18, see also 233; Beinhauer, *Humorismo*, 31; Raúl Porras Barrenechea, *Tres ensayos sobre Ricardo Palma*, 58.

19. Abrams, *Literary Terms*, 10; William Flint Thrall and Addison Hibbard, *A Handbook to Literature*, 71.

20. Highet, *Anatomy of Satire*, 190.

21. In this regard I have written articles entitled "Ricardo Palma and Francisco de Quevedo: A Case of Rhetorical Affinity and Debt" and "Ricardo Palma's Rhetorical Debt to Miguel de Cervantes."

22. In his literary portraits Palma regularly centers on the eyes, whether they be those of the attractive *limeñas* or, as we see here, of less satisfying reflection.

23. Merlin D. Compton, "Spanish Honor in Ricardo Palma's *Tradiciones peruanas*," 75. This thesis lays out in great detail the immense importance of honor in its many facets as found in the *Tradiciones peruanas*.

24. See Hatzfeld, *El "Quijote"*, 161.

25. Nimetz's study of Galdós' works unearths much satire rooted in *costumbrista* types. See *Humor in Galdós*, 39-40.

26. Ernest Stowell, "Ricardo Palma and the Legal Profession," 160.

27. See Highet, *Anatomy of Satire*, 224, in this regard.

28. See Dora Bazán Montenegro, *La mujer en las "Tradiciones peruanas,"* 35.

29. Eastman, *Sense of Humor*, 91.

30. See Nimetz, *Humor in Galdós*, 148.

31. See Leacock, *Humor*, 83ff.

32. Nimetz, *Humor in Galdós*, 148.

33. Alberto Escobar, "Tensión, lenguaje y estructura: las *Tradiciones peruanas*," 30-31. See also Bazán Montenegro, *Mujer*, 69-73.

34. See Eastman, *Sense of Humor*, 63-65; such exchanges of abuse "are sometimes called 'flyting,' from the old Scots word for scolding"—see Highet, *Anatomy of Satire*, 152.

35. Porras Barrenechea, *Tres ensayos*, 10.

36. See Highet, *Anatomy of Satire*, 16; see Nimetz, *Humor in Galdós*, 50-51.

37. See Oviedo, *Genio y figura*, 172; Luis Avilés, "La indisciplina de Ricardo Palma," 50, terms these bonding phrases "minute phrases that reveal to us a certain hidden hostility, a certain ironic indiscipline more sincere than incisive and bad." Walter J. Peñaloza, "Significado de don Ricardo Palma en nuestra cultura," 88, views the *tradiciones* as "more a copy of Palma's own epoch than of the viceroyalty."

38. Fredrick B. Pike, *The Modern History of Peru*, 124.

39. This reminds one of the "playful pain" theory espoused by Eastman, *Sense of Humor*, 11-19, wherein we laugh when confronted by a playful shock or disappointment. For Eastman's ideas on humor and hostility consult pp. 32-37.

40. Cited in Mariátegui, *Siete ensayos de interpretación de la realidad peruana*, 265.

41. This excerpt comes from Palma's collection of poetry entitled *Armonías*. I cite it only to remind the reader that such satire also characterizes the poetic creation of the author, particularly in this work and in *Verbos y gerundios*. See Ricardo Palma, *Poesías completas*, 95.

42. Note a similar comment by Cervantes: "Sepa que el primer volteador del mundo fue Lucifer, cuando le echaron o arrojaron del cielo, que vino volteando hasta los abismos." Miguel de Cervantes Saavedra, *Don Quijote de la Mancha*, edited by Martín Riquer I, 39.

(All future references will be to this edition and will appear in the text.)

43. Luis Alberto Sánchez, *Escritores representativos de América*, I, 312.

44. See Porras Barrenechea, *Tres ensayos*, 9-15; Edith Palma, p. xxii; Luis Avilés, "Al margen de las *Tradiciones* de Ricardo Palma," 64.

45. Lia Schvartz Lerner, "Creaciones estilísticas en la prosa satírica de Quevedo," 26, see also 134-39; see Leacock, *Humor*, 28-29; see Werner Beinhauer, *El español coloquial*, 59; see Hatzfeld, *El "Quijote"*, 195-206.

46. See Beinhauer, *Humorismo*, 101-102; see Eastman, *Sense of Humor*, 49.

Notes to Chapter 4: More Humor of Satire and Satiric Irony

1. Sturgis E. Leavitt, "Ricardo Palma and the *Tradiciones peruanas*," 352; David Worcester, *The Art of Satire*, 28.

2. Werner Beinhauer, *El español coloquial*, 248; Maren Elwood, *Characters Make Your Story*, 101-102; Wayne C. Booth, *A Rhetoric of Irony*, 22.

3. Angel Rosenblat, *La lengua del "Quijote"*, 81, see 79-94 for a fuller analysis; see Lia Schvartz Lerner, "Creaciones estilísticas en la prosa satírica de Quevedo," 24, 76.

4. Max Eastman, *The Sense of Humor*, 73; see Werner Beinhauer, *Humorismo*, 72-106; see Rosenblat, *La lengua*, 35, see also 81.

5. See Michael Nimetz, *Humor in Galdós*, 107; see Worcester, *Art of Satire*, 27-29.

6. Archer Taylor, *The Proverb* (Cambridge, Mass., 1931), 3, cited in Shirley L. Arora, *Proverbial Comparisons in Ricardo Palma's "Tradiciones peruanas*," 5, see also page 4.

7. Dora Bazán Montenegro, *La mujer en las "Tradiciones peruanas*," 65-66.

8. See William Russell Wilder, "The Romantic Elements in the First Edition of the First Series of the *Tradiciones peruanas* by Ricardo Palma," 433, 438-39.

9. Beinhauer, *Humorismo*, 73, alluding to Leo Spitzer's "Zur Kunst Quevedos in seinem Buscón," Archivum Romanicum, 11 (1927), 516ff.

10. Palma's use of *narigudo* and other similar terms—*desnarizadores* (123)—elicits recollections of Quevedesque wordplay: "desnarigado, narigano, narigudo, narigotas." See Antonio Papeli, *Quevedo*, 269.

11. Eastman, *Sense of Humor*, 54; Jean Lamore, "Sur quelque procédés de l'ironie et de l'humor dans les *Tradiciones peruanas*," 106.

12. D. C. Muecke, *The Compass of Irony*, 54.

13. See Lerner, "Creaciones estilísticas," 74, 148.

14. See Rosenblat, *La lengua*, 79-84, 158-67, and Hatzfeld, *El "Quijote,"* 173-76, for a complete study of comparisons and wordplay in Cervantes; Quevedo's entry, cited in Lerner, "Creaciones estilísticas," 148, from *El buscón*, see 158-63 for further examples; also Ilse Nolting-Hauff, *Visión, sátira y agudeza en los "Sueños" de Quevedo*, 240.

15. See Arora, *Proverbial Comparisons*, 63.

16. Bazán Montenegro, *Mujer*, 54-55.

17. Lerner, "Creaciones estilísticas," 133, cited from "Carta a una monja."

164 · Tradiciones peruanas

18. Beinhauer, *Humorismo*, 75.

19. See Rosenblat, *La lengua*, 93, and Lerner, "Creaciones estilísticas," 25, 84-85.

20. Ricardo Palma, quoted in José Miguel Oviedo, *Genio y figura de Ricardo Palma*, 55.

21. See Pamela Francis, ed. *Ricardo Palma: Tradiciones peruanas*, 100.

22. Arora, *Proverbial Comparisons*, 43, referring to José María Sbari, *Gran diccionario de refranes de la lengua española* (Buenos Aires, 1943), 58.

23. See Arora, *Proverbial Comparisons*, 137.

24. See ibid., 152, for commentary.

25. Ibid., 174, for a discussion.

26. Lerner, "Creaciones estilísticas," 79; see Rosenblat, *La lengua*, 74, 89-90.

27. Lerner, "Creaciones estilísticas," 81, cited from *El buscón*.

28. Arora, *Proverbial Comparisons*, 45, offers documented usages. Palma employs the same expression in "Haz bien sin mirar a quién": "con más ángel en la cara que un retablo de Navidad" (556).

29. From *El buscón*, cited in Lerner, "Creaciones estilísticas," 81: "hablaba como sacerdote que dice las palabras de la consagración."

30. See my article, "El arte de la caracterización en 'Don Dimas de la Tijereta' de Ricardo Palma," 157-63, for a full study of the techniques of character portrayal in this *tradición*.

31. From *El buscón*, cited in Lerner, "Creaciones estilísticas," 82.

32. Hatzfeld, *El "Quijote"*, 57.

33. Quevedo uses the same image in *Los sueños*: "Genova ha echado unas sanguijuelas desde España al cerro del Potosí, con que se van restañando las venas, y chupones se empiezan a secar las minas." Cited in Lerner, "Creaciones estilísticas," 91.

34. This recalls Don Lorenzo's comment to Don Quijote: " 'Verdaderamente, señor don Quijote, . . . que deseo coger a vuesa merced en un mal latín continuado, y no puedo, porque se me desliza de entre las manos como anguila' " (DQ II, 666).

35. See Lerner, "Creaciones estilísti-

cas," 147, 149, for reference to *Siglo de Oro;* Rosenblat, *La lengua*, 161, 167, see also Hatzfeld, *El "Quijote"*, 173-76; consult Nolting-Hauff, *Visión, sátira, y agudeza*, 226-45, and Lerner, 147-89, concerning Quevedo's ability with wordplay; see Leacock, *Humor: Its Theory and Technique*, 14.

36. Alvardo J. Moreno has produced a dictionary of *Voces homófonas, homógrafas y homónimas;* see Rosenblat, *La lengua*, 164, for examples of *diáfora* in *Don Quijote;* see Lerner, 150 and 153ff, for further clarification and examples. I use the Spanish terms for lack of sufficiently specific terms in English.

37. Lionel Duisit, *Satire, parodie, calembour*, 89, 90; Rosenblat, *La lengua*, 108.

38. See Roy L. Tanner, "The Art of Characterization in Representative Selections of Ricardo Palma's Tradiciones peruanas," 136-40, for a broader discussion on this point.

39. Beinhauer, *Humorismo*, 201. For ease in identification I shall underline the words involved in the pun in several of the examples in this section.

40. Leacock, *Humor*, 34.

41. Rosenblat, *La lengua*, 192.

42. Emilio Carilla, *El romanticismo en la América hispánica*, 196.

43. Cited in Hatzfeld, *El "Quijote,"* 219.

44. Francisco de Quevedo Villegas, *Obras completas*, 127.

45. Beinhauer, *Humorismo*, 25; see p. 126 for discussion of *paráfrasis;* see Rosenblat, *La lengua*, 68ff, and Lerner, *Humor*, 182-188.

46. Lerner, *Humor*, 182; see Henri Bergson, "Laughter," in *Comedy: Meaning and Form*, edited by Robert W. Corrigan, 475-76, and Beinhauer, *Humorismo*, 33; Leacock, *Humor*, 36.

47. Eastman, *Sense of Humor*, 8; Pascal and Kant are cited on pp. 152-53.

48. See Muecke, *Compass of Irony*, 19-21.

49. See Worcester, *Art of Satire*, 102-108, and Muecke, *Compass of Irony*, 62-63, 91-92.

Notes to Chapter 5: Other Modes of Humor

1. Albert Escobar, "Tensión, lenguaje y estructura: las *Tradiciones peruanas,* 27.

2. See Max Eastman, *The Sense of Humor,* 88ff.

3. Guillermo Feliú Cruz, *En torno de Ricardo Palma,* II, 353.

4. For a complete study of this point of style in Palma see my "Las expresiones alternativas y perifrásticas en la prosa de Ricardo Palma."

5. Werner Beinhauer, *Humorismo,* 39; see Helmut Hatzfeld, *El "Quijote" como obra de arte del lenguaje,* 167-173.

6. Dámaso Alonso, "Alusión y elusión en la poesía de Góngora," *Revista de Occidente* 19 (1928), 181, cited in Hatzfeld, *El "Quijote,"* 40.

7. Quoted respectively from Hatzfeld, *El "Quijote,"* 170 and Enrique Anderson Imbert, "La procacidad de Ricardo Palma," 271.

8. See Henry James, *The Future of the Novel,* 95-96, alluded to by Nimetz, *Humor in Galdós,* 6.

9. Osvaldo Crispo Acosta, *Motivos de crítica hispanoamericanos,* 47.

10. Cited in José de la Riva Agüero, *Carácter de la literatura del Perú independiente,* 178.

11. Escobar, *Tensión, lenguaje y estructura,* 34.

12. Wilder, "The Romantic Elements in the First Edition of the First Series of the *Tradiciones peruanas by Ricardo Palma,"* 241.

13. Respectively, Hatzfeld, *El "Quijote,"* 163; José Miguel Oviedo, *Genio y figura de Ricardo Palma,* 170-71; see Gilbert Highet, *The Anatomy of Satire,* 36-37, for historical context.

14. Alessandro Martinengo, *Lo stile di Ricardo Palma,* 66.

15. Leacock, *Humor: Its Theory and Technique,* 131.

16. Martinengo, *Lo stile,* 66.

17. Luis Alberto Sánchez, *Don Ricardo Palma y Lima,* 119; Martinengo, *Lo stile,* 59, tells us that "the anecdote and the insignificant event were an indispensable instrument" in Palma's jocose reconstruction of the viceroyalty and the colonial epoch.

Bibliography

I. Works by Ricardo Palma

Poesías completas. Buenos Aires: Maucci Hermanos, 1911.
Tradiciones peruanas. 6 vols. Madrid: Espasa-Calpe, 1930.
Tradiciones peruanas completas. Edited by Edith Palma. 6th ed. Madrid: Augilar, 1968.

II. Books and Articles on Ricardo Palma

Acosta, Tomás. "Palma y la historia." *Cuadernos Americanos* 12 (January-February 1953): 211-13.
Anderson Imbert, Enrique. "La procacidad de Ricardo Palma." *Revista Iberoamericana* 47 (1953): 269-72.
Arciniega, Rosa. "El 'volterianismo' de Ricardo Palma." *Cuadernos* 33 (November-December 1958): 25-28.
Arora, Shirley L. *Proverbial Comparisons in Ricardo Palma's "Tradiciones peruanas."* Folklore Studies 16. Los Angeles: University of California, 1966.
Avilés, Luis. "Al margen de las *Tradiciones* de Ricardo Palma." *Hispania* 20 (February 1937): 61-68.
———. "La indisciplina de Ricardo Palma." *Repertorio Americano,* vol. 46, no. 4 (1 February 1950): 49-54.
Bazán Montenegro, Dora. *La mujer en las "Tradiciones peruanas."* Madrid: n.p., 1967.
———. *Los nombres en Palma.* Lima: Ediciones de la Biblioteca Universitaria, 1969.
Carilla, Emilio. *El romanticismo en la América hispánica.* Madrid: Gredos, 1958.
Compton, Merlin David. "Spanish Honor in Ricardo Palma's *Tradiciones peruanas.*" Diss., University of California, Los Angeles, 1959.
Crispo Acosta, Osvaldo. *Motivos de crítica hispanoamericanos.* 4 vols. 1914. Reprint of *Motivos de crítica.* Biblioteca Artigas, 1965.
Díez-Canedo, Enrique. *Letras de América: Estudios sobre las literaturas continentales.* Mexico: El Colegio de México, 1944.
Escobar, Alberto. "Tensión, lenguaje y estructura: las *Tradiciones peruanas.*" *Sphinx,* vol. 15, no. 6 (1962) [Separata].

Feliú Cruz, Guillermo. *En torno de Ricardo Palma.* 2 vols. Santiago: Prensas de la Universidad de Chile, 1933.

Francis, Pamela, ed. *Ricardo Palma: Tradiciones peruanas,* by Ricardo Palma. New York: Pergamon Press, 1966, vii-xiii.

García Calderón, Ventura. *Del romanticismo al modernismo.* Paris: Paul Ollendorff, 1910.

Gómez-Gil, Orlando. *Historia crítica de la literatura hispanoamericana.* New York: Holt, Rinehart and Winston, 1968.

Lamore, Jean. "Sur quelque procédés de l'ironie et de l'humor dans les *Tradiciones peruanas." Bulletin Hispanique* 70 (1968): 106-115.

Leavitt, Sturgis E. "Ricardo Palma and the *Tradiciones peruanas." Hispania,* 34 (November 1951): 349-53.

Mariátegui, José Carlos. *Siete ensayos de interpretación de la realidad peruana.* 1928. Reprint. Mexico: Solidaridad, 1969.

Martinengo, Alessandro. *Lo stile di Ricardo Palma.* Padova: Liviana Editrice, 1962.

Miró, César. *Don Ricardo Palma: el patriarca de las tradiciones.* Buenos Aires: Losada, 1953.

Miró Quesada Laos, Carlos. *Rumbo literario del Perú.* Buenos Aires: Emecé Editores, 1947.

Oviedo, José Miguel. *Genio y figura de Ricardo Palma.* Buenos Aires: Editorial Universitaria de Buenos Aires, 1965.

———. *Cien tradiciones peruanas* by Ricardo Palma. Caracas: Biblioteca Ayacucho, 1977.

Peñaloza, Walter J. "Significado de don Ricardo Palma en nuestra cultura." *Tres,* no. 9 (September-December 1941): 73-95.

Porras Barrenechea, Raúl. *Tres ensayos sobre Ricardo Palma.* Lima: Librería Juan Mejía Baca, 1954.

Remos, Juan J. "El alma del Perú en las *Tradiciones* de Palma." *Revista Cubana* 21 (1946): 72-89.

Riva Agüero, José de la. *Carácter de la literatura del Perú independiente.* 1905. Reprint. In *Obras completas de José de la Riva Agüero.* Vol. I. Lima: Pontífica Universidad Católica del Perú, 1962.

———. "Elogio de don Ricardo Palma." In *Ricardo Palma: 1833-1933,* 17-42. Lima: Sociedad Amigos de Palma, 1934.

———. Ed. *Ricardo Palma: 1833-1933.* Lima: Sociedad Amigos de Palma, 1934.

Rodríguez-Peralta, Phyllis. "Liberal Undercurrents in Palma's *Tradiciones peruanas." Revista de Estudios Hispánicos,* vol. 15, no. 2 (May 1981): 283-97.

Rumichaca, Pedro. "Ricardo Palma 'tradicionista pero no tradicionalista.' " *Repertorio Americano* 48 (15 March 1954): 193-97.

Sánchez, Luis Alberto. *Don Ricardo Palma y Lima.* Lima: Imprenta Torres Aguirre, 1927.

———. *Escritores representativos de América.* 2 vols. Madrid: Gredos, 1957.

———. *La literatura peruana.* Asunción: Guarania, 1951.

———. *Nueva historia de la literatura americana.* 5th ed. Asunción, Paraguay: Guarania, 1950.

———. "Reactualización de don Ricardo Palma." *Revista Nacional de Cultura,* vol. 17, no. 106-107 (1954): 63.

Stowell, Ernest. "Ricardo Palma and the Legal Profession." *Hispania* 25 (May 1942): 158-60.

Tanner, Roy L. "El Arte de la caracterización en 'Don Dimas de la Tijereta' de Ricardo Palma." *Explicación de Textos Literarios,* vol 7, no. 2 (1978-1979): 157-63.

———. "Las expresiones alternativas y perifrásticas en la prosa de Ricardo Palma: una clava estilística." (To appear in *Cuadernos Hispanoamericanos,* 1985-1986).

———. "Literary Portraiture in Ricardo Palma's *Tradiciones peruanas.*" *The American Hispanist,* vol. 3, no. 27 (May 1978): 8-15.

———. "Ricardo Palma and Francisco de Quevedo: A case of Rhetorical Affinity and Debt," *Kentucky Romance Quarterly,* vol. 31, no. 4 (1984): 425-35.

———. "Ricardo Palma's Rhetorical Debt to Miguel de Cervantes." *Revista de Estudios Hispánicos,* vol. 17, no. 3 (October 1983): 345-61.

———. "The Art of Characterization in Representative Selections of Ricardo Palma's *Tradiciones peruanas.*" Diss., University of Illinois, 1976.

Umphrey, George W., ed. *Tradiciones peruanas,* by Ricardo Palma. Chicago: Benj. H. Sanborn, 1936, xv-lviii.

Webb, Kenneth William. "Ricardo Palma's Techniques in Re-creating Colonial Lima." Diss., University of Pittsburgh, 1951.

Wilder, William Russell. "The Romantic Elements in the First Edition of the First Series of the *Tradiciones peruanas* by Ricardo Palma." Diss., St. Louis University, 1966.

Xammar, Luis Fabio. "Elementos románticos y antirrománticos de Ricardo Palma." *Revista Iberoamericana,* vol. 4, no. 7 (November 1941): 95-106.

III. Books and Articles on humor, irony, or satire

Abrams, M. H. *A Glossary of Literary Terms.* New York: Holt, Rinehart and Winston, 1957.

Beinhauer, Werner. *El español coloquial.* 2d ed. Translated by Fernando Huarte Morton. Madrid: Gredos, 1968.

———. *El humorismo en el español hablado.* Madrid: Gredos, 1973.

Bergson, Henri. "Laughter." In *Comedy: Meaning and Form,* edited by Robert W. Corrigan, 471-77. Scranton, Penn.: Chandler Publishing Co., 1965.

Booth, Wayne C. *A Rhetoric of Irony.* Chicago: University of Chicago Press, 1974.

Duisit, Lionel. *Satire, parodie, calembour.* Stanford: Anma Libri, 1978.

Eastman, Max. *The Sense of Humor.* 1921. Reprint. New York: Octagon Books, 1972.

Feinberg, Leonard. *The Satirist.* Ames, Iowa: Iowa State University Press, 1963.

Gijón Zapata, Esmeralda. *El humor en Tirso de Molina.* Madrid: n.p., 1959.
Hatzfeld, Helmut. *El "Quijote" como obra de arte del lenguaje.* 2d ed. Madrid: Consejo Superior de Investigaciones Científicas, 1966.
Highet, Gilbert. *The Anatomy of Satire.* Princeton, New Jersey: Princeton University Press, 1962.
Hutchens, Eleanor N. "Verbal Irony in Tom Jones." *PMLA,* vol. 77, no. 1 (March 1962).
Knox, Norman. *The Word "Irony" and its Context, 1500-1755.* Durham, N.C.: Duke University Press, 1961.
Leacock, Stephen. *Humor: Its Theory and Technique.* New York: Dodd, Mead and Co., 1935.
Lerner, Lia Schvartz. "Creaciones estilísticas en la prosa satírica de Quevedo." Diss., University of Illinois, Urbana-Champaign, 1971.
Meredith, George. "An Essay on Comedy." In *Comedy: Meaning and Form,* edited by Robert W. Corrigan. Scranton, Penn.: Chandler Publishing Co., 1965.
Muecke, D. C. *The Compass of Irony.* London: Methuen and Co., 1969.
Nimetz, Michael. *Humor in Galdós.* New Haven: Yale University Press, 1968.
Nolting-Hauff, Ilse. *Visión, sátira y agudeza en los "Sueños" de Quevedo.* Translated by Ana Pérez de Linares. Madrid: Gredos, 1974.
Noriega Cantú, Alfonso. *El humorismo en la obra de Lope de Vega.* Mexico: Universidad Nacional Autónoma de México, 1976.
Onís, Federico de. "El humorismo de Galdós," *Revista Hispánica Moderna,* vol. 9, nos. 1 and 2 (1943): 293-94.
Papeli, Antonio. *Quevedo.* Barcelona: Barna, 1947.
Rosenblat, Angel. *La lengua del "Quijote."* Madrid: Gredos, 1971.
Thrall, William Flint, and Addison Hibbard. *A Handbook to Literature.* 1936. Revised by C. Hugh Holman. New York: The Odyssey Press, 1960.
Vilas, Santiago. *El humor y la novela española contemporánea.* Madrid: Ediciones Guadarrama, 1968.
Worcester, David. *The Art of Satire.* New York: Russell and Russell, 1960.

IV. Other Sources

Cervantes Saavedra, Miguel de. *Don Quijote de la Mancha.* Edited by Martín Riquer. 2 vols. Barcelona: Juventud, 1971.
Diccionario de la lengua española. 19th ed. 1970.
Elwood, Maren. *Characters Make Your Story.* Boston: The Writers, 1942.
Moreno, Alvaro J. *Voces Homófonas, homógrafas y homónimas.* Mexico: Porrúa, 1977.
Pike, Fredrick B. *The Modern History of Peru.* New York: Frederick A. Praeger, 1967.
Quevedo Villegas, Francisco de. *Obras completas.* 6th ed. Madrid: Aguilar, 1966.

Index